CLASS AND TENNESSEE'S
CONFEDERATE GENERATION

THE FRED W. MORRISON SERIES
IN SOUTHERN STUDIES

CLASS AND TENNESSEE'S CONFEDERATE GENERATION

BY FRED ARTHUR BAILEY

THE UNIVERSITY OF NORTH CAROLINA PRESS
CHAPEL HILL AND LONDON

FOR BONNIE, AMBER, ALEX, & STAN

Manufactured in the United States of America

Library of Congress Cataloging-in-Publication Data
Bailey, Fred Arthur
Class and Tennessee's Confederate Generation
(The Fred W. Morrison series in Southern studies)
Bibliography: p.
Includes index
1. Tennessee—History—Civil War, 1861–1865—Social
aspects. 2. United States—History—Civil War, 1861–
1865—Social aspects. 3. Veterans—Tennessee.
I. Title. II. Series.
E579.9.B35   1987   305'.90697'09768   86-1407
ISBN 0-8078-1703-1

Designed by Chris Wilkinson

CONTENTS

PREFACE

During the Depression of the 1930s, university sociologists became fascinated by the social structure of the American South. In their view, the region possessed peculiar social problems different from those of the nation as a whole. A host of scholars portrayed the modern South as a land dominated by a powerful, white, economic elite that lived in luxury while a significant population—white and black—suffered in deep poverty. They saw this situation as the heritage of an antebellum southern society dominated by aristocracy and slavery.[1] Having made a detailed study of caste and class in deep South cotton country, students of Harvard professor W. Lloyd Warner concluded in 1941 that in their subject community "life and labor . . . , as well as power and prestige, [were] based on relationship to land." They further noted that three-fourths of the country's acreage was monopolized by a tiny number of individuals whose ancestry could be traced back to Old South "planter-families." They affirmed that even as late as the third decade of the twentieth century, the states of the former Confederacy retained a highly structured class system with little social mobility.[2]

The portrayal of an aristocracy-dominated South offended southern historians during the 1930s, most notably Vanderbilt professor Frank L. Owsley. Dismissing modern social scientists as "sociologists and socialists," he determined to prove that the Old South was characterized by widespread economic and social democracy. His classic work *Plain Folk of the Old South*—as well as the writings of his graduate students—was intended to refute contemporary critics of the southern social system.[3]

Ironically, Owsley was not the first Vanderbilt professor to respond to the charge that the South was dominated by an aristocracy. In 1915 Gustavus W. Dyer, an eccentric professor of sociology and economics, developed a crude questionnaire and submitted it to surviving Civil War veterans. Although he collected only a small number of these questionnaires, his project was taken up seven years later by the energetic Tennessee archivist John Trotwood Moore. In the end,

1,648 veterans responded. Both Dyer and Moore expected the questionnaires to validate their belief that felicity rather than friction permeated the social structure. The responses contained a wealth of sociological information, but they were stored in the Tennessee State Library and Archives and remained largely unexplored until the early 1980s.[4]

This book is a detailed analysis of the Tennessee Civil War Veterans Questionnaires. It is a frank contribution to the debate over whether the South was a land dominated by aristocracy or a region characterized by democracy. Its conclusions should give comfort to the critics rather than to the apologists of the Old South.

ACKNOWLEDGMENTS

This work was made possible through the kind assistance of a number of friends and fellow historians. I especially appreciate Paul Escott and Vernon Burton who read the entire manuscript and offered excellent suggestions. Pete Daniel, John David Smith, Jerrold Hirsch, Ronald D. Eller, and John Robinson surveyed portions of the document. They all were most helpful. Early in this project my friend Bea Angelo at Freed-Hardeman College weaned me away from the stale jargon of the scholar and urged me to write in a style more acceptable to the general public. I hope I have followed her advice. At the University of North Carolina Press, Lewis Bateman encouraged me to expand my research into book form and Pam Upton professionally edited the manuscript, smoothing out many awkward sentences and making numerous suggestions for clarification. I am most thankful for their aid.

While developing this work, I taught at Freed-Hardeman College in Tennessee. Dean B. J. Naylor supported my efforts and somehow always found funds for my travels. In addition, this work required extensive computer time. For help in this mysterious field, I am thankful for David Russell, who understood that historians rarely speak computer language. He spoke English. Karen Walker and Redonna White were always on hand when the computer took a dislike to me and my project. At Freed-Hardeman, I had three student-secretaries who took tremendous interest in this endeavor. Working with Nancy Doss, Tonya Howell, and Nan Rhodes was a great joy. Near the end of this project, I was employed by Abilene Christian University in Texas. There Joe Booth went to great lengths to transfer my data from Tennessee to Texas.

Many others have been most helpful in matters great and small. Marilyn Bell at the Tennessee State Library and Archives called my attention to the Civil War Veterans Questionnaires, helped me secure them on microfilm, and responded generously to all my requests for aid. Jane Miller and Virginia Oliver at the Freed-Hardeman College Library and Delno Roberts at Abilene Christian University Library secured many of the materials needed. John Blassingame and John David Smith shared their knowledge of the abstruse Gustavus W. Dyer. Steve Ash furnished vital information on the desertion of John Johnston from the Army of Northern Virginia, and Jackie Goggin shared a letter from the Wendell H. Stephenson Papers that aided my understanding of Frank L. Owsley's reaction to his critic, Fabian Linden.

The Civil War Veterans Questionnaires were microfilmed for me by the Tennessee State Library and Archives. All materials presented here are drawn from the microfilm copies. At the same time that I was working on my book, Silas Emmett Lucas, Jr., of the Southern Historical Press in Easley, South Carolina, commissioned Colleen M. Elliott and Louise A. Moxley to transcribe the questionnaires for his press. They were published in 1985 and are available in a five-volume set. As a whole, they are excellent transcriptions, although they only extract materials such as newspaper clippings, letters from relatives, and memoranda from the library staff that were also included with the questionnaires.

Every scholar needs a first-rate spouse who understands the foolish urge to research and to write. I have such a wonderful person in my wife Bonnie. She and our children—Amber, Alex, and Stan—have always stood with me.

CLASS AND TENNESSEE'S CONFEDERATE GENERATION

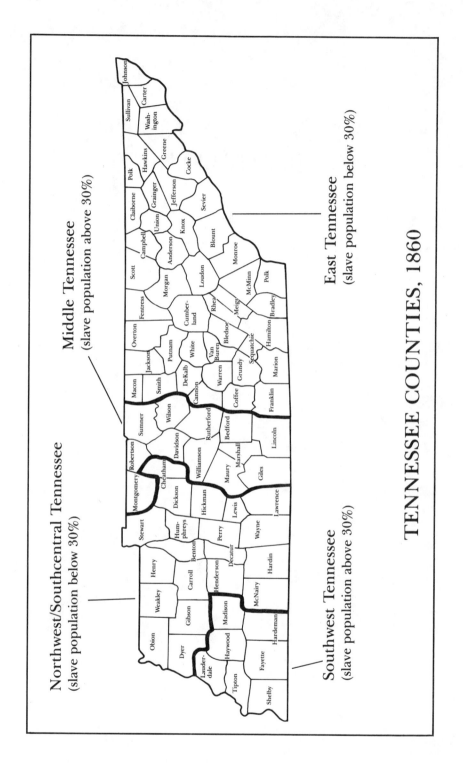

TENNESSEE COUNTIES, 1860

Northwest/Southcentral Tennessee
(slave population below 30%)

Middle Tennessee
(slave population above 30%)

East Tennessee
(slave population below 30%)

Southwest Tennessee
(slave population above 30%)

CHAPTER ONE

A TRUE HISTORY OF THE OLD SOUTH

This book begins with a tragic tale. As an eighty-one-year-old Confederate veteran who fought in the bloody battles of Seven Pines, Gettysburg, and the Wilderness, John Johnston was no stranger to violence. On his last Sunday, he may have worshipped with the Christian Church congregation in Watertown, Tennessee, and afterward lingered over the grave of a favorite daughter. Despairing over her death and conscious of the passing of so many Civil War comrades, he resolved to terminate his own life. On Monday, 9 October 1922, he demonstrated no unusual distress at breakfast. Nonetheless, at precisely 7:30 A.M., he walked to the picket fence in front of his home, inserted a shotgun stock between the slats, placed the barrel against his heart, and pushed the trigger with a stick. The old soldier joined those slain during the dreadful years of 1861 to 1865.[1]

Just thirty minutes later, the Tennessee State Library and Archives in Nashville received Johnston's response to the Tennessee Civil War Veterans Questionnaire. Reflecting on the autobiographical account encompassed by the questionnaire and the lamentable event connected with it, a secretary in the archives speculated that this was the last written legacy of the aged Confederate.[2] Johnston was one of 1,648 individuals who responded to Tennessee's unique attempt to preserve the memories of its Civil War generation.[3]

As late as the 1920s, Civil War passions still abounded in Tennessee. To be sure, the great leaders were now dead. Such Unionists as President Andrew Johnson, Congressman T. A. R. Nelson, and Governor William G. Brownlow rested beneath their monuments, comforted that they had vanquished the rebel cause. Secessionist Governor Isham G. Harris had become reconciled to the Union and went to his reward after a long—though undistinguished—career in the United States Senate. The Confederate commanders—Braxton Bragg, Joseph E. Johnston, and John B. Hood—had written their memoirs assuring posterity that their campaigns were strategically valid and morally justified. Politicians and generals had made peace with the past. When the conflict's leaders were gone, however, a younger generation of historians took up the cause, refighting the Civil War as partisans of the North or the South. These scholars largely ignored the wealth of information available from thousands of surviving veterans. Tennessee was a happy exception to this general rule. Between 1915 and 1922, the state gave its common soldiers the opportunity to share their perceptions of the Old South, the Civil War, and the postbellum world.

The respondents to the Tennessee Civil War Veterans Questionnaire were painfully conscious that they were the last remnants of a generation that knew firsthand both the Old and the New South. Seeing "the ranks of the gray becoming thinner day by day," wrote a Middle Tennessean, "serves to remind me that I . . . must soon lay aside this mortal coil." More despondent, Henry Dunavant described a celebration of Robert E. Lee's birthday in 1922. "I was the only old confederate there," he sadly remembered, "and felt so *lonesome* that I was sorry I went."[4] These aging veterans yearned to tell their stories.

Each questionnaire constituted a short, uniform autobiography of a Civil War veteran. It requested from each old soldier a description of his antebellum lifestyle: how much land his family owned; whether his family had slaves; what kind of house his family occupied and how many rooms it had; what kinds of activities were engaged in by his father and his mother; what type of work he did as a boy; and how much education he received. This descriptive section was followed by a series of questions soliciting the veterans' opinions concerning social-class relations: did white men respect manual labor; was there a friendly feeling between slaveowners and nonslaveowners, or were they antagonistic; was slaveownership a factor in politics; and were there opportunities for a poor man to advance economically? The respondents were then encouraged to relate their Civil War experiences. They were specifically asked to name their regiments, when and where they enlisted, and their first battle. Next they were invited to discuss briefly their military engagements, their camp life, and, if relevant, their experiences in hospitals or in prisons. The questionnaire concluded with a request that the veteran write a short sketch of his life since the Civil War, stating his occupation, where he lived, his church affiliation, and whether he held a civil office. In 1915 William E. Orr appended to his correspondence the inscription: "I hope you will be able to read what I have written and appropriate at leas[t] a part of it to the History of our beloved South-land." Seven years later, the barely literate Isaac Griffith finished his contribution and then prayed that he might "Live to Read A True Hisary of the Old South."[5]

The Civil War Veterans Questionnaires provide a rare opportunity to examine nineteenth-century social attitudes from the viewpoint of a variety of Tennesseans. To be sure, the questionnaires did not represent a scientific sampling of former soldiers. Officials at the state's library and archives simply mailed out blank forms, trusting the veterans to return them. As might be expected, wealthy (and well-educated) Tennesseans were overrepresented and impoverished (and undereducated) Tennesseans underrepresented in the responses.

The story that emerges on the following pages concentrates on 1,250 former Confederates from among the total respondents. Because only 115 Tennessee Unionists returned their questionnaires, they were not included in this study. In addition 263 non-Tennesseans and 20 individuals whose social status could not be determined from the information given were excluded. The men are divided into four categories: poor whites, nonslaveowning yeomen, slaveowning yeomen, and the wealthy elite. The poor consist of 243 men whose fathers were farmers and laborers owning no slaves and fewer than eighty acres of land. At the other end of the social scale, 286 individuals are characterized as wealthy. Their fathers were either planters with twenty or more slaves, or they belonged to the professional class—merchants, attorneys, physicians, academy teachers, and ministers—whose social status usually approximated that of plantation owners. Between these extremes are two other identifiable groups: 336 nonslaveowning yeomen and 385 slaveowning yeomen. The fathers of the men in both groups were nonprofessionals owning eighty or more acres of land. In addition, slaveowning yeomen families possessed between one and nineteen slaves (Appendix 2, table 1).

Geographically and economically, antebellum Tennessee was a microcosm of the entire South. Slavery flourished in two large regions. Seven southwestern counties—Shelby, Tipton, Lauderdale, Fayette, Hardeman, Haywood, and Madison—shared the plantation economy of the deep South. By the 1840s, the fertile soils of these counties had attracted settlers who engaged in cotton production. The per-acre yield of this crop was believed to equal or exceed that of similar regions in Mississippi and Alabama. Blacks made up a high percentage of the population, ranging from 35 percent in Shelby County to 64 percent in Fayette County.[6]

Slaves also constituted from 30 to 52 percent of the population in thirteen Middle Tennessee counties. The line of slaveholdings formed a column through the center of the state, beginning with Montgomery, Robertson, and Sumner counties along the Kentucky border; stretching south through Davidson, Wilson, Williamson, Rutherford, Maury, Marshall, and Bedford counties; and ending in Giles and Lincoln counties on the Alabama border. Cotton and tobacco plantations existed throughout this area, but the economy was dominated by midsize farms and small slaveholdings.[7]

Slavery was much less important in the mountain counties of East Tennessee and in the region sandwiched between Middle and Southwest Tennessee. The latter region consisted of those southcentral counties along the Tennessee River that were skipped over by settlers migrating to the rich cotton country farther west, and the northwest counties that were only just emerging from the frontier status in 1860. In this area, the majority of white farmers either could not afford or did not need slave labor.

These former soldiers, whose median age was seventy-nine, were old enough to remember the antebellum South (Appendix 2, table 2). To be sure, advanced years diminished the quality of many of their responses. The impoverished Samuel N. Reynolds, who described himself as an "old Rebel solger [and] a Jefsonian Dimercrat," wrote: "i dun the best culd [but] i am so nervus i cant rite with a pen i hop you can mak it out."[8] Other veterans demonstrated exceptional vitality. At age eighty, Robert L. Jones claimed that he continued to chop stove wood; at seventy-six, John L. McMurty could still recall from memory his company's muster roll; and at eighty-one, William Hunter bragged that "at Chickamauga the Yankees shot me five times and now I am hail and hearty." Few could match the ebullience of Joseph P. J. Hoover. "I attend all the [Confederate] Reunions," he boasted, "when I get out with the Boys I feel like a 2 year old I am very Active although nearing my fourscore years."[9]

When the aging veterans returned their questionnaires, they unwittingly contributed to a controversy as old as the antebellum struggle between northern and southern ideologues. The Civil War Veterans Questionnaires were intended to provide materials for the writing of a "true history of the Old South." Two chauvinistic southern scholars—Gustavus W. Dyer and John Trotwood Moore—hoped that these soldiers' testimonials would counter charges made by "neo-abolitionist" northern historians, who claimed that the antebellum South was a land where slave-rich aristocrats oppressed both the white poor and the slaves. Dyer developed the questionnaire during his brief tenure as director of the Tennessee Department of Archives and History from 1913 to 1915; Moore, who held a similar post from 1919 to 1929, gathered the majority of the responses. Their efforts resulted in a rich collection that made possible a comparison of the lifestyles and social attitudes of poor whites, plain folks, and planters. Interestingly, the "true history" that emerged from these documents is far different from Dyer and Moore's perception of the Old South.

Dyer was best remembered as an eccentric Vanderbilt University professor. Those who knew him in his last years recalled a rugged individualist, given to peculiarities of dress and to strong conservative views. In spite of a lecture style that could only be described as erratic, he was a favorite after-dinner speaker with Vanderbilt alumni, southern Chambers of Commerce, and various business groups. Depending on his mood—and not the appropriateness of the occasion—he might entertain his audience with his large "repertoire of 'darky' stories," or bore it with a dry lecture on Franklin D. Roosevelt's assaults upon the Constitution.[10]

Despite his later eccentricities, the younger Dyer was a scholar with potential. Born in 1867 in Henry County, Virginia, he grew up in the shadow of Confederate defeat. In common with many boys of his era, he delighted in hearing war stories spun by his father, a Confederate captain, and by the scores of veterans inhabiting his immediate neighborhood. His formal education included two years at Virginia Polytechnic Institute (1886–88), the bachelor of arts degree from Randolph-Macon College in 1891, and both the bachelor of divinity and master of arts from Vanderbilt University in 1894. Five years after his graduation, Dyer gained a position in Vanderbilt's Department of Economics and Sociology, where he remained until his retirement in 1942. He earned his doctorate in sociology from the University of Chicago in 1907.[11]

In 1905 Dyer published a small, controversial volume entitled *Democracy in the South before the Civil War*. This book was important both for its thesis and for its foreshadowing of the Civil War Veterans Questionnaires. In it Dyer denied that the South was dominated by a planter aristocracy and insisted that the region's small farmers possessed considerable political and economic power. His scholarship was inconsistent. Although the work's title referred to the entire South, Dyer focused on his native Virginia. He sometimes quoted impressive statistics gleaned from census data and local sources to bolster his ideas, but at other times he employed little more than biased rhetoric to support his beliefs.[12] In his review for the *American Historical Review*, Ulrich B. Phillips, renowned for his work on slavery, recognized the book's "very uneven value," but still praised Dyer's efforts "as one of numerous protests from the thoughtful youth of the South against the injustice done their people by the general American historians."[13]

The last chapter of *Democracy in the South* was a harbinger of Dyer's future interest in Tennessee soldiers. It was based upon his oral interviews with twenty-five former Confederates from the Virginia counties of Henry, Franklin, Pittsylvania, and Bedford. During the summer of 1902, he solicited responses to nineteen questions dealing with the men's occupations, their ownership of land and slaves, and their perceptions of social-class relations. From this small and unscientific sampling, Dyer concluded that economic "opportunities were good for a poor young man"; that "slaveholders, as a rule, were kind and sociable"; that "manual labor was held in high esteem" by all social classes; and that "at hotels, public meetings, etc., . . . there was no distinction made between big slaveholders and others."[14] Thirteen years later, he revised and expanded the same questions and sent them out to Tennessee's Civil War veterans.

For a brief period, Dyer was a respected, though minor, scholar. Several southern apologists, among them Ulrich B. Phillips, Wilbur J. Cash, and Fletcher M. Green, eventually cited Dyer's book as an authoritative source.[15] In 1909 Dyer contributed a chapter on social trends to the thirteen-volume series *The South in the Building of the Nation*. To a great extent, it was a panegyric to antebellum white egalitarianism. "Life in the rural South," he wrote, was "most favorable to the development of democracy, and the doctrine of equal rights to all." He pictured the home, the church, and the country store as the seedbeds for community leveling. In the country store, he asserted, "the people from all spheres of life—the rich and the poor, the educated and the uneducated, the cultured and the uncultured—often came together on a basis of absolute equality, and communed with each other as fellow citizens and friends." Mindful of the social problems of early twentieth-century America, Dyer longed for the South of old, which contained "no masses and classes, no problems of capital and labor, no strikes and lockouts."[16] He wrote romantically of a land that, in reality, had never existed.

Dyer's concern for Tennessee's Civil War generation developed during his short tenure as the director of the state archives in Nashville. Dyer was a Democrat—he was prominently mentioned as a possible candidate for the U.S. Senate in 1922 and for governor of Tennessee in 1932—but he departed from the faith long enough to support Republican Ben W. Hooper's successful gubernatorial campaign in 1912. Following Hooper's victory, Dyer received the archival appointment. Evidently his temperament was ill-suited to the methodical collecting and cataloging required by the position; he was only one of a number of mediocre, if not incompetent, administrators who held that particular political sinecure before 1919. When the Democrats regained the governorship in 1915, Dyer was soon ousted.[17]

Shortly before his removal, however, Dyer made his one notable contribution to Tennessee's heritage. On 15 March 1915, he sent out the first of the Civil War Veterans Questionnaires. "As a student and teacher of history," he explained in his cover letter, "I am convinced . . . that the leading history [sic] of the United States grossly misrepresents conditions in the Old South. . . . The true history of the South is yet to be written." He then urged the veterans to make "a real contribution to the land you love, and to the cause for which you have made many sacrifices."[18] Before more than a small handful responded, Dyer's job was terminated and the project was aborted.

Seven years later the quest for a "true history of the Old South" was taken up by John Trotwood Moore. A more substantial scholar than Dyer, Moore nevertheless shared with him an intense southern ethnocentrism. When Moore was appointed chief administrator in 1919 both of the Department of Archives and History and of the State Library, he had long been an established literary figure. His numerous poems, short stories, and novels glamorized the southern experience, and he was especially fascinated by the region's "plain folk." Two novels, *The Bishop of Cotton Town* (1906) and *Hearts of Hickory* (1926), romanticized Tennessee's common people.[19]

Moore's southern pride had a strong racist bite. In his correspondence, he boasted that whites living in the old Confederacy retained at least 96 percent pure Anglo-Saxon blood. By contrast, he believed, "The proud old State of Massachusetts [could] show only 46% of pure blood Anglo-Saxon . . . people." Racial purity, Moore affirmed, was the one gift "that Johnny Reb [was] going to hand back to the Union." Given this mind-set, he was highly sensitive to any perceived criticism of the southern heritage. Responding, in 1919, to an inquiry as to whether Moore had found any record of Puritan influence in his area, he retorted: "I am thankful to say that after careful search I have been unable to find any written evidence that Puritanism ever got into the South. I sincerely hope that you may be equally unsuccessful."[20]

Possessed of strong passions, deep curiosity, and considerable energy, Moore employed all those attributes in developing the Tennessee State Library and Archives into a meritorious institution. The legislature had established the State Library in 1854, but, before 1919, little effort had been made to secure adequate holdings or to make the library useful to the state's citizens. If anything, the archives were in worse condition than the library. Until just before Moore assumed responsibility for the state's records, they had been stored in the mildewed basement of the Capitol, and it was with considerable difficulty that one of his predecessors convinced the governor to move them to the building's attic. Moore's additional efforts at improvement were aided by a state legislature caught up in the patriotic fervor of post–World War I America and anxious to preserve this spirit for future generations. As a result, both the State Library and the Department of Archives and History obtained, for the first time, adequate funding and staff.[21]

Almost immediately after Moore assumed his duties as director of the library and archives, Governor Albert H. Roberts appointed him to chair the newly created Tennessee Historical Committee. In that capacity, he was charged with collecting "the 75,000 individual records of Tennessee's soldiers, sailors, airmen, and marines" who fought in the World War. He tackled the project with his usual enthusiasm. "Our Tennessee Historical Committee is gathering in the history of our great State bit by bit," he wrote a friend in Louisiana. "I lose myself so completely in it that I fail to do the creative things I long to do. But as soon as I get this well started . . . I hope to write some of the books I am thinking about." The World War project proved too massive even for the dynamic Moore. But in the process of gathering information on the returning doughboys, he became interested in another, smaller group of veterans—the aging survivors of the Civil War.[22]

Just when and under what circumstances Moore discovered Dyer's questionnaires is uncertain, as the two men were not well acquainted. However, at some point in late 1921 or early 1922, Moore copied his predecessor's work, making two modifications. The first was the printing in bold letters, at the top of the form, of the inscription: "Tennessee Historical Committee / Department of Libraries, Archives, and History / John Trotwood Moore, director"; the second was the addition of a line correcting Dyer's failure to ask the name of the subject's father. Moore's wife, Emily, succeeded him as director, and she took great pride in her husband's efforts to gather these unique Civil War records. Neither of the two appear to have left any documents crediting Dyer with the development of the questionnaire.[23]

Despite his failure to acknowledge Dyer's role in the project, Moore deserves praise for collecting a majority of the responses to the questionnaires. As a member of Tennessee's Confederate Pension Board, he had ready access to its files, and he supplemented this information with advertised appeals to Tennessee soldiers in the *Confederate Veteran* and with intensive follow-ups on additional names supplied by respondents.[24] He probably succeeded in reaching most of the state's living soldiers. Writing to Moore, William Harkleroad of Sullivan County noted that he knew "several veterans around here but think all of them have filled out blanks"; Richard Howell of Hardeman County observed that "all those . . . I know have received blanks like this one"; and James M. Jones of Fayette County reported that "most [old soldiers] I know of have recd letters from you." Little wonder that one former Confederate's daughter could express to Moore her confidence "that we have the right man in the right place. We are sure Tennesseans will be grateful for the store of information you have laid up for them."[25]

Both Dyer and Moore hoped that this "store of information" would lead to a "true history of the Old South" that would validate their view of the region as a land characterized by white solidarity. The interpretation that emerges from an analysis of the Tennessee Civil War Veterans Questionnaires differs significantly from the one anticipated by both men. Nonetheless, in collecting these documents they consciously participated in an intense historical controversy over the virtues of the southern social-class system.

To Ulrich B. Phillips, writing in 1929, the central theme of southern history was the problem of establishing harmonious relations between whites and blacks.[26] Before the passage of civil rights legislation in the 1960s, an uneasy racial status quo was maintained through the oppression of blacks. In the antebellum era, legalized slavery defined social boundaries; following emancipation, neoslavery was perpetuated by a harsh combination of custom, Jim Crow legislation, peonage, and violence.[27] Such an atmosphere roused severe critics, who condemned the South for its gross inhumanity, and equally defensive apologists, who pictured the South as a dominion of cotton, culture, and compassion. The internecine violence of 1861 to 1865 only briefly interrupted the war of words.

The rhetorical controversy between the North and the South involved not only the status of blacks, but also a dispute over the social and economic relationship between the white elite and other classes of whites. Antebellum abolitionists argued that slave-rich aristocrats retarded the prosperity and well-being of small farmers—a view occasionally bolstered by disgruntled yeomen.[28] In response, the elite assured both its antagonists and itself that class animosity did not exist. Such affirmations, however, were often shaken when aristocrats confronted discontented nonslaveowners. Class antagonisms were momentarily set aside during the early days of the Civil War. But as the conflict continued, small farmers saw little reason to die in order that the wealthy might own slaves. Nonslaveowning whites did not rebel, they simply went home.[29]

For many Southerners, the judgments of postbellum scholars compounded the indignity of military defeat. Called "prosecuting historians" by one student of American historiography, these writers worshipped the nation-state and condemned the slave-tainted South for causing disunion.[30] Among their many accusations, they resurrected the abolitionists' charge that planters oppressed the small farmer and the poor white. "Driven off the fertile lands by the encroachment of the planter," asserted James Ford Rhodes in 1892, the southern nonslaveowner "farmed the worn-out lands and gained a miserable and precarious subsistence." Compared with northern rural and urban laborers, he continued, "they were in material things abjectly poor; intellectually they were utterly ignorant; morally their condition was one of groveling baseness."[31] Hermann Von Holst, James Schouler, and John Bach McMaster echoed this assessment.[32]

Not until the end of the century did southern academics mount an effective counteroffensive. The most important thrust came from William Dunning's graduate seminars at Columbia University. Dunning drew around him a host of young southern scholars eager to return home and to reinterpret the Civil War and Reconstruction. The Dunning school assumed that most southern whites were socially homogeneous; its adherents castigated northern whites who, they believed, united with blacks to subjugate the South during Reconstruction. Dunning's disciples were essentially political historians little concerned with the basic social structure of the South.[33]

Gustavus W. Dyer, a trained sociologist, wrote his *Democracy in the South before The Civil War* hoping to counter Rhodes and others critical of antebellum social relations. Dyer wished to be numbered with the pro-South revisionist historians. Unfortunately for him, his uneven scholarship and erratic interests earned him little more than a footnote in the intellectual debate over North-South issues.[34] Another generation elapsed before southern scholars took up the question of antebellum social class attitudes. Coincidentally it was another Vanderbilt professor, Frank L. Owsley, whose *Plain Folk of the Old South* became the standard southern interpretation of antebellum white social relations.

Owsley and Dyer had much in common. Both were ardent defenders of the South; both taught at Vanderbilt University; and both believed that the southern social classes lived together in harmony. Despite these similarities, the two men probably were little more than acquaintances. No hard evidence exists that Dyer influenced Owsley's thinking. Blanche Clark Weaver, a student and a friend of Owsley, strongly doubted "if they had ever collaborated in any way on anything." During the 1930s and 1940s, Owsley was at the peak of his career, while Dyer had degenerated into a colorful character, rarely taken seriously by his colleagues.[35]

Owsley shared with Dyer and John Trotwood Moore a strong southern ethnocentrism. Born in Montgomery County, Alabama, in 1890, he grew up on a farm where his father rented land to black sharecroppers. In youth, he was impressed by the large number of Confederate veterans who were neither planters nor poor whites. After graduating with a degree in history from the Alabama Polytechnic Institute at Auburn in 1912, he entered the University of Chicago. There he studied under William E. Dodd; the two shared an identification with southern common folk and a distrust of northern industrialists. Owsley received his doctorate in 1924. From 1920 to 1949, he taught in Nashville, where he was intimately associated with the small colony of literary and academic figures known as the Vanderbilt agrarians. Their collected essays, *I'll Take My Stand*, published in 1930, were dedicated "to supporting a Southern way of life against what might be called the American or prevailing way." In his contribution to the anthology, Owsley praised William Dunning, his students, and other southern historians who "scorned the injustice and hypocrisy of condemnation of the South." He chided the North for "sitting in Pharisaical judgment upon the South," and pledged his essay "to point out the untruth of the self-righteous Northern legend which makes the South the war criminal."[36] Owsley remained an unrepentant southern apologist.

By the early 1930s, Owsley's reputation among southern historians was well established. Two major books—*State Rights in the Confederacy* (1925) and *King Cotton Diplomacy* (1931)—and his many journal articles were generally considered to be examples of solid scholarship. In 1936 he commenced a study of the antebellum southern social structure that culminated thirteen years later in *Plain Folk of the Old South*. Like Gustavus W. Dyer, Owsley believed that James Ford Rhodes and other late-nineteenth-century northern historians were little more than successors to the abolitionists. He abhorred their division of the South's population into wealthy slaveowners and poor whites; and he determined to present a humane picture of the forgotten Southerner—the antebellum small farmer.[37] In contrast to Dyer, Owsley possessed the intellectual merit and the personal stability to carry out a massive and painstaking project.

Owsley quickly confronted the problem faced by any historian interested in classes other than the elite—the paucity of written records. To overcome this difficulty, he pioneered the use of the federal manuscript census as a historical tool. He employed the population censuses of 1850 and 1860 to glean a wealth of information on farm sizes, personal property and real estate values, and slaveownership, and from these statistics, he attempted to draw a portrait of community life in the Old South. Owsley was assisted by his energetic wife, but he still found the project difficult. He soon surrounded himself with competent graduate students and assigned a particular state to each. Their work was both demanding and tedious. Over a fruitful fifteen-year span, 1942–57, their dissertations were turned into a small library of books and articles that reinforced the conclusions reached by the Vanderbilt scholar in *Plain Folk*. Owsley guided Blanche Clark and Chase C. Mooney through their explorations of social-class relations in Tennessee, and he strongly influenced both Herbert Weaver's study of Mississippi farmers and Harry Coles's discussion of Louisiana landholdings.[38] Owsley and his students assumed that because the poor, the small farmer, and the planter shared the same geographic neighborhood, they lived in harmony. He succinctly concluded that "to deal with the plain folk as a class-conscious group, bitter and resentful toward the aristocracy because of exploitation and neglect of the latter" was far from "reality."[39]

As a southern apologist, Owsley was highly sensitive to any work whose thesis differed from his own. In 1939 Roger W. Shugg wrote at length about white social relations in his *Origins of Class Struggle in Louisiana*. He found intense social cleavages. Louisiana, he affirmed, "was . . . a slave state policed by gentlemen; and the masses, having no real voice in government, received from it no benefit."[40] In a review for the *Journal of Southern History*, Owsley berated the book and accused Shugg of using inadequate statistical information to reach his conclusions; he then charged that Shugg had sinister political values. "One cannot avoid the feeling," wrote Owsley, "that the author has permitted his Marxian assumption to make him less alert in discovering or using data that would not conform to the theory of class struggle."[41]

Writing in the post–World War II atmosphere that gave birth to McCarthyism, Owsley and his associates recognized that his interpretations of antebellum social-class consensus had contemporary political overtones. In *Plain Folk,* Owsley stressed that the southern yeomen were "a closely knit people; . . . not class conscious in the Marxian sense."[42] In his mind, those critical of his interpretation were guilty of Communist sympathies.

Most notable among Owsley's critics was a young New York University alumnus, Fabian Linden. While doing graduate research on industrial slavery at the University of North Carolina, Linden became first fascinated by, and then skeptical of, Owsley's and his students' theories. In 1945 he submitted to the *Journal of Southern History* an extensive article questioning their methodology. Rejected by that periodical, it was later published in the *Journal of Negro History.* In January 1947, he also published in the *American Historical Review* a critical assessment of Herbert Weaver's *Mississippi Farmers, 1850–1860.* He noted that the book, originally a doctoral dissertation written under Owsley's direction, used raw census data from unrepresentative counties, contained significant statistical errors, and drew conclusions unwarranted from his evidence. "The utilization of basic census data for the rewriting of Southern history is a step in a very promising direction," Linden said. He regretted that Weaver's efforts were "scuttled by questionable techniques and untidy scholarship."[43]

Stung by Linden's article in the *Journal of Negro History* and the negative review of his student's work, Owsley strongly protested to the editor of the *American Historical Review.* "Mr. Linden damns by the simple process of assertion," he complained. "This is a familiar technique in propaganda today and it is disheartening to see it employed in historical criticism." Owsley and his students assumed that Linden was a Marxist but could not conclusively prove it.[44] Linden's later activities belied that assumption. After a brief flirtation with the historical profession, he turned to a career as an economic advisor to the U.S. Foreign Service in Vienna, Austria, then as a civilian consultant to the North Atlantic Treaty Organization, and finally as an active member of the pro-capitalist, New York-based Consumer Research Conference Board.[45]

Owsley fully appreciated the contemporary social implications of interpretive history. His admirers understood and endorsed the political applications of his work. One of them, M. E. Bradford, reflected in 1970 that the denial of southern antebellum class consciousness presented in *Plain Folk* had confounded the theories of "would-be Orwellian Rectifiers, Hamiltonians, and covert Marxists." In 1984 Clyde Wilson, a professor of history at the University of South Carolina, editorialized that Owsley's work remains "indispensable to the construction of any counter-leftist scenario of American history." He affirmed that "no more fundamental challenge than [*Plain Folk*] has ever been offered to the liberal conception of American history."[46]

Also writing in 1984, Grady McWhiney, the Lyndon Baines Johnson Professor of History at Texas Christian University, observed that Owsley's *Plain Folk* had "become part of the generally accepted interpretation of southern history." It is "a tribute to . . . his insight and his research," McWhiney continued, "that so many of his discoveries still inform and shape the history of the South." Turning his attention to Owsley's critics, McWhiney suggested that their efforts were "more assertive than assiduous, more willing to challenge him than prove him wrong." He claimed that they "have failed to follow up their challenges with solid research; no systematic refutation of *Plain Folk* has appeared in the . . . years since that volume was published." The reason, he believed, was that "Owsley's conclusions are valid. No researcher wants to spend time and energy trying to prove something wrong only to discover that what he had hoped to refute was after all correct."[47]

Owsley's use of the federal censuses of 1850 and 1860 was innovative, but it could not demonstrate all that he sought to prove. The census is effective for establishing wealth, slaveownership, and farm acreage for any given geographic area. Because the census marshall went from door to door collecting his information, it is also possible to determine the socioeconomic status of neighbors. Owsley and his students noted that an impoverished renter might live next to a wealthy planter, who in turn might reside next to a modest farmer. But the Owsley school exceeded their evidence when they assumed from these materials that these neighbors associated with a spirit of communal felicity. The census neither confirms nor denies that hypothesis. The southern small farmer and the poor remained inarticulate, their voices still unheard by historians. Even though he was an advocate of Owsley's conclusions, the eminent southern historian Clement Eaton lamented, in 1961, that it was "difficult to find journals and letters of nonslaveholders which give a realistic picture of the life of the yeoman farmer."[48] Ironically the Tennessee State Library and Archives was only a few city blocks from Owsley's office on the Vanderbilt campus. Housed in it was a rare and useful collection of primary source materials relating to the southern poor, yeomen, and planters—the Civil War Veterans Questionnaires.

Speaking before a special panel on Civil War historiography at the Organization of American Historians meeting in 1972, Eric Foner complained that "non-slaveholding whites are the least studied of all our social classes." The time had arrived, he admonished, for historians to "take a new look at the social and economic structure of the Old South." Two years later, Eugene D. Genovese echoed this challenge in an address before the Agricultural History Society's convention in Denver, Colorado. He hoped soon to see "a new wave of research" that would "pay close attention to the fundamental cultural as well as economic cleavages that separated the farmers of the up country from those of the plantation belt." Genovese urged historians to emulate those scholars who had recently studied another group of southern inarticulates—the slaves.[49]

Genovese had in mind recent explorations of the Works Progress Administration slave narratives. As one of the government-sponsored make-work projects of the Depression decade, young men and women were sent out to interview aging southern blacks about their slave experiences. Several historians—among them Genovese, John W. Blassingame, Paul Escott, and Leon Litwack—have explored the interviews in a rewarding effort to understand the peculiar institution from the slave's perspective.[50] Just as a careful analysis of these materials has shed light on antebellum race relations, a judicious study of Tennessee's Civil War Veterans Questionnaires can produce a model for interpreting the dynamics of nineteenth-century white social structure.

Blanche Clark, one of Owsley's students, briefly touched on these questionnaires in her study, *Tennessee Yeomen, 1840–1860*, but she emphasized that she employed them only "to give life to the dry figures of . . . Census statistics." While working on her dissertation, which was completed in 1938, Clark spent over a year scouring the Tennessee State Library and Archives for tax records and agricultural statistics. Only near the end of Clark's research did Emily Moore, now director of the library, inquire whether she might be aware of the questionnaires. Anxious to complete her project, Clark surveyed the records but did not make an extensive analysis of them. She did indeed refer to them in eight pages of her first chapter; however, she made little effort to distinguish between the social status or geographic location of the subjects. Although she acknowledged that the veterans expressed some discontent, she dismissed it as "a feeling of inferiority on the part of the poor man" and the snobbery of "the owners of one or two slaves." In the pages that followed her brief treatment of the questionnaires, Clark assumed that Tennessee's rural population possessed a unity of purpose. "As diverse as [the] various classes of the farming group may have been," she wrote, "there was one great bond holding them together: . . . the desire to improve the economic and social status of members of the agricultural population." After reviewing editorials in farming periodicals, speeches made at agricultural fairs, and articles in the public press, she concluded that wealthy slaveholding landowners "were considering the interests of the agricultural population as a whole, rather than those of their own particular class."[51] In common with both the antebellum planters and Frank L. Owsley, Clark assumed that the poor whites, the yeomen, and the planters shared a spirit of cultural solidarity.

Although most antebellum Tennesseans engaged in agriculture or related activities, class distinctions were more pronounced than the Owsley school assumed. Planters, plain folk, and the poor often occupied the same neighborhoods, but their social patterns were vastly different. Wealth, education, and family connections enabled southern elites to move in much wider circles than other whites. Given these advantages, Tennessee's planters and professionals (attorneys, physicians, academy teachers, and merchants) were vitally concerned with the defense of a southern culture based upon the peculiar institution. These were the important people. They fought the political battles, wrote the proslavery polemics, and defined the popular image of the South. Their community extended far beyond the confines of their immediate neighborhoods, and, in 1861, their united self-interest caused them to lead their fellow Southerners into a bloody confrontation with the North.

The fellow Southerners were primarily small landholders and non-slaveowning tenant farmers. Their worldview was much more restricted than that of their more affluent contemporaries. Lacking extensive formal educations and relying on subsistence agriculture for a living, the poor and the plain folk concentrated on the immediate needs of their families and their close friends. The broader worlds of commerce or state and national politics rarely intruded upon their daily routines. They were largely undisturbed by the nation-splitting debates over slavery and states' rights, focusing instead upon such community interests as crops, marriages, births, baptisms, and deaths. The emotional crisis of the Civil War soon gave southern nonelites a taste of the larger world's cruelties. The bitter truths of amputations, of dead comrades, and of impoverished wives and children made the poor and the plain folk painfully aware that their needs were in fundamental conflict with those of the planters and professionals. Class resentment resulted.

The composite story of these men who fought for the Confederate cause falls short of a "true history of the Old South." Modern scholarship recognizes the impossibility of writing an irrefutable account of the past. Certainly these men's testimonies contradict the "true history" envisioned by southern apologists. Nonetheless, the work begun by Gustavus W. Dyer and John Trotwood Moore has provided us with unique insights into the lifestyles and social attitudes of Old South Tennesseans.

CHAPTER TWO

★ ★

BROAD DISTINCTIONS OF SOCIAL CLASS

Tennessee's Confederate generation was conscious of the social differences that characterized the Old South. "There was a distinction and a *broad* one between the slave owners and others that had to do there own work," reflected Meriwether Donaldson in his Civil War Veterans Questionnaire. As he recalled, "there was quite an aristocratic spirit with most of the slave owners." Donaldson's father owned fifteen slaves. The sons of other and larger slaveowners also stressed class differentiations. John W. Wade lectured that "there is always some degrees in Society." Before the Civil War, he explained, "all were treated politely, but all did not move in the exact same circle." The son of a Maury County attorney with thirty slaves disdainfully remembered "a class of 'poor whites' . . . who hated those who owned any Kind of property." Veterans from less ostentatious origins shared a similar awareness of social discriminations. A Hawkins County brick mason's son wrote that slaveowners and nonslaveowners "went to the same Church and School, But Still didn't assoate with one another as they should"; a Monroe County small farmer's son complained that "all who owned as much as one negro seemed to feel that they were in a separate and higher class than the common people."[1]

Although there obviously were social distinctions in the Old South, historians nonetheless have had difficulty assessing the variations in lifestyle among the white poor, the yeomen farmers, and the affluent planters and professionals. The responses of Tennessee veterans to the questionnaires provide a canvas on which an analysis can be sketched. Although conditions varied from community to community and from region to region within the state, these materials supply a picture of three distinctive orientations. As a rule, each neighborhood was populated by the poor—largely landless farm tenants, propertyless artisans, and laborers without significant assets; by small farmers—landowners with or without slaves; and by planters and professionals—whose wealth, education, and family connections enabled them to move in wide social circles.

Differences in family wealth dramatically demonstrated the variation in lifestyles between the social classes. The Civil War Veterans Questionnaires requested old soldiers to estimate their fathers' personal assets. Among the poor, farm tenants possessed a median wealth of only $160, while impoverished blacksmiths and carpenters had personal assets of $0 and $300, respectively. Property owners were somewhat better off. The median wealth of nonslaveowning farmers was $1,000; of blacksmiths, $2,000; and of slaveowning yeomen and of carpenters, $4,000 each. Not surprisingly, planters and professionals had access to far greater capital. Physicians and merchants had a median wealth of $20,000 each, while attorneys were a little more comfortable at $30,000 each. Slave-rich planters were the most affluent of all, with a median wealth of $40,000 (Appendix 2, table 3). These figures demonstrate that antebellum Tennessee's resources were not evenly distributed. As a result, a tremendous social gulf separated the poor, who inhabited meager log hovels, and the rich, who resided in magnificent frame mansions.

Housing was the most visible symbol of class distinction in antebellum Tennessee. The quality of a dwelling indicated its owners' status in the community, their lifestyle, and the boundaries of their future expectations. The lives and worldviews of the poor and the yeoman classes were circumscribed by their limited physical surroundings. Their concerns centered around daily chores and seasonal activities; they were only vaguely aware of the world beyond their immediate geographic areas. Planters moved in wider circles, made possible by their affluence and education and manifested in their large frame mansions and the freedom from manual labor that slaveownership gave them.

Naturally the poor occupied the least desirable houses. As day laborers and tenants, they existed on the economic fringes of society. Francis Arnold wrote that his father, typical of this class, was "a renter and moved a great deal"; William Mays explained that his father "moved from place to place"; and William Archer testified that his family "lived at different places generly [in] one room log House[s]."[2]

The landless poor had neither the long-term interests nor the financial resources to improve their dwellings. Ninety-two percent of them inhabited crude log cabins and these characteristically contained no more than one, two, or three rooms (Appendix 2, tables 4 and 5). Their houses offered few comforts. Dirt floors and structurally hazardous "stick and dirt chimneys" denoted indigent circumstances. Within these cabins, wives prepared meals over open fireplaces—doubtless making them unbearable during summer's merciless heat and humidity. J. R. Miles vividly invoked the squalor surrounding destitute Tennesseans. In Weakley County, he and his mother struggled to survive in a "log Shack two Rooms with . . . cracks you could run your hands in."[3] Wesley Sheets's childhood home of brick would appear inconsistent with poverty, but his family demonstrated another aspect of the poor's marginal lifestyle. A landless blacksmith with ten children, Sheets's father maintained the brick house for its absentee landlord and was allowed to remain there as long as he paid its taxes. When the parents died, the house reverted to its owner.[4]

As landowners the small farmers, or yeoman class, lived in more substantial dwellings than did the poor. To be sure, the vast majority of nonslaveowners (78 percent) and a small majority of slaveowners (55 percent) constructed log cabins (Appendix 2, table 4). These structures usually contained two, three, or four rooms, plank floors, and relatively safe rock or brick chimneys (Appendix 2, table 5).[5] Several veterans described features characteristic of fairly stable construction. John Bittick proudly wrote that he grew up in a "four room double log house [composed of] Logs nicely hewn"; and Thomas Hightower noted with satisfaction that he was born in a house with "logs . . . hune very smoothe [where] the cracks [were] chinked and daubed with lime morter and [the] daubing was white washed."[6] Because kitchens were usually housed in a building separate from the main dwelling, yeomen enjoyed both the luxury of homes that were not overheated in summer, and the security of knowing that a cooking accident would result in only modest damage.[7] Despite some minor comforts, however, yeomen's homes were generally overcrowded. For example, the son of a McNairy County small slaveowner shared a two-room cabin with his parents and eleven siblings.[8]

Those who possessed a few slaves could often afford extra luxuries in their houses. Some slaveowning yeomen added frame extensions to their original cabins, others placed weatherboard veneer over their unadorned logs, and still others occupied unpretentious frame cottages (Appendix 2, table 4). Joseph Marshall's home in Williamson County illustrated how a plain log cabin could be expanded into a substantial dwelling. The initial building consisted of two log rooms built one on top of the other. In time a separate third room was constructed and then connected to the original by a roof to form a passage or "dogtrot." Later Marshall's father enclosed the passage, weatherboarded the structure, and built a frame addition. The completed house contained eight large rooms.[9] Although few slaveowning yeomen lived in as much comfort as the Marshalls, their houses were of considerably higher quality than those of yeomen without slaves.

The top caste of the social and economic structure—the wealthy—resided in relative opulence. Fifty-five percent lived in frame or brick mansions and 22 percent owned log buildings with either weatherboarding or frame additions (Appendix 2, table 4). John Osborne, whose father held twenty-two slaves and five thousand acres in Roane County, described his house as a brick structure "full two stories nine rooms [with] wide halls upstairs and down, wide porches back and front [and] full basement and attic." Thomas Neil boasted that his father's frame, eight-room house in Meigs County was "considered among the best in those days." Other affluent veterans pictured their habitations in succinct but descriptive terms. In Hardeman County, Christopher Robertson resided in "a seven room two story frame house"; in Rutherford County, Evander Lytle lived in a "large brick house—9 rooms"; and in Giles County, John R. McClelland's family owned a "Colonial, Frame—8 rooms."[10] Even those affluents whose domiciles were constructed of log inhabited impressive buildings. "We lived in a hewed poplar log house with four rooms and a 16 foot hall," recalled a small planter's son. "It had a rock fire place to each room. The house was weatherboarded, lathed and plastered and had ceder shingles."[11]

Despite the fact that living space was at a premium in antebellum cities, wealthy urbanites also lived in grand style. Day laborers, artisans, and clerks had to reside within walking distance of their employment and they crowded together on tiny city lots. Financially comfortable professionals, however, were able to avoid the miseries of overcrowding. In Bristol a prominent merchant's son, John N. Johnson, grew up in an "8 Room Frame dwelling [with] the kitchen[,] smoke house and servants quarters . . . of Brick . . . located in the

Yard." Relatives of Confederate General Thomas C. Hindman described the family's antebellum home as "a large brick residence on a plot of about five acres on what is now the principal street of Knoxville." In Nashville, Marcus Toney's parents retained three slaves to keep up his small estate in the Edgefield community; and in Memphis, Thomas Webb's family required ten slaves to maintain their seven-room frame house on Union Street.[12] Surrounded by slaves and pleasant gardens, the urban upper classes were isolated from the social blight surrounding them.

A few of the most affluent owned more than one habitation. Some in this category were aristocrats with several far-flung plantations, and others were professionals who owned both urban and rural dwellings. James A. Carnes owned a house and other property in Memphis and also had extensive landholdings in two Mississippi counties; William and Hewitt Witherspoon testified that their father kept up a ten-room frame mansion on their Madison County estate and a smaller six-room frame dwelling on their Arkansas lands; and John A. Pickard's father supervised his sixty slaves and his one thousand Maury County acres alternately from his frame country mansion and his brick town house in Columbia. James Sims of White County and Gideon Baskett of Rutherford County came from families of professionals with multiple abodes. Sims's father usually occupied an eight-room brick house next to his cotton mill, but he occasionally visited his more modest five-room log house, situated on his 1,500-acre farm. Baskett's father was a physician who owned fifteen slaves. His family divided its time between a substantial frame domicile in the rural district and a two-story brick house in Murfreesboro.[13]

Log hovels, small cabins, and great mansions punctuated the Tennessee landscape. Within their walls, some families subsisted in hopeless desperation, and others developed impressive aspirations. Each class contributed to the whole of Tennessee's culture, but each class did not prosper equally in society's rewards.

Tennessee's landless poor were cognizant of their disadvantaged condition. Slavery restricted their opportunities for employment and depressed their wages. "Them that was able had slaves to work," wrote the impoverished Robert Lankey, "but the poor class of People was al most slaves them selves. [They] had to work hard and live hard." Naturally this class accumulated few material possessions. In Monroe County, Daniel Webster explained that his family "owned Very little probly two ere three Hosses and a Cow or two"; and in

Jackson County, James B. West testified that his father had "nothing more than a milk cow." West emphasized: "we was very poor."[14] Lankey, Webster, and West were all part of Tennessee's large marginal population.

Among nonslaveowners on the eve of the Civil War, 45 percent of East Tennesseans, 40 percent of Middle Tennesseans, and 43 percent of West Tennesseans were landless, according to estimates made by Frank and Harriet Owsley.[15] The Owsleys concentrated their attention upon the landed majority and virtually ignored the sizable class that possessed neither land nor slaves. In every community, large numbers of families were dispossessed. Just who were they; and what was their perception of their place in the social order?

Thinking back on his youth in Williamson County, J. J. McCoy summarized the plight of his social class: "All my people have been very poor folk, [we] lived any where that we could get work." The little employment available provided only meager remuneration. "Wages [were] so low," complained Isaac Grimes, "I have worked . . . for $5.00 . . . a month and board." Other impoverished veterans recalled that laborers were fortunate to earn between twenty-five and fifty cents per day. As James Hodge of McNairy County observed: "$12.00 per month was considered High."[16]

Landless farmers lacked the economic and social independence that property afforded. They depended on the toleration and the patronage of large landowners who could always threaten to replace renters with slaves. "My father farmed some at home on rented land," recalled Robert Bayless, but he "also worked away from home for the land lord upon whose property we lived."[17] Other destitute Tennesseans were unable to rent and sought out whatever employment existed. Among these, George Payne's father was a "Day laborer"; Samuel Reynolds's father "lived at Publick works"; and J. T. Killen's father taught school. Although teachers might be considered a social and economic cut above others in the impoverished class, the elder Killen and those like him probably had few pedagogical skills. Despite his father's occupation, J. T. Killen reported, "I didnt have much schooling."[18] Whatever their economic pursuits, most of the state's poor could empathize with Julius C. Martin's lament: "We wer poor [and] we made our living by hard toil."[19]

Such conditions led indigent old soldiers to express class resentments. "A renter had no chance to save anything," remonstrated William Beard. "Slave holders were the only men that could make enough money to do anything." William Eskew complained that "Thire was no chance for a young poor man for his wages was so low. . . . [He was] discouraged by the Slaveholders." George Payne even accused the planter class of keeping the poor down "so they could make slaves of them," and A. J. Ferrell wrote with bitterness: "If [the wealthy] had not owned slaves a working man as I . . . could have secured better wages."[20]

Denied access to Tennessee's two major sources of wealth—land and slaves—the white poor lost out in the powerful laws of supply and demand. Unable to compete economically with black slavery, farm tenants and day laborers sank into the social background; they were largely ignored by both the yeomen, who toiled for survival, and the planters, who worked for riches.

Tennessee's yeoman class possessed an intense spirit of economic independence. James Walker boasted that his people were "working folks not office seakers nor preachers, lawyers[,] Doctors nor traders"; and Constantine Nance praised his father as "an energetic industrious farmer who reared a family of 12 children according to the injunction 'owe no man anything.'" In antebellum Bedford County, Flavius S. Lander's rural upbringing epitomized this autonomous disposition. "My Father was a man of all work," bragged the aged veteran. He "done his own carpenter work, [constructed] his own plows[,] made all the family shoes[,] . . . made his own grain cradles and made the first Buggy he ever owned."[21] Surrounded by his kin and familiar neighbors, the average yeoman was largely interested in his immediate community. He existed in a limited sphere, concerned with little more than enduring from one generation to the next.

The typical farmer managed between 100 and 250 acres. He, and often his entire family, were in the fields from sunrise to sunset. Each season had its demanding tasks; but the farmer usually measured his year from the springtime. Early in that season, he commenced the important job of plowing the land and planting corn, oats, and cotton. Hour after hour, throughout March and April, the yeoman followed his horse, mule, or ox over miles of broken earth. For the most part, Tennesseans employed only the bull-tongue plow, which had the advantage of cutting deeply into the soil but could not adequately turn or break the ground. Thus fields had to be crossed several times before the soil was sufficiently prepared.[22] Breaking new ground was especially unpleasant. Looking back on antebellum life, James Anthony testified that as a boy in Franklin County he frequently cultivated land full of roots and stumps. Many times, he complained, "have my shins been beaten blue by roots breaking and flying back."[23]

At April's end, the young corn, cotton, and oat plants pushed their way out of the soil, creating new chores. All during May and June, the farmer, his wife, and their children waged a campaign against threatening weeds in the cotton and corn fields. Oats and wheat were harvested in June. The ripe wheat, which had been sown the previous fall, allowed the farmers but a few days for gathering before the mature heads fell to the ground. The task required a cradle. This tool, which consisted of a long, slightly curved handle, a round blade, and a small container to receive the wheat stalks, enabled the farmer to both clip and bundle the sheaves with a single sweeping motion. Young family members then took the wheat sheaves to a cleared ground, where horses and other livestock threshed the grain by trampling over it until the outer covering, or chaff, broke away from the desired kernels. After several hours, the farmer removed the crushed, useless stalks and then completed the threshing by tossing shovelfuls of chaff and kernels into the air. A slight breeze separated the two, as the heavier kernels fell to the ground. Quickly bagged, these were ready for processing into flour by the local miller.[24] In much the same manner, and at about the same time, oats were also harvested and threshed. Set aside, they provided fodder for horses and mules.

July marked an important turning point in the yeoman's routine. About then the corn and cotton crops were "laid-by," and for the next two months the fields required little attention. Jeptha Fuston explained that in his Warren County community, farmers tried to finish their crop preparations in time for "the Baptist annual foot-washing," which took place the first Sunday in July.[25]

The lay-by season was far from an idle period. While younger children attended a few fleeting weeks of school, the farmer, his older sons, and—if he possessed any—his slaves, prepared for the coming winter. Day after day, they wielded axes and saws against large oaks and hickories. Once stripped of their limbs, these trees were dragged to a spot near the cabin, where they remained until they were cut into fire logs in the fall. The yeoman labored constantly, collecting and bundling corn leaves for animal fodder, repairing farm equipment, and attending to the ever-present chores that characterized subsistence agriculture. To be sure, this was a less demanding season than spring. In July and August, the yeoman frequently took time to fish and hunt small game, to visit neighbors, and to attend the numerous revivals held by the Methodist, Baptist, and Christian churches.

Intense activities resumed in early fall. Between the end of September and the hard freezes of mid-December, the farmer had to accomplish a number of vital jobs. Cotton picking required his children to abandon their studies and to assist their parents. Lacking the planter's large slave labor force, which made it possible to grow cotton as a cash crop, most yeomen grew only enough of the fiber for their own clothing. The majority of small farmers gained any surplus income from pigs. Throughout much of the year, the animals ran loose in the woods, grubbing acorns and other edibles. As the fall season approached, the yeoman collected his pigs and herded them into a fenced-off portion of his corn field. This benefitted the farmer in two ways: first, the hogs happily fattened themselves and saved the farmer the labor of gathering and hauling a part of his corn crop; and second, the animals' droppings fertilized the ground, preparing it for another season's planting.[26]

After apportioning a few pigs for breeding and selecting others for the family table, the farmer sold what remained to the hog drivers. These rustic entrepreneurs pierced the crisp fall air with their shouts and songs as they escorted swine herds across the mountains into Virginia, North Carolina, or Georgia, or down to the river ports of Clarksville, Savannah, or Memphis. Back on the farm, hog killing was an especially memorable day. The advent of cold weather in late November or early December sealed the pig's fate. Slaughtered, its hams, chops, ribs, and sausage provided the family's chief source of domesticated meat.[27]

The fall season afforded little time for recreation. As soon as possible, the family gathered the balance of the corn crop. They selected the best ears for seed corn, set aside the next best for the table and for milling into meal, and stored the remainder in the corncrib for the hogs. Once this chore was completed, the farmer again brought out his bull-tongue plow. After breaking up the ground, he sowed the wheat crop in anticipation of next June's harvest. As frigid weather approached, the farmer and his sons attacked the large oaks and hickories that had been cut in July and August. The brisk autumn air provided relief as their bucksaws whittled trees into small logs.

Although winter slowed the pace of labor on the farm, it also had its distinctive tasks. Because the weather was often too wet or too cold for outdoor work, the yeoman turned to tedious indoor projects. He spent hours carefully removing seed corn from its cob, he helped his wife and children separate seed from cotton fiber, and he aided his spouse in carding and spinning thread from cotton, wool, or flax fibers. One of the husband's main winter duties was making the family's shoes.[28] Any break in the weather allowed the farmer to venture outdoors. Barns and other outbuildings needed repairs, fences required upkeep, and almost invariably additional firewood had to be procured. Still winter had its more enjoyable periods. While warming themselves beside the hearth, families broke the season's monotony by roasting tasty corn ears or baking sweet potatoes. "In winter," reminisced Isaac Griffith of Scott County, "wee had Lots of Funn makeing maple sugar. Wee made Lots of it."[29]

A few chores demanded constant, year-round attention. The cow had to be milked, eggs gathered, water drawn, and, from time to time, young pigs castrated. The last was necessary to prevent a gamy taste when the mature hogs were slaughtered. All though the year, the yeoman family struggled for simple survival. The farmer did not possess the leisure time to consider abstract issues that had small meaning to his daily existence. A sweating plowman had little interest in the morality of slavery or the constitutional validity of states' rights. His principal concern was his family's continuance.

While the common Tennessee farmer was largely self-sufficient, his community included a number of other important people. Each neighborhood contained millers, blacksmiths, carpenters, tanners, and other artisans. In some parts of the state, the yeoman also had to contend with wealthy planters, whose ownership of large numbers of slaves and emphasis upon commercial agriculture conflicted with his needs.

When he had accumulated sufficient grain, the farmer sent his wheat or corn to the local miller. Every community had a small grist mill powered by waterwheel or by horse, and there the farmer traded a portion of his crop in return for having it ground into flour or meal. As the mill was often several miles from the yeoman's cabin, so that a single trip required the better portion of a day, younger family members generally were assigned to go there. Looking back on his boyhood in Gile County, David Bodenhamer recalled that he traveled four miles on horseback precariously juggling a sack of grain. "I would sit on the small end [of the sack] trying to keep it balanced," he wrote, "but the heavy end continued to give until the sack would fall off." He then waited impatiently for the appearance of an adult with the strength to lift the sack back onto the horse. Little wonder that Saturday trips to the mill were among the least favorite memories of many Old South youths.[30]

In a society that esteemed craft more than book knowledge, the blacksmith was a most respected citizen. Working with hammers, forge, and anvil, he constructed those tools that the average farmer could not make for himself. F. M. Copeland wrote that his father "did neighborhood blacksmith work, such as making nails, hoes, plows, and shoeing horses"; and Joe Rich recalled that his father "would make . . . and lay plows, make wagons and carts, . . . etc."[31]

The carpenter, another respected artisan, literally shaped the common Tennessean's culture. The carpenter felled his own trees and then employed his saws, hammers, and chisels to construct a wide variety of artifacts. In his questionnaire, Demarus Cunningham wrote with pride that, in Lincoln County, his father crafted all types of furniture including tables, cupboards, bedsteads, bureaus, and coffins out of "cherry and walnut timbers." In Madison County, James Dickinson's father specialized in spinning wheels, looms, and wagons.[32]

Because the farmer relied upon leather for many uses, the community valued the tanner's vocation. Not only was his product used in making shoes, but it was also needed for straps, whips, harnesses, and bridles. Normally a farmer traded with the tanner, giving him two raw hides for one side of leather. The artisan removed animal hair from the hide with lime. He then stacked the raw skins in a vat about four or five feet deep, alternating each skin with a layer of red oak chips. When the layers were covered with water and sealed for twelve months, the glue oozed from the skins, turning them into leather. The tanner completed his project by scraping the leather to a uniform thickness and blackening the fleshy side. Of necessity his shop reeked with foul odors; few people lingered there.[33]

Farmers, millers, blacksmiths, carpenters, and tanners formed a largely self-sufficient community. The yeoman traveled infrequently beyond his immediate environs, and only rarely did the issues and debates of the outside world intrude into his life. The broader spheres of commercial agriculture, southern literary endeavors, and politics were the domain of another group of Tennesseans—the slave-rich planters and professionals.

Affluence set the planters apart from all others. They owned the finest lands and possessed the slaves to cultivate them. Speaking of his father's 500 acres in Wilson County, John B. Masterson observed: "We were well fixed and could have sold the place for $60 per acre[.] We had lots of stock and plenty of hands to work it." In much the same manner, Thomas Yancey noted that his father's 400-acre estate in Gibson County "was Considered one of the finest in the country[.] I expect he could get 50 or 60 dollrs an Acre for it." James Sims had difficulty assessing the worth of his parents' 1,500 acres. "I have no

Idea what the value would be," he explained, but he crudely estimated that "it would amount to a great big pile."[34]

While the yeomen plowed their own land, the planters directed others in their physical toil. "Father 'managed' the farm," wrote William Johnston, "and negroes did the work." Other veterans gave virtually the same testimony. "My father had no time nor necessity for physical labor," recalled a Fayette County planter's son, "but [he] was . . . a very humane master and an exemplary christian." In Maury County, Andrew Webster candidly admitted that his father employed "good overseers [and spent] most of his time fishing and hunting"; and in Lincoln County, Louis Bledsoe rather cryptically observed: "Dad didn't do anything but hunt in the barns."[35]

The more prominent planters often traveled among their various plantations. Although each farm was under the immediate supervision of an overseer, the landed aristocrat felt compelled to make his presence known. Newton Cannon noted that his father hired a white man to manage each of his two farms in Tennessee and his 1,200-acre estate in Bolivar County, Mississippi. "He supervised all of them," the son explained, "seeing that the crops were properly tended[,] fences and houses repaired[,] etc." Every fall F. A. Turner's father left his 1,000 acres near Murfreesboro "to see after his Miss. Farm"; and Benjamin Hawkins's uncle and guardian was seldom at home because he was "busy overseeing his different farms and trading in negroes."[36]

These affluent Tennesseans often placed a high value on the leisure lifestyle. Reflecting on his father's patrician status in Fayette County, Joshua Mewborn boasted: "We were as good *as anybody* and had carte blanc in [the] best society famed for its high standard of morals[,] its culture, education and wealth." He also added: "We had some snobs [and] idle rich." Lee Billingsley agreed. "For ten or fifteen years just before the [Civil] war," he affirmed, "the larger land-and-slave-owners did not reguard manual labor as respectable for a gentleman." Robert Rogers was equally blunt. In his West Tennessee community, most large landowners "had slaves and hired overseers and took their ease."[37] Looking back on these circumstances, a non-slaveowning yeoman wrote that "a feeling of timidity" kept the laboring classes "somewhat aloof from the idle Rich."[38]

While some of the wealthy freely discussed their freedom from physical toil, others were more defensive. Although they admitted that slavery exempted them from manual labor, they also argued that it allowed them to pursue higher callings. "All [large slaveowners] were busy as Professional men or superintending their business," in-

sisted John Bell Tate of Wilson County.[39] Tennessee professionals—
attorneys, physicians, merchants, and academy teachers—maintained
a lifestyle and a social position that closely paralleled that of the
planters. Just as the miller, the blacksmith, the carpenter, and the
tanner were important auxiliaries to the yeoman farmer, the antebellum professionals provided vital services for the planter class. These
elites were integrated into a social whole whose worldview and expectations were notably different from that of the plowman.

Although the professional class rarely owned significant numbers
of slaves, the peculiar institution provided them with a comfortable
lifestyle. "As we lived in the city," pointed out a Nashville merchant's
son, "there was no necessity to own many slaves."[40] According to
information gleaned from the Civil War Veterans Questionnaires,
merchants owned a median of six slaves, and attorneys and physicians possessed a median of ten each (Appendix 2, table 6). Like the
planters, professionals could afford leisure. Writing about his father,
a Dyer County physician with six slaves, Gentry McGee explained: "I
never saw him do any manual labor except to plow and hoe the garden, and prune fruit trees; this he allowed no one else to do." The
same was true of a DeKalb County merchant with eight adult slaves.
"My father never done any plowing," reported John Fite. "He was
very fond of his garden and did a lot of hoeing in that."[41]

Attorneys, physicians, merchants, and academy teachers relied on
the patronage of the planter class. Because plantation owners were
often engaged in purchasing and selling land, slaves, and crops, they
valued an attorney's counsel. Deeds, contracts, and legal disputes
were an integral part of upper-class life. Furthermore Tennessee patricians wanted to perpetuate their families' wealth and influence
from one generation to the next. Lawyers helped by drawing up
trusts, executing wills, and establishing guardianships for minors.
Not surprisingly, most attorneys, as well as other professionals, came
from well-to-do backgrounds. Lewis Burchette McFarland, the son
of a physician and planter with twenty-five slaves, fondly recalled
the gentle chiding received after he made his career determination. "When I left Haywood [County]," he explained, the neighbors
"were afraid 'Burchette would spoil a good Farmer to make a poor
lawyer.'"[42]

Although antebellum physicians served the entire community, they
were especially solicitous of the planters. Few Tennesseans could afford a doctor's services. Most yeomen relied on folk remedies to combat their illnesses, and they turned to the medical profession under
only the most dire circumstances—to set a broken bone or to ampu-

tate a gangrenous limb.[43] On the other hand, the affluent not only possessed the financial means to secure medical care for their white families, but they also retained the doctor to look after their slaves. Despite his comfortable existence, the physician's duties were often characterized by hard work and self-sacrifice. During one prolonged epidemic in Middle Tennessee, Samuel Whitsitt reported that his father labored "for about 30 days without taking his clothing off."[44]

Merchants also relied heavily upon the planter's patronage. According to available account books, Tennessee merchants dispensed to the small farmer little more than whiskey, coffee, salt, sugar, tobacco products, painkillers (especially opium), and candy. Most transactions were on credit and barter was a frequent form of payment. C. Y. Gray, who managed an establishment near Union City, accepted in compensation such items as fruit, fish, and eggs. Under a ledger entry dated 9 December 1858, he noted that a customer by the name of Bloods North resolved his balance through "credit by work—$3.75."[45] In contrast to the yeoman, wealthy planters and professionals were able to indulge their taste for such commercial goods as manufactured cloth, furniture, firearms, and books. Not surprisingly, the country store became a social focal point for large land owners. Growing up in a Giles County village grocery, Edwin Gardner remembered that the planters hired overseers to do their work, which allowed them the freedom "to dine with the town people" and to "discuss politics, etc."[46]

Academy teachers were well-respected members of the planter community. Every county had one or more fairly substantial schools, housed in impressive brick or frame structures. There the planter's children received an education far superior to that provided for lesser whites. The instructors at such institutions were usually college trained and community spirited. James D. Jackson's son wrote that his father was not only an excellent academy teacher, but also was honored as "a good writer[,] a temperance speaker[,] a member of the Methodist Church and a full blooded democrat."[47]

The affluent also had more time to devote to politics. To be sure, an occasional yeoman held a civic office, but for the most part, community leaders came from higher economic backgrounds. They often exercised their influence for decades. Thomas Porter's father served as Maury County sheriff for twenty-four years, and Lee Billingsley's father was a justice of the peace for twenty-four years in Bledsoe County. The citizens of slave-rich Montgomery County retained their magistrates for significant tenures. Edward S. Bringhurst's father "was Mayor of Clarksville two or three times"; James

Nesbitt's father was a member of the county court for forty years; and Hervey Whitfield's father was elected county court chairman at age twenty-one and retained that post until his death sixteen years later.[48] Other elites were elevated to more important positions. Among them the fathers of James Carringer, James McNeilly, and James Warner served in the Tennessee General Assembly from the counties of Claiborne, Dickson, and Marshall.[49] James Monroe Jones proudly wrote that his father, Calvin Jones, was "Chancellor of the Western District of Tenn—1847–48"; and Arthur Deadrick recorded that his father, James William Deadrick, was elected to the "State Senate about 1852," then became "a member of the Supreme Court of Tennessee," and was eventually appointed chief justice.[50]

Often those of the wealthy whose fathers were not officeholders lived in families that were politically well connected. Nathaniel Harris was the son of a prominent Jonesboro physician. One of his paternal uncles served in the Tennessee legislature, Confederate Governor Isham G. Harris was a distant kinsman, and a maternal uncle was elected to the Confederate Senate. After the Civil War, Nathaniel Harris moved to Georgia, became politically active, and eventually served a single term as governor (1915–17). Two maternal cousins— Alf and Bob Taylor—became governors of Tennessee. John Hickman's ancestors were also influential. His father was a wealthy attorney whose political ambitions were crushed by an injury that left him paralyzed for thirty-eight years. Hickman's great-grandfather, Robert Weakley, fought as a colonel in the American Revolution and later represented Tennessee in the U.S. Congress. His maternal grandfather was the eminent Cave Johnson, who, after eighteen years in Congress, became the U.S. Postmaster General under President James K. Polk.[51]

A combination of slaves, wealth, education, and family connections gave planters and professionals options not available to Tennessee's poor and yeomen. Some enjoyed their leisure, others strove to increase their fortunes, and still others dedicated themselves to community and civic affairs. Whatever their approach to life, these were the men who led Tennessee out of the Union in 1861, who provided its officer corps, and who, in the years following Confederate defeat, saw their sons move into prominence in the New South.

Social distinctions were especially intense among Tennessee women. Often stranded on isolated farms and plantations, wives and mothers experienced prolonged periods of loneliness and depression. Their work was tedious and largely devoid of gratification.

From the wealthy to the impoverished, their domestic routines required weaving cloth from cotton, flax, and wool; sewing it into coats, dresses, and trousers; cooking meals over open fires; milking cows; feeding chickens; and much more. The hard labor was supplemented by the discomforts of repeated pregnancies, the demands of young children, and the intense agonies of gynecological irregularities.

Quantifiable differences existed in women's lifestyles. According to information found in the Civil War Veterans Questionnaires, 93 percent of impoverished wives and 88 percent of other nonslaveowning wives performed their own chores. In addition, 4 percent of the poor women hired out to other families and 10 percent of the nonslaveowning yeomen employed either free or unfree labor to assist their spouses. Given the drudgery of women's duties on antebellum farms, slaveowners usually directed one or more blacks to work with their wives. Sixty-seven percent of the small slaveholders and 90 percent of the wealthy kept domestic servants. In both classes, 2 percent of the families hired others to help with household tasks (Appendix 2, table 7).

Most nonslaveowning women—poor and yeoman—contributed to the family's self-sufficiency. Their lives were focused on each day's momentary concerns. Week by week and season by season, their activities varied little. Although a bit sentimental, Harrison Farrell's account of his mother describes what was probably a typical woman's routine:

> Mothers duty as a farmers Wife [was] to Keep the house in good order [She did] the cooking . . . the washing and Scouring. The children [were] Kept in order. . . . She carded and spon Wool and cotton she would make cloth of Several Kinds . . . Plain cloth for sheets for Beds and Blankets. she made several kinds of jeans and then she made What was called sister cloth the Best of all to wear. . . . she made quilts and fine pleted Bossom shirts With her hands. . . . when the crop got behind and needed work she would take us children out. . . . she would hoe [and] make us Pull Weeds. . . . Sunday she would fix us [and go to the church] meeting you might hear her sing one mile, But [now] mother [is] gone to a Better world than This.[52]

From the scores of shorter discussions of their mothers' lives contributed by other veterans, it is clear that the nonslaveowning woman's experience was one of almost unmixed toil. In addition to her other activities, C. W. Hicks's mother daily "milked two or three cows, raised the chickens, [and] carried water 100 yards" to the house. Benjamin Swafford remembered that his mother "worked by fire blaze till late Bedtime every winter Knight to make close for the family."[53]

Impoverished wives sometimes worked outside the home to add to the family income. In Maury County, William Aydelott's mother served as a midwife; in Lincoln County, Charlie Blackwell's mother "cut and made Clothes for the Family and for other People"; and in Dickson County, John Welch's mother would weave cloth for other women. No doubt, in Tennessee's tradition-bound culture, seeing the wife and mother leave her family to serve beyond the home was a difficult adjustment for both husband and children. A strong hint of resentment appeared in Samuel Reynolds's bitter lament that his mother "Sode for the Rich Peeple."[54]

Unlike the poor, a few fortunate nonslaveowning farmers were able to employ domestics. "My mother superintended the house work, haveing . . . a negro woman hired to help her," wrote a Middle Tennessee yeoman. The Kirkham family of Grainger County retained "no regular servants [but] occasionally [secured] some woman or girl to assist . . . in [the] busy season or illness"; and the Sullins family in McMinn County "usually hired a colored man and his wife from [the] slave holders."[55] Nonetheless, most nonslaveowning women relied on their own families for support. The questionnaire respondents reported that their sisters usually aided their mothers, and they frequently admitted that they were also impressed to do household chores. "We boys took our turn in the kitchen," testified Jeptha Fuston, "as well as bed making, sweeping, etc. I spun, spooled, filled quills and carded bats."[56] Lacking slave labor in the fields and in the house, the yeoman family used all its resources to survive.

These yeomen who possessed slaves generally assigned one or more to assist their spouses. This help rarely freed the wife from all of her responsibilities, but at least it exempted her from the most odious tasks. Samuel Adams's mother left the weaving of cloth to her slave, James Shofner's mother "kept a cook most of the time," and Powhatan Pullen's mother relied on "a girl to take care of the Baby." While the ownership of a few slaves relieved yeoman wives from some domestic burdens, it failed to give them a lifestyle equivalent to that of planter women. Doubtless many yeomen could empathize with the Levi London family. They owned "one negro women [who] worked some in [the] house when not at work in [the] field."[57]

A vast gulf separated the wives of planters and professionals from all others. Wealthy sons typically described their mothers as "managers" or "supervisors" in the domestic sphere. William Taylor explained: "My mother superentended the Negro women and children and looked after spinning, weaving, and making ther clothing and that of our family." Isaac Rainey reminisced that his "Mother had well trained house servants who were devoted to her and her children"; and Lee Billingsley reported, more harshly, that his "Mother saw that each negro woman did her part of the work and did it right."[58]

Several of the former soldiers provided impressive lists of servants that often included both black slaves and poor whites. "My mother superintended the housework," wrote John Fite of DeKalb County. "The negro women did the spinning and weaving . . . and very often my mother would hire a white woman to make the clothes." Hampton Cheney cataloged his parents' servants as "two cooks, two washerwomen, one dining room servant, two seamstresses, one house girl, one house boy, one carriage driver, one hostler, one gardner, [and] one errand boy, all under the supervision of my mother." In addition to their sizable retinues of black domestics, the Sims family of White County usually "hired Some poor white girl to do the weaving"; the Yancey family of Gibson County kept a "White Lady" at their mansion to sew clothing; and the Lipscomb family of Maury County payed their live-in white servant ten cents a yard for her cloth.[59]

In contrast to the poor and the yeoman wives, many affluent women succumbed to a leisure ethic. "My mother did no manual labor except serving [and] Knitting," wrote Gentry McGee. "On the few occasions when I saw her on the loom bench [she] was only instructing the servant." In Lincoln County, L. H. Russe noted that his "mother never did any work, except fancy needle work"; and in Rhea County, John Crawford's mother and grandmother passed their hours "knitting, sewing, and [making] fancy quilt work." Crawford emphasized: "My mother worked only as she wanted to." Certainly the slave-rich lifestyle of the Oglesby family in Williamson County was far different from the hard-toiling yeoman's existence. "Mother never cooked but one meal," recalled the son, "and declared she would never cook another."[60]

The social distinctions among Tennessee women led to occasional resentments, as recalled by two Middle Tennesseans, Marcus Vesley and James Thompson. Vesley remembered that, in Wilson County, women with slaves "Had little to do with poor people"; and Thompson concurred that, in Davidson County, "females seemed to have a distant feeling toward each other." A Chattanooga tailor's son recorded in his questionnaire that "some times I have heard the women folk say . . . 'Oh she is stuck up because she has a negro.' "[61]

Tennessee's antebellum youths also experienced the broad distinctions of social class. While the poor and the yeoman's children were early introduced to adult chores, those of the planters and professionals enjoyed the luxuries of a prolonged childhood. "As we had so many slaves," reflected Andrew Webster, "it was not necessary for me to work."[62] At the other end of the social scale, yeoman boys went to the fields as early as age four, five, and six and usually carried the full responsibility of plowing by the time they were anywhere from eight to eleven years old. George Porter of Lincoln County, R. P. Lanius of Wilson County, and Gilbert Harrell of Coffee County recorded that they commenced plowing at age eight; Thomas Whitfield of Williamson County took the plow handles at age nine; James Rogers of Dickson County did the same at age ten; and Mark Anderson of Putnam County boasted: "I did a man's work with [a] plow after I was eleven years old."[63] The wealthy had a different concept of maturation. As William G. Lillard explained in his questionnaire, "when a young man became 21 years old his father would set him up either in some profession, merchant business, or place him on [a] Farm."[64]

From their youths, impoverished boys understood their inferior status. Simple economic necessity required many of them to seek out employment beyond the home. A. T. Bransford recalled with sadness that he "ploughed, hoed or did any kind of work there was to do, barefooted and in rags." He bitterly added: "Some who owned a number of slaves felt their importance kindly like the present time." One of seven illegitimate children born to a destitute mother, John Hank was hired out to local farmers for two dollars per month. Reflecting on his conception, he cursed: "The man that was said to be my father had negroes and property and never did anything for me." John T. C. Fergus stated that he "was a hireland . . . for [the] M & C RR"; Timothy Leigon "worked on farm[s] as [a] hired boy in several states"; and William Eskew reported that he was employed "on the farms of Rich Men." "All the rich men who owned negroes did not work," Eskew wrote with anger. "Thire was no neighboring with the poor man and rich man."[65]

The sons of yeomen emphasized their toil. "I worked from early morning until after sun down," explained C. W. Hicks. "Prior to the civil war," he continued, "the few farming tools in use were clumsy, slow and inefficient." George Washington Willing also testified that, from dawn until sundown, he worked "with [a] bull tongue plow and [a] home made eye hoe."[66] Although most men boasted of the physical demands made by antebellum farming, at least two Tennesseans refreshingly admitted to youthful indolence. William Needham of Hardeman County acknowledged: "I . . . done as little [as] I could get by with"; and A. M. Bruce of Campbell County testified: "I never liked [work] any too well but I always had to do my part or take a limbing. . . . when it came to hoeing I generally had the cleanest row if it was not quite so long."[67] Needham and Bruce were exceptional. Few yeomen fathers could afford to tolerate sloth in their sons.

Slaveowning yeomen's sons generally worked in the fields with their fathers' slaves. "I was only a lad," wrote Josiah Hinkle of Robertson County, "but with my brothers and the negro boys . . . [I] made a capable 'hand.'" Baxter Hoover bragged: "I Kept up my end of [a] Row with the Negroes," and Turner Johnson believed that his "father owned me Just as he did the negro boyes."[68] Despite their shared fraternity of labor, racial differences separated white sons from black laborers. "I done the Same kind of work our negros did," explained Ridley Brown, and he ate "the same kind [of] grub they did but not at the Same table."[69]

Frequently small planters employed their sons in the fields. In Smith County, Elijah Knight's father sent his four boys and twenty slaves out to cultivate corn, wheat, and oats. The son explained that in his father's absence an older slave, "Uncle Daniel," was "our boss— that of course was when we were small boys." When school was not in session, Augustine Atkins and "a negro boy went to the mill every Saturday"; and Robert Taylor was required to do the same type of work as his father's slaves.[70]

Affluent children spent far more time pondering in the classroom than plowing in the field. Slavery and wealth freed the planters' sons to pursue their studies. When the Civil War began, observed William Lillard, "I was a student at College and did no work regularly." McCage Oglesby bluntly stated that he "Didnt work—went to school"; and Robert L. Morris reflected that he was busy "getting an Education, [I] was Just fourteen years old at the outbreak of the war."[71] In the same way that slavery widened their fathers' options, it gave financially comfortable adolescents much greater freedom of choice in their activities than other young whites had.

Like their elders, Tennessee's upper-class youth enjoyed a leisure ethic. James Morey recorded that he "hunted and fished like other boys, but did no special work." William Anthony of Haywood County,

Charles Mison of Montgomery County, and F. A. Turner of Rutherford County made similar testimonials. While on vacation from
school, Anthony went on "pleasure trip[s] and visiting." Mison wrote
that "being an orphan I was petted and done but little work." Turner
happily recalled that, during summer breaks from school, "we Had a
big time playing Ball and giving Picnics." Writing in the same spirit,
Herman M. Doak fondly remembered summers spent hunting bear
and deer, fishing for trout, and "dancing on [plank] floors with
mountain girls"; and Louis Bledsoe wrote: "I worked a little with a
plow and a hoe but most often time I was over seeing on the farm
or stilling—making whiskey."[72] Naturally, the disparity in adolescent
lifestyles between the elites and the other classes led to resentments.
As the indigent James Hodge complained, "the Slave Holders [and]
especially their sons . . . hunted[,] fished and went to school."[73]

Growing up within the framework of the peculiar institution,
planters' children quickly grasped that they were in positions of command. Many, like Lee Billingsley of Bledsoe County and Sam Davis
of Rutherford County, had black boys assigned to them as personal
slaves. Others soon learned that their parents' slaves would quickly
cater to their young wills. The orphaned Benjamin Hawkins romantically recalled his Old South boyhood. He "was not forced to work"
and instead frequently accompanied his uncle's slaves on trips to
hunt rabbits or possums. "When I got tired [the] negroes would carry
me on their shoulders for hours," he wrote in his questionnaire.
"They loved me well enough to care for me." Preston Hill of Wilson
County shared a slightly different childhood vignette. Recalling the
first ten cents he ever earned—remuneration for shelling corn—he
explained that after payment he "had one of the Servants Sadle a
horse" and then rode to town to purchase candy.[74] Given such an
environment, planters' children often developed the arrogance that
comes with power at an immature age. Seeing this, less fortunate
whites could be most critical. "Slave holder boys did not work any,"
charged one impoverished Tennessean. "They would even make a
negro slave hand [them] a drink of water."[75]

The peculiar institution was an ever-present factor in Tennessee's
antebellum social-class system. Landholding and slaveownership determined both the individual's social status and his worldview. Given
Gustavus W. Dyer and John Trotwood Moore's racist views, the questionnaires solicited little information about slavery as understood
by Tennessee whites. Nonetheless a few former Confederates volunteered descriptions that demonstrated interesting social-class differences.

As might be expected, the planter class presented the softest images of slavery. Hampton Cheney left a good example. Born in Louisiana, at the age of five he moved to Davidson County, Tennessee, with his widowed mother. Both his father and his stepfather were exceptionally affluent. Thinking back on his youth, Cheney recalled felicitous "evenings . . . spent in the negro quarters . . . witness[ing] the scenes of jollity with the banjo twanging and the fiddle making the little darkies cut all sort of capers. . . . Even the older [slaves] looked cheerful and bright, as they discussed the latest news from the adjoining plantations, and not one had the sad, distressed, dissatisfied look that our northern brethren were wont to picture." Under these circumstances, he affirmed that "when I contrast the lives of . . . master and slave . . . I am constrained to believe the slave must have been the happier."[76]

Despite this positive image, Cheney's questionnaire was the only one to contain a reference to a slave rebellion. The aborted uprising occurred before Cheney's birth on his father's Louisiana plantation. In Cheney's account, a young, male, domestic servant named Louis emerged as the hero. He warned the white community of impending doom, and the elder Cheney and his neighbors quickly captured the rebellious blacks. They then "hung thirteen of the most bloodthirsty to the nearest trees without judge, jury or trial." Cheney chose to focus his account on the loyalty of Louis rather than upon the desperation of the rebels. Louis received his freedom, but, fearful of retribution from the community's black population, he fled to Mexico. There he settled, purchased a small farm, and married. Cheney seemed untroubled by the rebellion as a harbinger of slave discontent.[77]

Almost all the former Confederates were reticent to discuss mistreatment of slaves by whites. Elijah Hassell, himself from a nonslaveowning family, observed that, in Williamson County, "some would drive their Slaves and treet them rough." W. A. Rushing, from neighboring Rutherford County, recounted a nasty instance of inhumanity. On one occasion, the slaves in a Shelbyville pork-packing plant were offered the incentive of a fine hat, to be awarded to the individual who most exceeded his assignment. To their horror, the winner's rate then became the daily quota and, in Rushing's words, "the negroes were worked to death."[78] None of the other respondents gave specific examples of harshness to slaves. However some used the peculiar institution as a measure to discuss negative white social relations. Planters, complained A. J. Childers, "didnt treat white men any better than slaves."[79]

A few aging soldiers hinted that slavery caused friction among antebellum whites, especially among East Tennessee slaveowners. Lemuel Beene of Marion County and Jeremiah McKenzie of Meigs County believed that, shortly before the Civil War, the "abolitionist idea" was agitated in their communities. John Mitchell thought that "a few men in White County . . . oposed slavery"; and Ephraim Riddle of Green County grumbled that "Some non Slave Holders was always medling in Slave Holders Business." Such individuals, he continued, were "not though[t] much of by Slave Holders [because] they wer all way trying to get Slaves to do Something wrong."[80] Beene, McKenzie, Mitchell, and Riddle may have failed to distinguish between East Tennessee Unionism and true abolitionism. Nonetheless a small number of the former Confederates were from homes opposed to slavery. In McMinn County, Aaron Brook's religious views forbade keeping slaves. William Herbison of Dickson County, Flavius S. Landers of Bedford County, and J. P. Funk of Jefferson County testified that their fathers were against slavery. Herbison and Landers both stressed, however, that their fathers were strongly loyal to the South.[81]

Two of the respondents to the Civil War Veterans Questionnaires had a special appreciation of the peculiar institution—they were slaves. While such a small sample precludes sweeping observations, these two individuals provide some insight into slavery from the perspective of southern blacks. Colman Davis Smith and Peter Collman experienced bondage at different levels. Smith was a domestic body servant from childhood; Collman was a field hand and a runaway.

Colman Smith's early life was intertwined with Captain Sam Davis, who has been immortalized in Tennessee folklore as the "boy hero of the Confederacy." Smith and his parents were purchased by Lewis Davis and brought from Virginia to his plantation near Smyrna. The elder Smith worked in the fields, his wife cooked, and his child, Colman, became a "play fellow" to Davis's son Sam. The two grew up together and evidently developed close affections. When Sam Davis volunteered, Smith accompanied him as his servant. In 1863 Davis was captured near Pulaski, Tennessee, tried as a rebel spy, and hanged. His slave remained with him throughout the ordeal. "I begged him to tell what the Yankees wanted," Smith explained, "but he said no. I asked him to let me tell [but] he said no." Following his master's execution, he was welcomed home by the Davis family, remained with them until the late 1860s, and then spent the balance of his life laboring as a hired man on white farms in Tennessee and Mississippi. He lived in dread that some day he might be punished for his association with a Confederate spy. In 1926 the poor man was destitute and, with great trepidation, sought help from H. C. Featherstrum, a Senatobia, Mississippi, philanthropist. With Featherstrum's encouragement, Smith applied for and received a small pension from the state of Mississippi for an "Indigent Servant of a Soldier or Sailor of the Late Confederacy." The environment of slavery had left Colman Smith tragically inadequate for the pursuit of prosperity.[82]

Peter Collman was of sterner mettle. Although born into slavery, he resisted the institution, volunteered for the Union Army and, in his old age, remained defiant of white society. When asked about his parents, Collman responded "i Have Not Had No father," but he speculated that he might have been the son of Peter Atkins, who lived near Paris, Tennessee. Recalling his youth, he resented the fact that, under slavery, white men "was the Boss," and observed that "thay was a difference Between" those whites who owned slaves and those who did not. The planter class, he believed, sought to discourage the ambitions of nonslaveowning whites. At some point before 1861, he fled to Illinois. During the first summer of the Civil War, he joined Company A of the Twenty-ninth Illinois Volunteers—probably as a servant. Despite the fact that blacks could not legally serve with Union forces until 1863, Collman claims to have fought at Shiloh and later at Vicksburg. After the Confederate defeat, he settled on a farm near Whiteville, Tennessee, but he never was comfortable with the white community. Collman enclosed with his questionnaire a letter giving his bitter assessment of southern race relations. The black man's labor, he protested, "aunt worth nothing by white Say and we aunt aloud to Say what we are worth[.] we Just work and the white people pay Just what they want. . . . So we Just can make Enough to get Something to Eat and By the white people old clothes[.] Sometimes cant do that." Peter Collman found Tennessee whites less than benevolent.[83]

An analysis of the Civil War Veterans Questionnaires suggests that labor—both free and unfree—was an important key to understanding the dynamics of Tennessee's antebellum social-class relations. The nonslaveowner was almost totally dependent upon his family's toil. The husband, the wife, and all the children of sufficient age combined their efforts to cultivate crops, to accomplish daily chores, and to complete domestic responsibilities. This unremitting labor placed them at a distinct social and economic disadvantage to most slaveowners. In their struggle for survival, the landless poor were especially conscious of the problem. Slavery restricted their opportunities for employment and depressed their wages. Although nonslaveowning yeomen were economically more independent than the poor, they shared with them a reliance upon familial labor. Because the children of yeomen were particularly affected by the necessity for constant work at home, their formal education was severely retarded.

By contrast slavery provided many white Tennesseans with the ability to grow crop surpluses, the time to assume civic responsibilities, and the luxury of exempting their children from labor and thus allowing them to obtain quality educations. The differences in schooling received by Tennessee's antebellum youths constituted one of the greatest inequalities between the social classes. Unequal education not only served as a symbol of class status, but it also ensured that the class structure would remain relatively constant from generation to generation.

CHAPTER THREE

CASTE AND THE CLASSROOM

Responding to the Civil War Veterans Questionnaires, William C. Dillihay reproached the quality of education available during his childhood. "The fragments of interest and the little amount of money appropriated for public schools," he complained, "leaves a blot on the history of the state."[1] This bitter statement arose from an antebellum educational system that favored society's privileged classes and inhibited rather than encouraged social mobility. The result was a caste-like system in which the combination of a youth's social position and his access to classroom instruction virtually predetermined his adult status. James K. Clifton of Dickson County explained simply: "True wealthy slaveholders were able to give their sons advantages in the way of education . . . which the poor man could not."[2]

This assessment varies significantly from the views of Frank L. Owsley and his student, Blanche Henry Clark. Writing in *Plain Folk of the Old South*, Owsley asserted that "the opportunity of acquiring an education [was] the gateway to the professions and success was quite favorable for ambitious youth, however poor he might be." He affirmed that those young men "who *desired* an education" could secure it in one of the more than 2,500 Old South academies. Clark, whose study concentrated on Tennessee, agreed with her mentor. She concluded that if the yeoman class failed to profit from their abundant opportunities for an education, "it was due to their own negligence."[3] Doubtless Owsley and Clark's interpretation was influenced by the traditional American idea that mass education provided the individual with opportunities that more than compensated for the disadvantages of birth into a lower socioeconomic class.

Some recent theorists have suggested that education in fact perpetuated the class structure. In a provocative essay published in 1972, Samuel Bowles argued that, in the nineteenth century, an individual's "status, income, and personal autonomy came to depend in great measure on one's place in the work hierarchy." In turn the social division of labor became "associated with educational credentials reflecting the number of years schooling and the quality of education received." With this in mind, high-status parents secured for their children quality schooling that prepared them for positions at the top of the occupational ladder. Children from lesser-status families generally obtained an education that was inadequate for significant social advancement.[4] As the South east of the Mississippi River changed from a frontier region to a settled society, good agricultural land became difficult to obtain. Young Southerners began to look to the professions for social and economic advancement, but those with deficient educations found the door of opportunity firmly shut.

The testimonies of respondents to the Civil War Veterans Questionnaires described a dual education system in Tennessee. The poor, the yeomen, and, to a lesser extent, the small slaveowners gravitated to short-term public and subscription schools of indifferent character that convened during the few short weeks between crop cultivation in spring and early summer and crop harvest in the fall. The more affluent planter-professional class, for the most part, attended high-quality academies. Largely undisturbed by the routines of farm society, these institutions operated for ten months out of twelve. Social statistics gleaned from the manuscript of Tennessee's 1860 census suggest the disparity between the schools. Comparable information was lacking for several counties, but it appears that the yearly per capita expenditure for children attending an academy was $25.93 as compared to a per capita expenditure of only $2.02 for children attending the public and subscription institutions (Appendix 2, table 8). The picture presented by these statistics is somewhat misleading, as some children never graced a classroom; others attended public schools but supplemented that schooling with additional months of subscription instruction; and a few of the most wealthy had private tutors.

Tennesseans attending public or subscription schools received an education that was decidedly inferior to that provided by the private academies. By the time of the Civil War, almost all counties received state revenues for the education of white children. In many communities the parents supplemented the state funds with a small tuition, usually one dollar per month for each child, and in a few cases parents paid the whole tuition. These institutions, hereafter termed "common schools," assembled from mid-July to early September and occasionally met for a few weeks in January or February; in colloquial terms, they ran from the time when corn was laid by until fodder-pulling and wood-hauling time.[5] Even these brief terms were constantly interrupted by the demands of farm life. Gilbert Harrell remembered that he rarely studied more than "a month or so" each year, because he had "to stop to help [his] father"; James Frazer remarked that he "went [to school] when it wasnt work time on the farm"; and Reuben Moore reported that he "went to school after crops were laid by, if there was a school."[6] Several veterans commented that young girls remained in the classroom while their brothers dropped out to perform chores.[7]

The makeshift nature of common schools demonstrated their lack of quality. Both Robert Holman and Carter Upchurch recorded that they pondered the mysteries of knowledge in abandoned tobacco barns, and others met classes in community church buildings, empty stores, or deserted log houses.[8] Most did assemble in buildings constructed for educational purposes, but the facilities suggested that learning was not a high community priority. The structures were often made of rounded, rather than hewed, logs. Such "pole log" houses were easily constructed but highly temporary. Within their drafty walls, students sat on uncomfortable split-log benches, walked on dirt floors, and warmed themselves by fireplaces that had dangerous stick and mud chimneys. James Carroll described his school as an "old log House [with] cracks in it a fellow could throw a Dog through," and Arthur Davis wrote that in winter his teacher dug a pit in the floor to make a fire. Doubtless these men would agree with Francis McKnight, who pictured the common school in his Rutherford County community as a "Sorry little log hut and poorly furnished."[9]

Common school instructors were as lacking in quality as their buildings. Most were farmers of modest academic attainment. Less often they consisted of widows, unmarried young women, or college students on summer vacation.[10] Faced with reluctant scholars, these teachers were more often appreciated for their ability in maintaining discipline than for the learning they inspired. James Anthony explained that his neighborhood rarely hired female teachers because "women were not supposed to be able to control big boys." James

Trusty described his teacher as "a very strict man"; N. B. Nesbitt studied under "a man who treated the little folks brutally"; and James Tyner painfully remembered an instructor who beat him about his head until his ears bled.[11] Because teachers received little more than eight to ten dollars per month—less than the wages of a farm hand—few individuals of ability found such work rewarding. "The first school I went to," grumbled Samuel Matthews of Maury County, was "taught by a woman [who] couldnt spell toBaker." Some teachers were social misfits. Robert Austin wrote that his fellow students often threw their drunken teacher into a creek, and Sam Ralls related that "after Mr Ashbrooks (a methodist preacher) was Through Teaching, he Stol my Neighbors wife and Eloped." Putting it succinctly, William Briggs characterized his Hickman County instructors as "Verry common and Sorry Teachers."[12]

Both the curricula and the instructional methods of common schools indicated their limited value. Teachers did little more than lead their students through *Webster's Blueback Speller*, augmenting it with "Fowlers" or "Smiles" arithmetic and an occasional geography textbook.[13] In one-room buildings that housed an average of forty-seven children—though the number of pupils often approached one hundred or more—would-be learners recited their lessons in clamorous unison. Joseph Sullivan reminisced that all shouted out their spelling "at the same time making as much noise as a gang of geese." David England believed that anyone in his community "could have heard us a bout Six hundred yards off getting our spelling lessons and even further . . . when the teacher Said . . . take your dinners." England added: "I was [a] dullard and did not learn much."[14]

Under these circumstances, the overburdened instructors instilled in their students little more than a crude phonetic ability to spell. Usually little children were taught the vowel and consonant sounds with the hope that they would approximate the correct letter groupings of words. Nineteenth-century personal correspondence and diaries are filled with examples of this method's shortcomings, and the Civil War Veterans Questionnaires abundantly demonstrated the common school's limitations. Julius C. Martin wrote out "Jenerly" for "generally" and "chool" for "school." Julius A. Vernon reported that he studied "rithmatick" and "geogryfy." Instead of attending a "subscription school," James Aiken mistakenly wrote that he went to a "prescription school."[15] Such academic blunders were understandable. As George Wray explained, "in those days [there] were just comon schooll[s] where you could learn to spell[,] read[,] write and figure a little."[16]

If names indicate social worth, then the common schools possessed decidedly plebeian designations. Children attended institutions with such unpretentious names as Muddy Branch, Ball Creek, Possum Hollor, Little Tick, and Flyer's Lick.[17] Given the physical conditions, the inferior teachers, and the inadequate curricula of these common schools, few Tennessee youths achieved more than minimal literacy.

Tennessee's academies stood in magnificent contrast to the humble public and subscription institutions. While the latter could assemble only during the brief lulls from the farm routine, the academy was free from such restraints. Traditionally classes commenced in September and continued until the end of June. For ten months, young scholars studied within the confines of impressive brick or frame buildings. Such an environment inculcated its inhabitants with a sense of intellectual superiority over their less fortunate neighbors.

Academy teachers established standards of excellence. Several veterans recalled with pride their instructors' academic accomplishments. Among them John Crawford wrote that all teachers at Washington Academy in Rhea County were "graduates of colleges and universities"; and William Greaves boasted that all the teachers in his Haywood County academy "were well educated in the classics and English branches." In Fayette County, Berenes Carter studied under "D. M. Quarles a graduate of the University of Virginia"; in Lake County, Meriwether Donaldson matriculated under a Yale alumnus; and in Cannon County, John Wharton attended an academy taught by "a northern teacher from Tufts college." James Morey noted that his father, an academy teacher in East Tennessee, possessed a masters degree from the University of Vermont.[18] These men were well paid. In Athens, Tennessee, the president of Forest Hill Academy received an impressive $1,300 per annum. Doubtless his faculty, including a "Prof[.] Kaube from Belgium," received incomes sufficient to maintain comfortable lifestyles.[19]

Throughout Tennessee academies offered courses ranging from the basics in reading, penmanship, and spelling to advanced studies in mathematics, rhetoric, philosophy, Greek, and Latin. Joshua Mewborn, a Fayette County planter's son, proudly noted that his education not only included classes "in Greek, Latin, and the English branches," but also "French as a polish."[20] The upper-class community took tremendous interest in its children's accomplishments. On Friday afternoons in aristocratic Williamson County, residents assembled at the local academies to hear the South's future leaders display their skills in oratory and spelling.[21]

Antebellum academies demonstrated their elitist orientations by adopting impressive names and by instilling in their students an elitist spirit. In Tennessee these schools boasted such patrician nomenclatures as Mt. Vernon Academy, Fort Hill Academy, Jefferson's Academy, and Columbia Athenaeum.[22] An aura of honor pervaded these institutions. Hampton Cheney noted with pride that, in Nashville, boys from rival academies often fought to defend the reputation of their school. At "about 12 years old," he bragged, "I became quite a warrior, having fought so many battles with [other] boys." On a less belligerent note, William Pollard proudly explained that Union Academy in Williamson County was sufficiently attractive to draw "pupils from many of the Southern States."[23]

In addition to common schools and academies, three other educational options existed for Tennesseans: no school, public schools supplemented by subscription classes, and private tutors. By the 1860s, few children lacked access to a classroom, however crude it may have been. Nonetheless veterans from impoverished households complained that they were deprived of an education. "I only went to school 3 days in my life," wrote John Welch. "I never had an opportunity to go to school." He also observed: "Them that was able to pay the tuition attended regularly." Another destitute old soldier poignantly testified that he "Did not go enough to learn the alphabet."[24]

At the upper end of the social scale, some of the most wealthy Tennesseans received their instruction at home. The children of Drury Dance, a Gibson County planter with between fifty and one hundred slaves, were instructed by private tutors. Dance rarely required his sons to engage in farm labor, insisting instead that they devote their efforts to study. In East Tennessee, Herman M. Doak remained at home, where he boasted that by age ten he had mastered "Burn's low Scotch and Chaucer's old English" and by age twelve he was translating Greek, Latin, and French. Doak also became proficient at the piano and violin, but a hand wound at Shiloh put an end to his musical proclivities.[25]

In those communities where academies were unavailable, financially comfortable families sent their children to public schools and then supplemented this training with additional periods of subscription instruction. A clear class distinction existed under such circumstances. The poor white, the yeoman, and the planter associated during the brief weeks of public education; however, when the free school ended, the less affluent turned to home responsibilities while their more fortunate contemporaries continued their quest for knowledge. After the "common free school," wrote Eli Hinson, a subscription class commenced. With regret he pointed out: "i never got the advantage of them." A small slaveowner's son made a similar statement. David Bodenhamer recorded that, at the close of the public session, teachers provided for a fee "advanced work fitting students for college and professional life." "Those in deep poverty," he continued, "could go to school only when not needed at home."[26]

This description of Tennessee's antebellum educational structure illustrates a simple dichotomy between poor-quality and high-quality education. The common schools were lacking in significant worth, and obviously the absence of a good school denied a child adequate access to knowledge. On the other hand, those studying at academies, with private tutors, and at public schools supplemented by subscription instruction received an education that held out reasonable expectations for achieving high-status positions.

A statistical comparison of the Tennessee Civil War Veterans Questionnaires demonstrates noticeable class divisions within this instructional dichotomy. To be sure, a few of the poor attended academies, and a few wealthy children attended only the common schools. For the most part, however, children were segregated into institutions associated with their social standing. Across the state, 59 percent of the planter and professional class received high-quality instruction, compared to 10 percent of the poor, 9 percent of nonslaveowning yeomen, and 24 percent of small slaveowners (Appendix 2, table 9). The slightly higher percentage of poor attending academies, as compared to the yeomen, is misleading. A second statistic showing the number of years of schooling puts the relationship between class and education into perspective. The average length of academy study was two years for the poor, five for both the slaveowning and nonslaveowning yeomen, and an impressive nine years for the planters and professionals (Appendix 2, table 10). While the poor and the yeomen's sons sweated in the fields, their wealthier contemporaries pondered in the classroom. To be sure, the Civil War cut short several veterans' studies. As one unrepentant Confederate observed: "When I ought to have been in school, [I] was shooting yankees."[27]

Both the Tennessee Social Census for 1860 and the Civil War Veterans Questionnaires showed that academy attendance was higher in the more wealthy and slave-rich sections of the state. In the two regions where blacks constituted 30 percent or more of the population—Middle and Southwest Tennessee—academies were more prominent than in the valleys and mountains of East Tennessee or the northwest and southcentral counties sandwiched between the state's slave concentrations. According to census information compiled from those counties with adequate statistics, 8 percent of Tennessee school children studied at academies. When the statistics were adjusted regionally, they showed that only 5 percent of school-going children went to academies in the northwest and southcentral counties and only 6 percent did so in the eastern mountains. By contrast, 21 percent of Middle Tennessee schoolchildren and 32 percent of Southwest Tennessee schoolchildren were enrolled in academies (Appendix 2, table 11).

The questionnaires confirmed the regional differences in educational attainment and emphasized a social-class distinction. Among the 437 Middle Tennessee veterans, 67 percent of the planters and professionals obtained high-quality schooling, compared to 13 percent of the poor, 16 percent of the nonslaveowning yeomen, and 27 percent of the slaveowning yeomen. From Southwest Tennessee, 115 former soldiers responded. Of that number, a quality education was received by 25 percent of the poor, 31 percent of the nonslaveowning yeomen, 38 percent of the slaveowning yeomen, and a notable 74 percent of the wealthy (Appendix 2, table 12).

Possibly because many less affluent East Tennesseans sided with the Union, the region's Confederates who responded to the questionnaires were slightly better educated than their contemporaries who were surveyed in the 1860 census. Still they did not obtain the level of instruction available in the major slave regions. In the mountain and valley counties, 45 percent of the planter and professional class benefited from high-quality instruction, compared to 9 percent of the poor, 6 percent of the yeomen without slaves and 19 percent of the yeomen with slaves. Former Confederates from the northwestern and southcentral counties more nearly conformed to the expectations derived from the 1860 census. In this region, all the poor were limited to inferior educations, and only 3 percent of the nonslaveowning yeomen were able to supplement their public schooling with subscription instruction. Slaveowners' sons fared much better. Eighteen percent of the yeomen and 41 percent of the planters' and professionals' sons received quality schooling (Appendix 2, table 12). As a general rule, wherever slavery was prominent, each segment of the white social structure had more access to quality instruction than in less affluent areas. But in every section of the state, high-status individuals had significantly greater opportunities than other elements of the white community.

Colleges were an elitist's preserve. None of the poor attended. Although 2 percent of the nonslaveowning yeomen and 7 percent of the slaveowning yeomen had better educations, a respectable 29 percent of the wealthy attended institutions of higher learning (Appendix 2, table 13). As one impoverished East Tennessean observed with resentment, "rich men Sent there boys to college."[28]

Planters and professionals were well aware of the relationship between education and economic success, and they possessed the financial means necessary to pursue that course. The Civil War appears to have had little negative effect upon their ability to pay for higher education. Among those veterans who attended colleges and universities, 53 percent went before the conflict, 36 percent studied following it, and 11 percent left school for the army and then returned after the Confederate defeat (Appendix 2, table 14). The war did have a sobering influence upon their educational emphasis. Before 1861 college youths preferred a liberal arts curriculum over professional training by almost a three to one margin. Matured by combat, 65 percent of the veterans pursued studies in the professions of law and medicine after the war (Appendix 2, table 15). Their fathers' prosperity and social connections propelled these young Confederates to the top of postbellum professions and politics. One former soldier reflected with pride on his parents' insistence that he enter the University of North Carolina. Thomas Webb explained that "my Father was a strong advocate of education and told us wealth was precarious and education was the safest fortune."[29]

Southern colleges, by and large, failed to liberalize the worldviews of their students; instead they reinforced the narrow cultural values that separated the upper classes from lesser whites. These institutions were little more than finishing schools that conditioned young aristocrats to assume command of their society. Herman M. Doak, whose father was a professor at Washington College, near the East Tennessee community of Jonesboro, exemplified the class consciousness bred by these schools. "Ambitious young men," he explained, graduated from Washington College and then "went west or south [to] Georgia, Alabama, Arkansas, or Texas." By contrast, he believed that North Carolina and East Tennessee furnished thousands of "the lower classes" who emigrated to Illinois and Indiana. Mocking their dialect, he condescendingly described their response to the questions "where are you from?" and "where are you going?" as "Come fum Nawth Caliner, gwyne ter the Eelinoy—Gimme a chaw o' terbaccker."[30]

The inequality of education among the various social classes was nowhere better revealed than in their respective views of the role that education played in their daily lives. The yearly routine of the poor and the yeomen—slaveowning and nonslaveowning—revolved around the farm rather than the classroom. Financially secure youths, on the other hand, focused their attention on studies, with other activities receiving a lower priority. To be sure, anomalies existed in every community. Each morning John K. Roberts, the son of a slaveless yeoman, pasted onto his plow handle the "leaves out of 'Webster's Blueback Spelling' book" and thus combined labor with learning. A wealthy Middle Tennessee merchant's son was equally exceptional. "My father being of Dutch descent," complained Edwin Gardner, "he did not believe in a liberal education and would send word . . . to let me study only reading, writing, and arithmetic."[31] Both Roberts's and Gardner's experiences were atypical.

The poor and the yeomen stressed that, for them, agricultural responsibilities took precedence over education. William Orr stated that as a "farmers boy my Educational opportunities were quite limited." Flavius Landers noted that he attended classes "when not making crops," and James Sain pointed out that, in Bedford County, children "were not made to go [to school], besides there was work to do."[32] The sons of planters and professionals also proclaimed that they labored. Nonetheless they frequently prefaced their claims with the phrase "when not in school," indicating which portion of their youth was the more important. "When not in school," wrote Newton Cannon, "I helped to feed the Stock [and] went on errands." "During summer vacations from school," testified James McNeilly, "I worked on the farm, hoeing, and plowing." "When not in school," explained William Timberlake, "my father required me to work with his negro laborers."[33] Still other wealthy veterans stressed that they did not labor. Dero Mills bluntly observed that he did "No farm work [and] was in school when war began." In a similar vein, James McColgan mused that he "was in school most of all the time, sometimes may have worked in the garden [but] never ploughed or made a Field hand." When asked what type of activities he engaged in as a boy, the son of a Wilson County attorney responded with "school."[34]

Tennessee patricians frequently recorded that their families helped the poor secure quality educations. Only a small number from the other classes confirmed that claim. Wealthy men, wrote McCage Oglesby, "saw that children of poor people had their tuition paid." Two Fayette County residents agreed. George Baskerville remembered that his father always sent "some poor boy . . . with us from home as one of the family," and Robert Rogers affirmed that "Many Slave owners Sent Poor Boys to School[,] clothed them [and] payed [their] Tuition." Rogers exaggerated when he concluded: "the Poor Boys had a better chance than the Rich."[35] Few among the wealthy veterans were as candid as Marcus Toney of Nashville. He stressed that opportunities for an education were "not very good" for the impoverished due to the fact that "all schools were private and [families] had to pay for an education."[36]

Despite the paternalistic testimonials of the planters' and professionals' sons, other Tennesseans recalled that tuition was a barrier to their educational opportunities. Given the cashless economy of the antebellum yeoman, even the small fee of one dollar per month for each student charged by the common subscription schools was a hardship. In Gibson County, a slaveowning yeoman's son wrote that "the school being . . . pay . . . the poorer children did not go regularly, and many others but lit[tle]," and a renter's son complained that "the poor honest young man had very small chance of getting an education [because] there were no free schools." William Eskew explained that in Sumner County the "poor could not pay the price per head"; Elijah Barnes noted that in Sullivan County school attendance was "Just tolerable . . . owing to How much [people] Had to pay"; and Burl Flemming emphasized that in Rutherford County children went to school "Eregular on account of mony to pay."[37]

The perceptions of whether children attended school regularly or irregularly also differed according to social class. Writing in his questionnaire, James C. Giles observed that only "Those whose parents were able to do without their childrens labor attended regularly."[38] Among the veterans who received only common school instruction, 36 percent of the poor and 31 percent of the nonslaveowning yeomen recalled moderate to significant absenteeism. Slaveowners going to these schools were less conscious of the problem. Their awareness of chronic truancy declined to 27 percent of the yeomen and 17 percent of the wealthy. John F. Cole understood the discrepancy in attendance. In his West Tennessee community, most youths dropped out of school to do farm work except for the children of "them that o[w]n Slaves [and] som few others."[39]

The tragic circumstances of orphans provided another example of class disparity in education. Among the poor and yeomen, a father's death automatically terminated his children's studies and dictated that they work at home to help support the family. As John M. Patrick sadly reflected: "my father died when I was 12 years old [and] that ended [s]chooling."[40] The sons of financially comfortable planters and professionals were able to weather the same tragic events with little effect on their formal learning. Robert Morris lost his mother when he was six years old, and his father, a Nashville merchant, died five years later. Raised on his uncle's Davidson County plantation, Morris wrote that, before the Civil War, he spent his energies "getting an Education." The same was true of James Shivers, a native of Shelby County. Orphaned and living with his grandmother on a plantation near Bolivar, he usually occupied his time with studies, but he remembered that he "sometimes worked on the farm when not at School."[41]

Most of the veterans demonstrated an awareness of class differences in antebellum education. The poor and yeomen resented the privileged instruction secured by wealth. "I didnt attend no school as there wasnt no school to attend," complained the impoverished William Barnes. "The rich class of people harred thair own teachers." Similar testimonials were made by John Fergus of Rutherford County and William Eads of Loudon County. Writing that he received nothing better than common free instruction, Fergus added with bitterness: "There was a school on Stewart's creek that Slave holders attended." Eads simply stated that "Slave holders had a better chance to Educate their boys."[42] This disparity in quality instruction was reflected in relations between the social classes. As one indigent veteran expounded: "At school and public gatherin, some slaveholders seemed to think themselves a little better than the non-slave holders."[43]

Upper-class veterans were also aware of class differences in academic attainment. "There was some distinction between the slaveholders and the non-slaveholders," admitted Daniel Long. "The more intelligent and cultured class owned slaves while the shiftless and ignorant had none."[44] Other affluents claimed that few social differences existed in their communities, but they then included qualifications based on education level. John Osborne suggested that, in Roane County, all men and women associated freely "if refinement and education were equal." In Maury County, wrote Isaac Rainey, "a mans social standing was based on moral and intellectual merit rather than on the amount of his property." A West Tennessean agreed. Christopher Robertson affirmed that slaveowners and non-slaveowners intermingled but continued: "Of course they classed themselves along educational lines."[45] The son of a West Tennessee planter, M. B. Dinwiddie, illustrated this view. Benefiting from an impressive academy education, he later read medicine under a "Dr. Elexander" and then volunteered as a surgeon in the Confederate Army. Looking back on his antebellum community, he recalled that the better folk remained aloof from that "certain breed of white people, drunks and thugs that the slaves themselves would not associate with." He then lectured: "honest white men, . . . teachers and Preachers that did not own slaves" received equal respect within planter society.[46]

Nineteenth-century Tennesseans had highly uneven access to education. This fact gave great rigidity to a class system based on wealth, education, and family influence; it virtually perpetuated an elite class from one generation to the next. "A boy with out [an] edgieation," wrote the impoverished G. W. Miller, "had a Slim chance."[47] To a great extent the upper classes accepted the status quo as the natural order of things. Other whites who completed thier responses to the Civil War Veterans Questionnaires demonstrated significant resentment toward the Tennessee gentry. Just as members of the Confederate generation grew up experiencing different lifestyles and educations, they also developed contrasting attitudes toward the justice of the social system.

CHAPTER FOUR

CLASS CONSCIOUSNESS

John Clayton and William Johnston shared membership in Tennessee's Confederate generation, but little else. While Clayton's family was among the state's poorest, Johnston's was among the most affluent. In Shelby County, Clayton's father struggled to survive as a blacksmith, without benefit of land or slaves. In Madison County, Johnston's father prospered from the labor of thirty slaves who cultivated his six-hundred-acre estate. Though separated by a vast social and economic gulf, the two men concurred on one issue: class strife was pronounced in antebellum Tennessee. "Those that *didn't* owned slaves hated those that did," declared Johnston in his Civil War Veterans Questionnaire. He further stressed that "Antagonistism was mostly the fault of the non-slave holder." Clayton's perspective was different. He agreed that conflict existed, but blamed the slave-owners. Local aristocrats, he wrote, "passed and repassed but did not mingle freely with those who didn't" have slaves. "They was generally considered better than the non-slave holders," he grumbled, "because they was rich."[1] Johnston's and Clayton's testimonies refute the notion of an antebellum southern white solidarity.

Although they are crude by modern standards, the Civil War Veterans Questionnaires were intended as an instrument to measure the degree of social-class conflict in antebellum Tennessee communities. In developing the form, Gustavus W. Dyer was governed by the contradictory influences of his scientific training as a sociologist and the cultural biases of his southern heritage. Although he attempted to phrase his questions in an objective manner, his patrician upbringing led to the employment of prejudicial words and phrases. Essentially he requested that the veterans address four subjective topics: (1) to what extent was there social-class conflict or consensus in antebellum Tennessee; (2) to what extent did slavery influence the southern white work ethic; (3) to what extent were economic opportunities available for Tennessee's poor; and (4) to what extent did slaveowner-ship influence politics. Dyer biased his questions with references to "honorable men"; to "honest toil" and "honest work"; and to "poor, honest, industrious, young men who were ambitious to make some-thing of themselves." When he asked the old soldiers to describe their farm work as youths, he reminded them that "certain historians claim that white men would not do work of this sort before the [Civil] war."[2] To that the son of one wealthy Tennessee planter responded: "It was a Yankee lie that Southern boys (white boys) wouldnt do that kind of work."[3]

Given Dyer's slanted questions, Southerners' strong sense of ethno-centrism, the South's legendary sensitivity to criticism, and the fact that these former Rebels had risked their lives for the "lost cause," it would have been remarkable had there been many negative re-sponses to the questionnaires. As a small slaveowner's son ex-pounded: "It would be doing a gross inJustice to our parents to even intimate that social inequality" existed in his community. This was echoed by another small slaveowner's son from Maury County. "We did not make the [social] difference," responded J. G. Williamson, "as charged by our northern friends."[4] A review of all the former Con-federates' statements revealed that many individuals affirmed abso-lute social equality in their neighborhoods, others exposed subtle class distinctions, and still others testified to the prevalence of social-class antagonisms.

Dyer approached the topic of social-class relations by soliciting from the veterans answers to three direct questions. "Did the men who owned slaves mingle freely with those who did not own slaves," he inquired, "or did slaveholders in any way show by their actions that they felt themselves better than respectable, honorable men who did not own slaves?" He then asked whether at "the churches, at the schools, [and] at public gatherings in general . . . slave-holders and non-slave-holders mingle[d] on a footing of equality?" Finally, he bluntly questioned: "Was there a friendly feeling between slave-hold-ers and non-slave-holders in your community, or were they antago-nistic to each other?"[5] In response a majority of all the old soldiers proclaimed that absolute social harmony existed in their communi-ties. A significant minority, however, reported moderate to intense social conflict, and even those who argued for class felicity demonstrated subtle distinctions.

Statistics gathered from the Civil War Veterans Questionnaires provide one indication of the extent of social disharmony. Across county and class lines, 27 percent of the former Confederates acknowledged moderate to significant resentment in their communities (Appendix 2, table 16). Refining the figures by class and by geographical areas demonstrated some trends. On a geographic basis, discontent was mildest among those living in the mountains and valleys of East Tennessee. The intensity of class ill will became more pronounced through the moderate slaveholdings of Middle Tennessee and into the frontier-like regions of Southcentral and Northwest Tennessee, and it was most severe in the cotton country of Southwest Tennessee.

In the state's eastern regions, class consciousness among the former Confederates appeared to be relatively low because many yeomen expressed their discontent by joining the Union cause. Because slaves constituted a relatively small portion of East Tennessee's population, its white inhabitants were well aware that their region was culturally distinctive from the remainder of the state. Oliver P. Temple, a prominent Unionist and Knoxville attorney, observed in 1912 that the "overpowering influence of slavery [and] the fear of falling under the condemnation of the mighty oligarchy of slaveholders, to some extent paralyzed the minds" of many in his region.[6] Many Confederate veterans also recognized the social importance of Unionism in their communities. As William Morelock pointed out, in upper East Tennessee the classes were "antagonistic at [the] beginning and close of [the] war . . . the community was divided in Sentiment Federal and Confederate." A Jackson County aristocrat concurred. In his neighborhood, "about half of the non-slave holding class went off with the Federals and it was several years after the war before harmony was restored."[7]

As Unionists who responded to the Dyer questionnaire were not included in this sampling of East Tennessee Civil War soldiers, relatively little variation appeared among the social classes' awareness of antagonisms. That awareness ranged from a low of 20 percent for the slaveowning yeomen to a high of 28 percent for the nonslaveowning yeomen (Appendix 2, table 17). Those who did respond negatively revealed in deceptively simple language the frustrating slights received from the upper classes. William Jones of Smith County remembered that the "slave holder children . . . made fun of the nonslave holders"; George Willing of Jefferson County emphasized that the wealthy "felt their selves above the common people"; Johnson Spurlock of Jackson County noted that the slaveowners and non-slaveowners "were not the best of friends"; and James King of Sullivan County stated "Some thought because they owned slavs they were better than any body." James Kinsley of Cocke County did not fully comprehend the dynamics of his social environment. The classes "did not mingle," he wrote, but "I do not no why."[8]

Middle Tennessee Confederates were more class conscious than their compatriots to the east. Although slaves constituted from 30 to 53 percent of the population in this region, there were relatively few large planters. In contrast to the plantation and cotton economy of Southwest Tennessee, the state's middle section was characterized by modest farm holdings worked by small numbers of slaves. Despite this fairly comfortable environment, a significant portion of the veterans recalled social-class disharmony. Throughout the region, one out of three respondents noted conflict. The poor were the most negative; 47 percent reported class strife. Similar feelings were expressed by 31 percent of the nonslaveowning yeomen, 24 percent of the slaveowning yeomen, and 26 percent of the wealthy (Appendix 2, table 17). Those at the top of the social scale often assumed that class distinctions existed but doubted that they seriously disturbed the social fabric. "There is always some degree in Society," lectured John W. Wade. "All were treated politely, but all did not move in the exact same circle." More to the point, William Lillard claimed that while the social classes were amicable, "the laboring white man did not visit the aristocratic girls." Writing for her husband, Mrs. Henry Rogers remembered some minor tensions. All in her community were mutually respectful except for a few nonslaveholders who "were influenced by a feeling of envy."[9] One small slaveowner's son from Maury County recalled that social-class relations were "Jest tolerable."[10]

The counties designated as Northwest and Southcentral Tennessee showed the sharpest differences among the social classes in their awareness of discontent. A majority of the poor (56 percent) and a significant portion of the nonslaveowning yeomen (31 percent) reported negative associations. By contrast only 12 percent of the slaveowning yeomen and 10 percent of the planter-professional class remembered disharmony (Appendix 2, table 17). This difference can be accounted for, in part, by the region's settlement pattern. The section was made up of those counties along both banks of the Tennessee River's western cut through the state and a tier of counties that stretched along the state's northern boundary, from the Tennessee River to the Mississippi River. In the 1830s and 1840s these counties were skipped over by the cotton entrepreneurs, who were drawn to the more fertile soils of Southwest Tennessee, and were settled instead by the yeomanry, who owned few if any slaves. By the time of the Civil War, however, the plantation culture, with its emphasis on slavery and commercial agriculture, had begun to spread into the area. Intent upon increasing their landholdings and establishing their social ascendancy, the newly arrived patricians were largely insensitive to their impact upon the already established yeoman society.

Confederate veterans from Tennessee's Northwest and Southcentral counties were more vocal about the social conflict between yeoman and planter. The impoverished John Welch explained that in his community the owners of one or two slaves were reasonably friendly, "but those that owned several seemed to think them selves a little better than the men that did not own slaves." In Weakley County, Francis McClure recalled, most of his neighbors mingled together "except [for a] few aristocrats," and in Houston County, Elijah Hassell complained, the wealthy appeared "stuck up over property." James C. Hodge, the son of a McNairy County renter with no slaves, was extremely blunt. Local patricians, he wrote, held "them Selves above those that did not own slaves." He remembered "Just one man in east Tenn that . . . associated with the poor class." In his area, the social classes "gathered together but [slaveholders] showed a distinction especially in schools and to a great extent in church." Little wonder that one Dickson County yeoman's son could write with bitterness that his father would not "hav anything to do with" slaveowners because they "thought they wer Better than the Poor People and would not have anything to do with the poore clas."[11]

The seven southwestern counties of Shelby, Tipton, Lauderdale, Haywood, Madison, Hardeman, and Fayette most closely resembled the familiar southern cotton and plantation culture. Throughout this region, wealth was concentrated in the hands of a few large planters and class antagonisms were pronounced. While the poor were the most negative (56 percent), the other social classes also recognized discontent. Thirty-three percent of the nonslaveowning yeomen, 32 percent of the slaveowning yeomen and 21 percent of the planter-professionals referred to class conflict (Appendix 2, table 17). In Madison County, the indigent John I. Bruce complained that slaveholders "considered theirselves superior." Arthur Davis, also from Madison County, saw the same point in more positive terms. The son of a yeoman with five slaves, he proclaimed that the planters "showed they were better." The region's aristocrats were highly sensitive to any perceived criticism of their class. One Fayette County planter's son averred that absolute social solidarity characterized his community "except [when] some one wanted to stire up strife."[12]

The voice of discontent was spread across the state of Tennessee. In the antebellum South, those with vested interests in the peculiar institution developed an arrogance of command. Aristocrats could order slaves to cater to their needs, and they grew to expect deference from lesser whites as well. Rather than fostering a spirit of democratic solidarity among whites, slavery drove a wedge between those who enjoyed its benefits and those who performed their own toil. "The laboring class," explained a Williamson County yeoman, "was looked by a few of the Richest people as being a low class." John S. Luna complained that slaveowning "kins folk did not mingle much" with nonslaveowning relations; John M. Patrick resented that "once an awhile [a slaveowner would] turn up hise nos at a Pore man"; and a wealthy resident of Davidson County remembered: "There was a caste in my Section . . . the slave owners kind held themselves above the non Slave holding class." C. W. Hicks of Monroe County reflected the feelings of a significant portion of Tennessee's Confederate generation. "Some of the slave owners," he pointed out, "showed a patronizing air toward the non slave holders. That they considered themselves to be in a separate class . . . was shown by their visits and close friendships being mainly with slave holding families."[13]

A majority of the old soldiers claimed that social harmony was the general rule. Richard Beard, whose father was a professor at Cumberland University in Lebanon, noted that, in Wilson County, "there was no such thing as aristocracy, poor as well as rich, generally met on the level." In Davidson County, Robert Moss reflected, "Only two real wealthy slave holders [lived] in this neighborhood and [they] never 'put on airs.'" Benjamin Bates was ebullient in his assessment of social-class relations. He believed that, around Murfreesboro, there existed "Nothing but [a] friendly feeling and a warm hand shaking and [an inquiring of] how is the old woman and the children."[14]

Those former Confederates who argued for an antebellum class harmony pointed to the social intercourse of patrician and plain folk during times of both community celebration and community crisis. The son of a Fayette County planter argued that "you could not tell the diference at a Pic nic or fish fry . . . the non slave holder was considered as good as anybody." The wealthy Theodoric Lipscomb of Middle Tennessee wrote that "the land . . . and slave owner would meet the poorer man at a 'Turkey shooting' and Shake hands and be as friendly as Can be"; and the impoverished William Patterson claimed that "at corn shuckings[,] Log rolings[,] and House raiseings . . . the slaveowner was just one of us." Patterson added, however, that in the contest of wits "the intellectual advantage fell to the non slave owner."[15] Other veterans remembered slaveholders who loaned their slaves to neighbors in periods of need. A Gibson County slaveowning yeoman's son proudly recalled that "if a poor man got Sick [and] not able to work, [the] Slave holder Sent hands to work out his crop"; and a Macon County planter's son wrote that on frequent occasions his "Mother sent negro girls . . . to stay with a sick neighbor."[16]

William Allen, whose father was a nonslaveowning yeoman in Rhea County, gave one of the strongest testimonials to class harmony. From his own experience, he asserted that both rich and poor worked in the fields, that at parties impoverished boys courted affluent girls, and that the social classes often intermarried. To illustrate his perspective, Allen pointed to his own wedding: "I married into a Slave owning fam. my wife, Miss Mary E. Thomisen, associated with Daughters of Slave owners. My wife had one beau who owned 40 slaves and [another] 10 slaves. My best man had no slaves, my wife['s] best young Lady had 30. . . . their was 80 invited gest[.] Rich and poor were invited."[17] Approximately three decades after Allen returned his questionnaire to the Tennessee Historical Committee, Blanche Clark, in her book *Tennessee Yeomen*, assumed that his observations typified social conditions within the state.[18] In reality Allen's statements reflected only the peculiarities of his local environment. Rhea County had a black population of only 12 percent, and planters made up a negligible portion of the county's whites.[19] In such areas, there were too few planters and professionals to form an exclusive elite society. Under such conditions, the social classes came into frequent contact with one another, and conflict was muted.

Many Tennesseans resided in communities where slavery was a relatively insignificant social factor. "So Few . . . owned slaves," wrote a DeKalb County yeoman, that "you could not Tell much Difference in the mixing and visiting with each other." Few blacks inhabited such upper East Tennessee counties as Sullivan, Hawkins, and Scott. William Cox of Sullivan County recorded that "few owned slaves near me"; Harvey Chase remembered little class antagonism because "there was no one close to me that own slaves"; and William Harkleroad explained: "As a rule there wasent any ill feeling between slave holders and non slaveholders as there wasent any slave holders."

Samuel Moulock of Hawkins County affirmed that "in my community slavery was not known," and Isaac Griffith of Scott County noted that "their was no Negro in that Country At that time." Even in counties with sizable slaveholdings, some isolated neighborhoods were virtually free of the peculiar institution. In hilly Sumner County, F. G. Durham recalled little class friction because: "Their were verry few slave-holders this side of the ridge." James Agnew believed that, in his section of Giles County, "all seemed to be equal, [because] not ma[n]y slaves [were] owned in my community"; and John Leonard emphasized that, as a rule, in his Marshall County neighborhood the classes "wer Social as there was a very few that held many slaves."[20]

A small number of the former Confederates came from sections where most white families possessed human chattel. Robert Dew reported that in his part of Weakley County "the great majority of our Community owned a few negros; few families owned from 25 to 100 Negros but as a rule each . . . [had] from about 5 to 10 Slaves and all worked together white and black." Marshall Jones recalled little class conflict in Shelby County, "for most all owed a few slaves"; and for Maury County, John Frierson echoed this assessment because "there were very few non slave holders in my community." Aristocratic Williamson County contained the state's second-largest population of blacks. Among the respondents from this area, Joseph Marshall explained that "the greater part of the men in the community owned slaves"; Robert McAlister stated that "most . . . in the community were Slave holders"; and Robert Herbert noted that "every neighbor was a slave owner."[21] Because they had little contact with nonslave-owning yeomen, individuals from such neighborhoods were limited in their cultural values and had little understanding or awareness of the roots of class conflict.

Despite their assurance of class consensus, some wealthy Tennesseans so rarely associated with the yeomen and the poor that they developed the patronizing attitude indicative of a lack of sensitivity toward their nonslaveowning peers. "As far as I know [the classes] were very friendly indeed," wrote the son of a Rutherford County planter with one hundred slaves. "My Father always kept an overseer and trusted every thing to him." Robert Herbert remembered that his father "hired a poor white man," who "worked with the Slaves [and] ate at the family table." A well-to-do merchant's son from Columbia was especially confident that there existed "a free mingling of slaveholder and nonslaveholder." As proof he declared: "I attended school at Jackson College and I am sure some of our teachers, possibly all of them, did not own any slaves." "If people were educated and refined and of good character," he explained, then "Slave ownership was not considered."[22]

Although fervent in their attestations to social equality, upper-class Tennesseans judged other whites by their own elitist code of honor. Patricians would associate with nonslaveowners provided they were "gentlemen," or "honorable," or "respectable," or "honest and upright." "If they were gentlemen," wrote a wealthy slaveowner from Shelby County, then "no difference" was shown toward those without slaves. Amos Jones and John Reid of Madison County and Harrison Randolph of Robertson County stressed the importance of being an "upright honest gentleman" in social relations. John Lipscomb, whose father owned between forty and fifty slaves and 1,200 acres in Franklin County, well expressed this patrician concept. "Where they acted right," he lectured, the men who did not own slaves "could see no difference in there treatment." M. B. Dinwiddie, who was raised in Henry County, emphasized that "gentiely and principal led all associations, male and female."[23]

Substantial numbers of white Tennesseans failed to live up to the aristocrat's standards of gentility. "Men who did not own slaves . . . were well-received by the planters as their equals," reflected Hampton Cheney, provided "they were well bred, honorable men, who conducted themselves properly, and were not offensive in their opposition to slavery." Several affluent veterans discussed the relationship between honor and class. Jeremiah McKenzie assured posterity that while the inhabitants of Meigs County "were in separate and distinct classes, . . . the southern gentleman owning slaves always recognized worth and merit under all circumstances, and mingled freely with those who were respectable and honorable regardless of property." Given the patricians' positive perception of their own cultural values, they could only conclude that critical yeomen were motivated by either ignorance or maliciousness. A Middle Tennessee planter's son argued that "Honest and Upright" men associated freely. Despite this, he noted: "There was envy then as now, by some who were not very successful."[24]

In an apparent contradiction, Tennessee aristocrats often acknowledged some class discontent and at the same time proclaimed social felicity. This double-think was achieved by characterizing dissident yeomen and others as "poor white trash." Almost without exception, only planters and professionals employed this term. In Southwest Tennessee, James Hill, whose father owned two blacks, complained that "large slaveholders felt themselves better than the poor white trash as they called [nonslaveowners]"; and in Middle Tennessee, the wealthy Lee Billingsley remembered "hearing some families referred to as 'poor white trash.' "²⁵ Patricians vicariously used their slaves to condemn nonconforming yeomen. "There was no distinction between slave owners and non slave owners," reported John Johnson, "but the servants (whom I consider the best Judges of respectability) often made distinctions." In Dickson County, Edward Martin boasted that "on account of there gracious maners and social qualities," local slaveowners "were termed true aristocrats." These men associated on an "equal footing" with "honorable non slaveholders." As a result, he averred, "there was no antagonism existing between the two classes except [for an] indolent non working Clas whom the Slaves called po white trash." In the same spirit, Lemuel Tyree pointed out that in Maury County "there was in every neighborhood poor white trash as the negro called [them] . . . that gentle people did not associate with."²⁶ Yeomen took umbrage at these condescending attitudes. Among them, Robert Mosley resented the fact that Williamson County aristocrats would call his family "clod hopers."²⁷

Tennessee planters were socially ethnocentric. They, and those who sympathized with them, assumed that their cultural values were the southern norm. Confident of their community status, busy in their pursuit of commercial success, and insensitive to their impact on less prosperous neighbors, the elite saw themselves as virtuous, and they neither appreciated nor understood resentment on the part of lesser whites. Zachary Dyer, the son of a Giles County overseer, identified with local aristocrats and demonstrated little sympathy for those critical of the antebellum social system:

> As a General thing the Slave owners mingled freely [with] all honorable men upon a common level socially[.] The poor class as a general rule wer to blame for what nonsociability existed in my section. . . . I lived in one of the best communities Gods sun ever Shone upon. They were nearly all Slave holders but Christian people remember[ed] Christ words . . . the poor you have with you always. . . . the non Slavehold[er] Seemed to envy the Slaveholder to some extent the same as the people are to day the rich are envied by the poor to Some extent.²⁸

Whether the nonslaveowners were envious or resentful of the wealthy was a matter of perspective. But regardless of interpretation, it is clear that the poor, the plain folk, and the planters were class conscious. This was inevitable in a culture where the vast majority of the white population gave high social value to manual labor, while a minority disdained such efforts as not befitting gentlemen. From their early youth the poor and the yeomen exercised their own muscles to till the earth, to hoe crops, and to chop wood. Fathers taught their sons to work hard and judged their neighbors by their degree of industry. These people were offended by the image of an idle aristocrat growing wealthy from slave labor. Scores of old soldiers voiced their discontent in the Civil War Veterans Questionnaires.

One of Dyer's aims in developing the questionnaire was to ascertain the level of respect for manual labor in the Old South. Conscious of pro-North historian John Ford Rhodes's accusations that there was a southern leisure ethic, Dyer hoped to prove the opposite. He asked several pointed questions: "How was honest toil—as plowing, hauling, and other sorts of honest work of this class—regarded in your community? Was such work considered respectable and honorable? Did the white men generally engage in such work? To what extent were there white men in your community leading lives of idleness and having other men do their work for them?" Born into a society that valued labor as a test of male virility, the old soldiers overwhelmingly responded that everyone in their community worked. Eighty-one percent agreed with Harrison W. Farrell's testimonial: "Every Since I can Remember . . . all Worked Except [a] few Drones . . . called sore Back quality . . . and [there were] very few of them" (Appendix 2, table 18).[29]

The defensive phrase "everyone worked" was a natural response to Dyer's questions. A small number of veterans stressed that slaveowners went into the fields with their slaves (6 percent) and an even smaller number pointed out that slaveowners performed important functions other than manual labor (2 percent). Only 4 out of 1,223 former Confederates condemned the poor white for their idleness.

Each class evaluated its culture's commitment to labor by its own peculiar standards. A hard-toiling yeoman naturally assumed that others in his community shared his work ethic. On the other hand, many impoverished Tennesseans resented the leisure enjoyed by the elite, and significant numbers of upper-class veterans candidly acknowledged their freedom from drudgery. Twelve percent of all the former Confederates claimed that slaveowners took their ease. Those at either end of the social scale most often made that observation—19 percent of the poor and 14 percent of the wealthy (Appendix 2, table 18).

The sons of planters and professionals frequently acknowledged that members of their class did not feel compelled to perform manual labor. Work "was honorable but not generally done by slave owners," reflected Marcus Toney. "It was done, but mostly by the Negroes[.] The slave holders generally had the Negroes [to work and] . . . if not enough we hired the poor whites." Remembering his father's seventy-five slaves, Creed Haskins declared that "as a rule Slave owners did very little hard work"; and the affluent James M. Johnson wrote that "the majority [of slaveowners] lived lives of ease." Both Robert McAlister of Williamson County and William Greaves of Haywood County made strong distinctions between their class and other whites. "Those who had plenty did but little" manual labor, explained McAlister, but "the more unfortunate ones had too." Greaves stated simply: "The poorer class [worked] the better class didnt."[30]

Yeomen—both slaveowning and nonslaveowning—also distinguished between their work ethic and the planter's leisure lifestyle. "There were a few who owne[d] several negroes and . . . did not look upon work as being very exalting," recorded Isaac Day of Madison County. His father owned two slaves. "I suppose those who owned several slaves thoug they were a little better than other people," he wrote, and then added: "our people did not so consider." Samuel Clemmons concurred. "Where only a few Negrows in a family," he explained, "negrow Boys and white all went to work together but in families with [a] large amount of slaves the white as a rule did very little work." As a result, he believed that planters often caused "men that had no slaves to feel a little unpleasant." The son of a Maury County yeoman with two slaves resented the fact that the wealthy "did not have to work" and instead "speculated on different things Such as land and colored people"; and the son of a Haywood County nonslaveowner complained that "Quite a number of rich men had boys that did not [work]."[31]

Indigent Tennesseans were especially harsh in their assessment of the elite's leisure ethic. William Vardell, who was raised in Rutherford County, proudly wrote that "we were taught we should live by the Sweet of the brow [and] all reasonable men new that it was honest and right." Except for a "few worthless slaveholders," everyone in his neighborhood measured up to that standard. Isaac Broyles of Rhea County listed among his community's idlers the "Merchants, Lawyers, Doctors, the majority of slave holders, Preachers, School teachers, and live stock traders." The son of a Sullivan County day laborer noted bitterly that those who "owned Slaves did not work and did not have their children do any work." "Negroes and poor white men did the work," explained Ezekiel Inman of Perry County, while "Slave holders [felt] above working people" and "Spent their time in hunting and fishing and riding around."[32]

Each class—the planters, the plain folk, and the poor—viewed the concept of work from a separate vantage. A vast difference existed between the gentry, who lived within the social and economic environment of commercial agriculture, the yeomen, who engaged in subsistence farming, and the impoverished, who often depended upon the gentry for survival. The affluent were engaged in supervising their holdings, purchasing land, and trading slaves. Still their wealth made leisure possible. Herman M. Doak, an East Tennessee patrician, claimed that all in his social class worked. Of course, he remembered, a few "Drones [existed] in every hive. I suppose there were some of us. I can't recall any [but there were] a few fox hunters of which I was one."[33] The yeomen often interpreted "fox hunting" and other such sports as idleness.

The subsistence farmer largely depended upon his own labor and that of his family, and each season was a struggle for survival. He looked with disapproval on the leisure of the upper classes and chafed at the knowledge that planters had slaves to do their work for them. Although the social classes resided in the same communities, for the most part the yeomen rarely came into direct economic and recreational contact with the planter. On the other hand, because day laborers and renters relied upon the elite's patronage for their subsistence, they directly associated with the upper classes. On a daily basis, they were able to compare their degraded condition with the wealth of the gentry, and the resulting feelings were often bitter. As the sister of an impoverished veteran complained: "There was a social line drawn between the men who had to work, and the ones who did not."[34]

In his questionnaire, Dyer assumed that the nineteenth-century South abounded in economic opportunities. He asked for a response to two statements that suggested a southern version of the Horatio Alger ethic. "Were the opportunities good in your community," he inquired, "for a poor young man, honest and industrious, to save up enough to buy a small farm or to go into business for himself?" This was followed by the query: "Were poor, honest, industrious young men, who were ambitious to make something of themselves encouraged or discouraged by slaveholders?" Given this obvious reference to the American belief that economic prosperity was available to any diligent individual, no matter how humble his origin, only the most disillusioned or cynical of the aged veterans replied with negatives.

In the Old South, success was largely contingent upon the possession of two properties: land and slaves. Naturally those born into families with one or both of these assets gave the most positive responses. Across the state, 82 percent of the nonslaveowning yeomen, 88 percent of the slaveowning yeomen, and 93 percent of the planters and professionals believed in economic opportunities for all white men. About four out of ten, or 38 percent, of the poor—those who had no access to either land or slaves—returned negative answers to Dyer's question (Appendix 2, table 19).

As would be expected, the wealthy were the most enthusiastic in their assessments of economic opportunities. "Every non-slaveholder was working to become a slaveholder," asserted the son of a wealthy Memphis merchant, "and the existing slaveholder helped him to make the money to buy slaves." Andrew Miller confidently stated that in Wilson County "almost all of the successful men of that day started poor"; and Elisha Taylor claimed to have known men who [began work] at 25 cents per day" and eventually "left to their heirs Land worth Fifty thousand [dollars]." Joshua Mewborn's father owned forty-eight slaves and 2,100 acres of Fayette County land. When asked whether economic opportunities existed for the honest poor, he declared: "Yes! Yes! Yes! with all the emphasis I can give it."[35]

The wealthy's faith in the possibility of financial advancement was based on two premises: first, that land was both inexpensive and abundant; and second, that their class paternally helped the worthy poor. "There was a virgin soil and cheap land," wrote Meriwether Donaldson of Lake County. As a result, he believed that "industry and economy was rewarded." Pressley Conner agreed. Writing about Lauderdale County, he explained that "Lands were cheap and very fertile and ... *many young men did well.*"[36] Other planters' sons pointed out their class's altruistic behavior toward the indigent. "I have known rich men with numbers of slaves," testified Amos Jones of Madison County, "to assist poor young men to buy a farm or to be educated and [to] assist them in a number of ways too numurous to be mentioned." Thomas Webb affirmed that in Shelby County "many young men came who had not a dollar and were helped along to success." Frequently, he emphasized, these ambitious young Southerners "married the daughters of the rich and became the most prominent and useful men we had." On a more personal note, Hervey Whitfield wrote: "I remember as a boy when my father offered to pay [the] first payment on a tract of land for a man that had nothing."[37]

Planters and professionals viewed their own success as the criteria by which to judge others. They assumed that those whites who failed to measure up to their standards were either unambitious, lazy, or ignorant. Blessed by wealth, family connections, and quality educations, they could not appreciate the perspective of the impoverished. Those who saw economic opportunities from the bottom up painted a far different picture.

A significant portion of the poor and a few from the other social classes expressed strong negative attitudes. William Barnes of Madison County pointedly stressed that "a poor man or boy didnt have no opportunities to own a farm"; Joe C. Brooks of McNairy County believed that it was "emposibal for a young man to own land"; and J. W. Keaton simply stated that "times were hard." "Land was very cheap," remembered Nimrod Reed, "but money was very hard to get hold of."[38] These veterans cast doubt on the fabled planter paternalism and often accused the gentry of selfishness. A few of the poor recognized that slave labor contributed to their disadvantaged condition, and others perceived that their limited educations precluded their entering the professions.

While some poor admitted that an occasional planter helped less fortunate whites, they did not recognize such happenings as commonplace. "If the youn[g] man was a relative or a personal friend of a slave holder[,] he would help him," observed John Welch. "If not[,] he didn't pay much attention to him." James Carroll of Hickman County was more harsh. "If the Slave holder could See a few Dollars in it for him," he believed, the poor were assisted. "If not [the planters] dident take no intrust." Carroll continued that in "Them Day[s] the Peopel were generaley Poore [and] they Dident have no Chance." Other veterans noted that the wealthy were merely indifferent to the aspirations of the impoverished. Responding to the question concerning whether slave owners encouraged or discouraged the industrious poor, John Dunavant explained that "there wasent much interst taked eather way." Still other veterans claimed that patricians actively worked against the ambitions of less affluent Tennesseans. J. W. Bradley complained that "wages [were] 25 to 40 cts per Day and . . . the Slave holder never gave the poor young man but little encouragement." James Coop thought that "the policy of most slaveholders was to acquire all the land they could for themselves"; J. M. Davis believed that local aristocrats "all waise tride to down the pore Boey all they cood"; and Ezekiel Inman grumbled that "No encouragement was given by the Slave holders to others out side of their own class."[39]

A small number of former Confederates recognized that the peculiar institution worked counter to their interests. They were aware that slavery enabled the wealthy to receive a higher-quality education than other whites and at the same time that it depressed the laboring man's wages and committed him to an enduring cycle of poverty. "A poor man had a hard time to qualify him Self for business," wrote James Gross of Grundy County, because "our free schools never went longer than two months in a year." Similarly Edward Gannaway took note of both his community's insufficient academic facilities and the unfortunate pay received by common school teachers. Due to the fact that "money [was] mighty scarce," he recalled that few could afford an education and even "the young man that had the learning cold hardly get enough to pay his board [on a teacher's] salary of $10 per mo."[40] Slavery was at the root of the poor's limited opportunity. William C. Dillihay observed that "negro Emancipation placed white people on a more equal footing causing much better opportunity for young men"; and Marcus Toney bluntly declared that in rural neighborhoods the poor had little chance "against slave labor." Having grown up in a one-room cabin on rented land, Lewis Hayes was especially caustic. "The slave holders could get the slave for almost nothing," he murmured, "and the poor young man like myself could not get a job."[41]

Dyer's inquiry concerning economic opportunity assumed that the poor and the yeomen among Tennessee's Confederate generation frequently moved into the planter and professional class. This was unlikely. As subsistence farmers, the yeomen probably assumed that mere survival from generation to generation constituted success. Wealth, extensive lands, and slaves were the concerns of those who moved in different and wider circles. As for the poor, they were locked into a hopeless lifestyle that deadened ambitions. To be sure, a few young men employed strict economy and made persistent efforts to migrate to a higher social level. Reflecting on these, one Maury County yeoman quoted a plebeian proverb: "Like Lawyers going to Heaven, [they were] few and far between."[42]

Hoping that his questionnaires would create the source material for a "true history of the Old South," Dyer tried to ascertain whether civic democracy was extant in antebellum Tennessee. "In a political contest in which one candidate owned slaves and the other did not," he asked, "did the fact that one candidate owned slaves help him any in winning the contest?" The question's wording was unfortunate. It suggested that in any given contest for public office, slaveownership was an issue. Overwhelmingly the Confederate veterans denied that assumption. Nonetheless those who did claim that owning slaves helped a candidate followed predictable class lines. Twenty-four percent of the impoverished responded in the affirmative. This figure fell to 12 percent of the nonslaveowning yeomen, 11 percent of the slaveowning yeomen, and a meager 6 percent of the planters and professionals (Appendix 2, table 20).

Most former Confederates argued that slaveownership was a negligible factor in a person's candidacy. In a typical affirmation, Ford Adams of Robertson County wrote that people usually "voted for the most capable man regardless of slaves." Some of the wealthier respondents even claimed that the indigent had the upper hand. David Watkins, whose father "owned between 50 and 75 slaves—old and young," declared that "generally the poorer man was elected"; Thomas Webb, whose father was a cotton broker with 25 slaves, believed "the fact that a candidate was a poor man and needed the job was one of the strongest appeals to the voters"; and William Witherspoon, whose father owned in excess of 125 slaves and extensive acreage in both Tennessee and Arkansas, affirmed that "the none Slave holder had the advantage, as [voters] thought he needed the office worse."[43]

A minority of Tennessee's Confederate generation believed that slaveownership was a determining factor in politics. "The man that owned slaves," wrote a Rutherford County yeoman, "always won." The impoverished John Duke of Wilson County shared that view. He thought that owning slaves "helpt the canidate in most every case." Three veterans—Johnson Spurlock of Jackson County, Sam Smithson of Williamson County, and John Foster of Gibson County—described antebellum politics in terms of a class struggle. Spurlock contended that in a race "the Slave holders generally did all [they] could for the Big man and the poor man went for the poor man"; Smithson remembered that "slave owners usually voted for the democratic ticket [and] the non slave holders voted the whig ticket"; and Foster propounded: "Those that had no slaves fought much harder to win a contest than those who did for they knew the influence of slaveholders."[44]

In reality slaveowners, especially the planters and professionals, were more likely than nonslaveowners to attain political office. Before the Civil War, 23 percent of the wealthy veterans' fathers and 17 percent of the slaveowning yeomen's fathers held either local or state positions. In comparison offices were held by 11 percent of the nonslaveowning yeomen's fathers and 4 percent of the poor's fathers (Appendix 2, table 21).

A look at the posts held by the veterans' fathers suggests that slaveowners usually presided over the local decision-making process. Sixty-one individuals served as county court members. None were poor. Fourteen were from among the nonslaveowning yeomen, twenty-six were from among the slaveowning yeomen, and twenty-one were from among the planter and professionals. Five of the affluent were clerks of the county court. The same position was also held by three slaveowning yeomen, and one each from among the nonslaveowning yeomen and the poor. Those at the bottom of society fared a little better as justices of the peace. Five poor men attained that position. Eleven nonslaveowning yeomen, twenty-three slaveowning yeomen, and eleven wealthy also secured this office. Given the isolated nature of most rural communities, the justice of the peace officiated over minor judicial matters. In those districts with little slaveownership, the local justice would naturally come from the yeoman class. Filling out his Civil War Veterans Questionnaire in 1922, an indigent veteran from Williamson County pointed out that "the line between the . . . classes was more strictly drawn then than now. . . . slave holders generally held most public offices, [but] Some of the small county offices, constable, clerks, etc., were held by the poor whites."[45]

Slaveowners dominated local law enforcement. Thirty-two of the veterans' fathers were either sheriffs, deputies, or constables. Two-thirds of these owned slaves—ten planters and professionals and eleven yeomen. Nine nonslaveowning yeomen and two poor held positions in law enforcement. This work was hazardous. William Mabry sadly wrote that his father "was Sheriff of Wilson County—When he was killed."[46] All state judges and, with one exception, all other state offices were held by slaveowners. The exception—John W. Lowry of East Tennessee—was a poor schoolteacher who was elected to the general assembly in 1861 to oppose secession.[47]

Although slavery played an important role in Tennessee's antebellum politics, there was rarely a direct contest between the slaveowning and nonslaveowning communities. Rather the affluence made possible by the peculiar institution provided for the upper classes—and to a lesser extent the yeomen—the basic elements needed to hold office: wealth, leisure time, education, and family connections. Some veterans recognized this. Charles Faris of Rutherford County declared that "Non slave holders seldom rain for office [because] they were generally poor people and renters." Napoleon Abbott accused the wealthy of buying "votes, with liquor and cigars"; James Tyner remembered that only slaveowners could afford "big barbacues during times of Elections"; and John Allen stated that in politics "money always has its influence."[48]

Not only did affluence help a person gain an office, but it also helped in other ways. William Moss believed that financial comfort gave slaveholders "more time to devote to political work"; and Marcus Toney recalled that "nearly all the candidates I [knew] were slaveholders and men of wealth who could buy an education."[49] Because, as a general rule, local aristocrats socialized among themselves, they encouraged members of their own class to seek positions of civic trust. John Brawner thought that in Weakley County "Slave holders appeared to support each other"; and Samuel Reynolds responded that in Dickson County "it Seamed that Birds of a fether wood flock to gether."[50] William Davis of Marshall County summarized the situation well. In politics, he wrote, "it seemed that the slave holder had the firepower."[51]

Class consciousness did exist among antebellum Tennesseans. Most individuals were cognizant of their own status as well as others'. To a great extent, however, social segregation prevented extensive conflict. As long as the activities of local aristocrats did not work against the needs of the yeomen and the poor, the latter pursued their humble lives untroubled by the gentry's dealings in slaves, land, and politics. Because of the various class differences in lifestyle, education, and cultural perspective, however, pre–Civil War Tennessee was more a land of social cleavages than social concensus. The dreadful events of 1861 to 1865 further strained the relationship between plebeians and patricians. Thrown together in the comradeship of combat, the wealthy, the yeomen, and the impoverished shared both the hardships of camp and the carnage of battle. Under these circumstances, the Confederate generation gradually awoke to the fact that the classes possessed fundamentally diverse social values and significantly divergent stakes in the conflict.

CHAPTER FIVE

★ ★

SOCIAL CLASS AND CIVIL WAR

The Civil War created a common ground for the members of Tennessee's Confederate generation, for whom the war years constituted a demarcation between the Old and New South. The deprivation, destruction, and death associated with the conflict blighted their lives. Few cherished romantic ideals. "I have experienced that war is hell on earth," lamented William Duggan. "The Devil is at the head of it and I hope I will never see any more." Because the vast majority of the aging soldiers filled out their questionnaires in 1922, their memories of the tragic carnage may have been heightened by the recent World War. John Wilson prayed that he "could Just pull back the Curtain and show . . . a true picture of the dead[,] dying and wounded and Suffering of the civil war." Carroll Clark spoke the sentiments of thousands of his peers. "I went through the war from start to finish," he explained, "and could not tell all the hardships I endured. It would take a book of several pages to contain what I . . . suffered."[1]

In spite of measurable class strife during the antebellum era, most white Tennesseans entered the conflict fairly united in their support of secession. To be sure, a majority of East Tennesseans, as well as a substantial number living near the western cut of the Tennessee River, sided with the Union.[2] Most of the remainder enrolled under the Confederate banner. Youths volunteered, emboldened by patriotic fervor, excited by the prospect of adventure, and blinded to the slaughter of combat. Whole communities enlisted; dissent was associated with treason and failure to join was attributed to cowardice. Class antagonisms were momentarily set aside in the moment of cri-

sis. "To arms!" admonished a Hickman County colonel in his recruit-
ing circular. "Our Southern soil must be defended. We must not stop
to ask who brought about war, who is at fault, but let us go and do
battle . . . and then settle the question who is to blame."[3]

United in rebellion, the poor, the yeomen, and the wealthy were
forced to live on more intimate terms in the Confederate army than
they had in civilian life. Some veterans thought that this verified the
existence of class harmony. Walter Jennings, whose father owned fifteen slaves, boasted that out of his regiment "of more than 725 men
more than ⅔ . . . of the very best of them were non slave holders."
Similarly a Dyer County physician's son remembered "little distinction among intelligent, decent people. . . . There were more non
slave holders in the Confederate Armies than there were slave holders."[4] Despite these testimonials, the South's military forces reflected
the culture's aristocratic tint. While both plebeian and patrician
shared in the initial euphoria of war, eventually the poor and the
yeomen grew weary. In camp and in combat, social differences were
abundant. Often small differences were a sign of social patterns and
a portent of greater difficulties to come.

Few Tennesseans were conscious of the major issues of the war,
and fewer still had any real concept of the South's goals. Rational
thought and cold calculation of self-interest were rarely part of the
decision to enlist. Caught up in the pageantry of war, adolescents
yearned for the ultimate rite of passage—combat. In almost every
Tennessee community, public meetings and dinners on the ground
gave politicians the opportunity to inflame passions. Unaware of the
consequences, parents and young girls urged their sons, their brothers, and their beaus to do their duty and to bring home honor.[5]

Across the state, academies closed and teachers encouraged their
youthful scholars to enlist in the cause. Mill-Wood Institute near
Sycamore faced a serious crisis when its principal revealed his northern sympathies. The assistant principal promptly mutinied and soon
enrolled "all young students of proper age . . . in the Confederate
Army." Events moved more smoothly at Mt. Vernon Academy near
Lebanon. Its chief administrator, Sam Freeman, put aside his academic duties to organize an artillery battery. In November 1864,
he—and no doubt some of his former students—died at the vicious
Battle of Franklin.[6]

Even in the middle of this early war euphoria, social-class differences were already evident. Both the choice of army service—infantry, calvary, or artillery—and the attainment of rank—from private to

general—were determined by class distinctions. Although a majority of soldiers from each social level marched in the infantry, the cavalry had a disproportionate share of wealthy Confederates. Forty-two percent of the affluent served under the commands of Nathan Bedford Forrest, Joseph Wheeler, John Morgan, and other cavalry commanders, while only 32 percent of the slaveowning yeomen and 31 percent of the nonslaveowning yeomen were cavalrymen, and only 26 percent of the poor rode horses into combat (Appendix 2, table 22). Whatever their branch of service, Tennessee Confederates obeyed officers with personal commitments to slavery. Only 3 percent of the poor and 5 percent of the nonslaveowning yeomen held the ranks of lieutenant or captain. A significantly larger number of slaveowners received commissions—12 percent of the yeomen and 19 percent of the wealthy (Appendix 2, table 23).

Tennessee's aristocrats, having been raised to dominate slaves and to receive deference from lesser whites, were prepared to lead in combat. Several rushed home from college to raise companies and drill troops. William Carnes resigned his appointment at the U.S. Naval Academy and returned to his Memphis home, where he was commissioned a first lieutenant and assigned to train an artillery unit; within a few weeks he was commanding, as captain, a battery at New Madrid, Missouri. By the end of the war, he commanded a small coastal vessel in the Confederate navy. David Crockett Brown left Virginia's Emory and Henry College to organize an infantry company in his native White County. He and his father scoured the countryside collecting arms and encouraging enlistments.[7]

The fortunes of war enabled some young aristocrats to move up rapidly through the ranks. John Fite, the son of a DeKalb County merchant, captained Company B of the Seventh Tennessee Infantry. When the regiment was reorganized outside Richmond, Virginia, in April 1862, he became the ranking captain. Just before the Battle of Seven Pines his colonel was promoted to brigadier general and Fite rose to major. A few days later the unit's lieutenant colonel died in a charge at Gaines Mill. Fite replaced him. In a matter of weeks, the colonel had resigned due to ill health and Fite found himself in command. In just over a year, he had moved from captain to colonel.[8]

Tennessee's poor and yeomen were also caught up in the initial martial spirit. Their positions were usually more humble than those of the elite; their stories were often touching. Carroll Clark, the son of a small farmer without slaves, wrote that he volunteered "on the 15th day of May 1861 at Spencer, Van Buren County. It was on Wednesday a beautiful clear day. I kissed mother good by and went to war." Jesse Green naively left home to enter the war "for three weeks and was gone for nearly three years"; and sixteen-year-old John O'Neal ran away from his parents to join with his five older brothers "in the Service." Impoverished William Beard sadly remembered that he left behind a "mother and two sisters all alone without anyone to support them."[9] Beard's experience paralleled that of many others; the situation soon became a vital problem for the Confederacy. The poor and the nonslaveowning yeomen relied on the labor of husbands and sons for their livelihood. When the men abandoned the farms, their families suffered intensely. As the war dragged on, desperate farmers wavered in their commitment to the rebellion and began to desert, thus hastening the defeat of the Confederacy.[10]

Even during the excitement of the war's first spring and summer, dissident voices were heard. A few Tennesseans resisted the stampede to secession. Although Richard Winn fondly recalled that in Montgomery County "it took very little urging to get volunteers," he also added: "Some of course didnt like the Idia of with drawing from the union." The anti-Confederate spirit was especially strong in eastern Tennessee. As a region with little commitment to slavery, a majority of its inhabitants were reluctant to fight for the property rights of other Southerners. Elias Montgomery believed that slaveowners in Bedford County "felt above those who did not own slaves" and he recalled that social antagonisms grew as "the war clouds gathered." In Smith County, G. W. Lamberson thought social problems became worse when "the war talk started"; and Jeremiah McKenzie affirmed that at "the breaking out of the war" social-class relations in Meigs County "became tense."[11]

In 1861 volunteering was in vogue and young male Tennesseans were caught up in patriotic fervor. Death, gore, disappointment, and adversity lay before them. Few comprehended this. Only gradually, in the months and years to come, would the Confederate generation develop a full appreciation of the bitterness of war.

Whatever romantic images the fledgling warriors harbored of heroic charges and brave stands, reality consisted of dreary periods of inactive camp life. Relatively few days were spent on the march and even fewer involved combat. Like soldiers in most wars, young Confederates endured boredom, lice, and disease. The dreary and repetitive tasks of collecting firewood, cooking rations, and constructing shelters gave them plenty of time to reflect on their situations and on the social protocol of the camps. Confederate camps mirrored southern society as a whole. Although to some degree rich and poor shared common discomforts, in several ways the aristocrats enjoyed advantages made possible by wealth, slaves, and family connections. Camp diseases, inadequate food, and poor shelter knew no class boundaries. Nonetheless, Tennessee's elites were better able to endure these conditions because they possessed better clothing and body servants, and they often drew the choicest military assignments.

Hundreds of Tennessee youths perished before they ever met the Yankees. Because commanders and common soldiers alike were woefully ignorant of basic hygiene, training camps were notorious breeding grounds for communicable diseases. Soldiers pitched their tents on swampy ground and dug latrines next to wells; the ill were rarely, if ever, quarantined. Measles, mumps, and whooping cough became epidemic, and many survived these only to be swept away by secondary infections and pneumonia. Looking back on several distressing weeks at Camp Trousdale near Gallatin, Tennessee, W. L. Shofner painfully wrote: "we went th[r]ough a scourage of Measles and lost a good many Soldiers."[12]

Harrison W. Farrell graphically illustrated the horrors of "measels, . . . mumps, pneumonia, and Brain fever" associated with early Civil War camp life. Shortly after Company A of the Forty-fourth Tennessee Infantry marched into Bowling Green, Kentucky, in December 1861, the inexperienced captain bivouacked his troops on low ground. It promptly flooded. In short order, one-third of the company—including Farrell—was incapacitated with intense chills. With men dying every day in the camp's crude infirmary, the survivors were ordered to Nashville. Herded into drafty freight cars, they received no medical aid en route and were abandoned at the Nashville depot in the midst of a sleet storm. "Wet and chill[ed] Beyond Reason," Farrell wrote, several "fainted and Died Befor they got to their hospital."[13] The nightmare had only begun.

In the capital, Farrell and his fellow sufferers were confronted with appalling incompetency and inhumanity. Among other things, they lacked adequate food. "In the hospital . . . our allowance was [designed] to starve one to Death," he recalled: "1 cracker[,] 2 table spoonfull[s] of chicken water [and] 1 gill [of] coffee water twice a Day. . . . It was awfull to See [the sick] Begging for something to eat [and] Die hungry." Fortunately for Farrell, David Brooks, a compassionate friend, smuggled baked sweet potatoes to him. "We had to watch when we ate of our private grub," he said, because "the Nurses and Warden would find it" and consume it themselves. After several visits, the friend was struck by a fatal fever. Although paralyzed in one arm and extremely weak, Farrell secured permission to accompany Brooks's corpse home. Once there, Farrell never returned to the army.[14]

In a few short months, most raw recruits developed immunities to the more common communicable diseases, but other maladies continually plagued the hapless soldiers. Mid-nineteenth-century Americans lacked basic knowledge about balanced diets, the importance of cleanliness, and bacterial infections. Throughout the conflict, there was as much death and suffering from typhoid fever and diarrhea as from combat. "Sanitation of the camps was bad," remembered a private in the Twenty-seventh Tennessee Infantry. "Disease ran riot among the soldiers taking more than were slain by bullets." William Hunter agreed that "Chronic Diarhea was the most dreaded desease in the Army." William Wakefield and others in his company were constantly "troubled by the itch and body lice." Typhoid fever took a dreadful toll. It prematurely ended the military careers of John Lusk of Sevier County, William Crihfield of Lauderdale County, and John Tate of Wilson County. Lieutenant Calvin Crook volunteered for his brother's regiment in August 1861 but rarely saw combat because he was "sick all [the] time." Plagued by recurring bouts with diarrhea and other camp illnesses, he resigned in December 1862. During his military service, he had lost nearly half his body weight.[15]

A few Tennesseans described better camp conditions. "I had a good tent [and] a cot to sleep on," bragged David Sullins, whose father was president of Odd Fellow College in Jonesboro, Tennessee. "We had fair rations," he continued, and noted that he was "not much exposed to hunger and disease." Significantly Sullins was an officer assigned to the quartermaster's corps. Far more typical was the testimony of Sims Latta, who recalled spending unhappy nights exposed to rain and sleeping in the mud or "on the frozen ground." On other occasions, he and his fellow Confederates "marched bare footed[,] ragged and half frozen." Thomas Kinser complained that, in camp, the Second Tennessee Infantry lived "like hogs on the ground."[16]

Shortages of food and shelter contributed to the soldiers' misery. "Sometimes we had a good meal," reflected D. P. Chamberland, "but generally we . . . had to buckle up our belts to find whether we possessed stomachs." Throughout the questionnaires, the Confederate veterans grumbled about eating little more than "blue beef," rough milled corn, and dried peas. Cooking facilities were crude. Holes covered with oil cloths became mixing bowls; "corn dodgers" were roasted on the ends of sticks; and one Williamson County soldier remembered that, in his company, "an old skillet with the handle off" served eight men. By late in the war Confederate troops, weakened by hunger, disregarded regulations and stole food from southern farmers. Of Hood's desperate Tennessee campaign of November–December 1864, William Key wrote: "We shore had the sheep and Hog[s] on the sly."[17]

Shortages of tents and other shelters left Tennessee troops subject to the whims of nature. "We were exposed to such weather as came," remembered Erasmas Osgatharp. "We were not protected any." Edward Doe often awoke covered by snow "or drenched with rain"; Ben Moser piled fence rails over mud for bedding; and Lorenzo Sanders constructed windbreaks of cedar brush for relief from winter storms. Suffering caused by freezing temperatures was intense, and shivering Confederates would often burn brush and logs over the frozen soil, scrape away the coals, and then spread their bed rolls on the warmed ground. Recalling this experience, Robert Bowden explained that several comrades would huddle together on one blanket while another spread additional blankets and pine branches over them. When finished the last individual was allowed to "root up in the middle of [the] men."[18]

The soldiers' youthful immaturities, combined with the brutal environment of war, frequently created hazardous camp atmospheres. Boredom and tension encouraged the playing of stupid and dangerous practical jokes, and occasionally tempers would flare, with tragic results; an added danger was the constant threat of the Union army. William Tucker recounted the murder of his close friend, Masey Trull, during a card game. Angered over a disputed poker hand, the assailant "thrust a knife into [Masey's] breast" and then escaped. Isaac Griffith, while eating breakfast, looked on in horror as "some fool" struck a dud shell with "a Day iron." "It Exsploaet," he wrote, and killed three men. As Demarus Cunningham and his company divided their meager morning meal, "a stray ball from the enemy" crashed into a crowd. Wounded along with several others, Cunningham testified: "James F. Grant [took] my arm off leaving only 1½ inch stump."[19]

Few Tennessee soldiers were left with romantic images of their Civil War camp life. Even the passage of nearly six decades failed to soften the veterans' bitter memories. Writing to the Tennessee Historical Committee, William Yates of Shelby County highlighted some of the discomforts he endured in his constant struggle for basic cleanliness and warmth: "[I] had vermin so bad at one time [that] I took [my clothes] . . . and burnt [them] to . . . get rid of the lice. . . .

when we were ordered to spend the night in quarters that others had just vacated[,] the place seemed alive with them. One night it was so cold and I had so little to keep warm with[,] I lay . . . close to the fire[.] when I awoke I found part of the tail of my coat (the only one I had) was burnt off." On another occasion, he braved a snowstorm to wash the filth from his only shirt. As he explained: "Clothes were pretty scanty."[20]

Clothing constituted one of several notable differences between the sons of planters and professionals and most other young Confederates. The wealthy naturally dressed better than others. Most veterans received almost all their clothing from home, with predictable results. "Our uniforms were uniform in one respect only," reminisced James Anthony. "We were uniformly ragged! We had rags of all sizes, . . . Rags of all colors textures and makes; Rags of bright colors and gloomy ones."[21] Tennessee patricians, especially officers, felt compelled to be "more neatly and smartly dressed." When General Braxton Bragg's wagon train was captured at Perryville, Kentucky, Hampton Cheney lost his entire wardrobe. Upon his arrival at Knoxville, Cheney purchased a new uniform for $2,500, a new hat for $100, a pair of boots for $1,500, a pair of corduroy pants for $100, and a new sword for $700.[22] Doubtless the sight of finely attired, aristocratic officers occasionally provoked contempt on the part of more shabbily dressed enlistees. When those same privates marched in the snow with bare, bleeding feet, class distinctions became even more acute.

An appalling scarcity of shoes was another detriment to Confederate morale. While Tennessee country boys might easily adjust to barefoot summer campaigns, unshod marches in winter were agonizing. William Hartsfield vividly remembered Braxton Bragg's torturous retreat through Cumberland Gap, Kentucky, in late 1862. "It snowed on us," he wrote, and "we could track the boys by the blood . . . from their bare feet." Both Theodore Harris and Alax Underhill affirmed that the army's lack of shoes caused profound suffering following the wintertime Battle of Murfreesboro, and several other veterans looked back with pain on Hood's invasion of Middle Tennessee during one of the century's bitterest winters. As Robert Holman and others of his company neared Nashville, they were "almost barefooted"; Hamilton Hennessee declared that "when Hood came to Tenn. I [marched] barefoot till I had blood blisters on the bottom of my feet." Henry Guthrie watched shoeless Confederates struggle past his home in the "snow and sleet." Taking pity upon them, Guthrie's wife and mother bound their battered feet with rags.[23] By the war's fourth winter, many young soldiers must have questioned whether the cause justified their personal afflictions.

Despite the diseases, discomforts, and deprivations associated with Confederate camp life, Tennessee patricians enjoyed some benefits made possible by slavery and family connections. Wealthy Confederates brought their personal servants along on campaign. After "fair-[ing] Sumptuosly" in their first winter quarters, however, J. F. Osborne and his fellow aristocrats in Company D of the Thirty-third Tennessee Infantry were abruptly deprived of their creature comforts. On the march south from Columbus, Kentucky, they were ordered to send their "negro cooks and Sunday clothes home." Others managed to retain their servants throughout the conflict. "My father sent with me . . . a negro boy of my age," wrote John Dance, "and [he] stayed . . . during the entire war." Charles Rice was less fortunate. Over a half century after the Civil War, he remained indignant that the Yankees forced him to surrender his personal slave following the Confederate defeat at Vicksburg.[24] Whenever slaves were unavailable, the upper classes drafted the enlisted men for personal service. Milton Rowell, whose father owned no land and no slaves, recorded that he saw little combat because he was detailed to cook for his officers.[25]

Confederate commanders usually selected their personal staffs from members of their own social class. The sons of planters and professionals frequently gained the privileged positions of aides and couriers. Closely associated with the colonels and the generals, they were often isolated from some of the more distasteful aspects of camp life. Among these fortunate affluents, James McColgan became the private secretary to his regiment's colonel, Samuel Whitsitt was "detailed as courier to Col. Smith" of the Eleventh Tennessee Infantry, William Johnston was employed first "as General Loring's escort" and later "on Gen. Rucker's staff," and Hampton Cheney was "appointed adjutant . . . to Gen. John C. Brown" during the war's last two years. Thomas Aldrich, whose father had twenty slaves and a small Davidson County plantation, illustrated the benefits of such assignments. "I was with General N. B. Forrest 13 months of Staff duty," the old veteran recalled. "He was my best friend in all the war [and] he took care of me."[26]

A few wealthy fathers used their influence and personal connections to secure safe positions for their sons. In March 1862, William Lillard's father had his son appointed as clerk of the commissary department at Griffin, Georgia. His efforts were foiled, however, when the youthful Lillard ran away to join his uncle's cavalry company. Robert Parker was more obedient. Following the directions of his father, a prominent Memphis merchant, he spent the last three years of the war keeping records for the Confederate ordnance bureau.[27]

Social distinctions in the Confederate army were no more pronounced than they had been in civilian life. But there was an important difference. Before the war, the classes were largely segregated and therefore their contrasting lifestyles were only occasionally obvious. The army thrust the wealthy, the yeomen, and the poor into constant and close association. A hungry, ragged private huddled next to his meager fire could not help but note the more comfortable status of aristocrats. They were better dressed, they possessed obliging servants, and they often partook of the honor associated with command. By the latter part of the war, the poor and the yeomen felt far less committed to the southern crusade than their more affluent peers in Tennessee's Confederate generation.

Civil War battlefields were gruesome. As a haze of spent gunpowder shrouded the landscape, a macabre atmosphere haunted the surviving combatants. Wounded animals dumbly bellowed, maimed soldiers screamed for mercy, and the silent dead littered the soil with their gore. In their Civil War Veterans Questionnaires, Tennesseans vividly remembered the war's horrors. Several recalled that the grim contest at Chickamauga epitomized the devastation of battle. An aging cavalryman recorded that he "walked on dead boddies for a mile"; a Sullivan County infantryman testified that he waded through a creek "stained Pretty Bad with Blood"; and a former dispatch bearer recalled the dying screams of fifty injured soldiers trapped in a burning house. Thomas Corn defended a Confederate artillery battery in the same bloody event. Dead Union soldiers "and confederates mingled . . . to gether around the guns," he recounted, and "it was a gas[t]ly Sight."[28]

Death was the constant companion of armed combat. The old soldiers confronted their enemies and witnessed the slaughter of relatives and friends. William Orr killed his first Yankee as the surprised victim scurried out of his tent at Shiloh; and William Lucy shot a sniper at Raymond, Mississippi. As Lucy recalled the incident, the Yankee "shot one man on each side of me [and] while he stoped to load his musket[,] I killed him[.] he was loading to get me next." Many of the aging Rebels, regretting the terrible violence, could sympathize with John Mason's forlorn prayer. "I fired a cannon," he wrote, "I hop[e] I never kill[ed] any one."[29]

The violent demise of brothers, cousins, and boyhood friends haunted many veterans. Describing the moment when his comrade, Ches Chatman, was struck by a cannonball, G. W. Lamberson graphically wrote: "It hit [his] hed and solders and tore [them] off and throwd meat in my face." At Shiloh, William Tucker saw a minié ball impact just above his cousin's ear. "I asked him how many times he had [been] shot," the veteran stated, but "he did not have time to answer." Lee Sadler grimly obeyed the instructions given by his elder brother. Just before the battle of Murfreesboro, his sibling warned: "If you get hurt . . . I cant stop to take care of you. If I get hurt or killed, you go on." Within days Lee Sadler rushed passed his brother's mutilated body.[30]

Brutalized by war's incessant disregard for human life, mid-nineteenth-century youths grew insensitive to the sufferings of others. John Johnston remembered a nasty scrimmage when he and other retreating Confederates were overwhelmed by Union cavalry. Just before he was knocked unconscious, he saw "two yankey's . . . hacking at [his mess mate] with their sabers." Left behind when the battle moved on, Johnston awoke to find his friend striking a wounded cavalryman with a large rock. "The yankey was begging him to stop saying he was shot," the veteran reported, but the "mess mate replied you wouldent stop when I was begging and I wont stop for you." Throughout the rest of his life, Christopher Robertson remained embittered at the callous treatment accorded his dying brother. A participant in Forrest's raid on Memphis in 1864, the brother "was mortally wounded through the bowls" and abandoned during the withdrawal. "The yankees went about hauling away the dead," Robertson explained, "and when they came to my brother two men took this eighteen year old boy by his wrists and ankles and . . . threw him into the waggon on top of . . . dead men." Horrified, a compassionate civilian prevailed upon the Union commander to surrender the writhing soldier to his care. Young Robertson died that night.[31]

Even in death, differences persisted among Tennessee's social classes. The poor and yeomen who were struck down in battle were all too often interred with little concern or ceremony. Patricians received more attention. Two soldiers—Wesley Sheets and Phillip Weems—provide examples of the differing treatments. Both fell during the Civil War and had their questionnaires completed by relatives. Shot down at Shiloh, the impoverished Sheets was buried anonymously in a crowded trench. In 1922 his sister wrote: "When I get to thinking of that I am bitter with hatred as I was in the sixties." The aristocratic Weems's story was told by his nephew, the family's genealogist. Weems grew up in the resort community of Bon Agua Springs, where he was pampered by his parents' thirty slaves. "Being young and having been brought up in more or less luxury," the nephew commented, "he seemed to have been high strung, gallant, and wild." At the outbreak of the war, he raised an infantry company composed of Hickman and Dickson County volunteers, and in July 1864, he led these men in a charge before Atlanta. Struck by seven bullets, he lingered two days before he died. In recognition of his honorable sacrifice, Brigadier General George W. Gordon mailed to his grieving family a personal note of condolence and enclosed a lock of the youth's hair.[32]

In one important category, little statistical difference existed in the Confederate generation's military experiences. Union bullets and shells cared little for socioeconomic status. Twenty-one percent of both the poor and the wealthy, and 24 percent of all yeomen, were wounded (Appendix 2, table 24). Missing limbs and mutilated bodies became lifelong reminders of war's cruelty. "I was 16 years old when I Joined the army," lamented a Marshall County veteran; "I got my arm shot off before I was 18 years old." H. C. Cole reported that he "lost his right leg at Cassville, Ga."; James C. Fly's left arm was amputated at Chickamauga; and Harrison Neece specified that his right arm was removed during "the battle of Atlanta the 22nd day of July 1864." James Moore bluntly stated: "I was discharged at Chickamauga Sept 19, 1863 and still carry my discharge in my left Shoulder." That same day, James Coop was deprived of an eye. After filling out his questionnaire, William Key apologized for his wretched printing. Due to a wound at Nashville, he said, "I have only two fingers on my rite hand."[33]

Some soldiers were wounded more than once. Jesse Short, a veteran of the battles at Shiloh, Murfreesboro, Atlanta, and Franklin, was shot on five separate occasions. Richard Colville had a finger blown off at Murfreesboro and received a serious leg injury at Chickamauga; and Hiram Hawk was wounded first at Shiloh, again at Chickamauga, and yet again at Franklin. "I was shot through the right thigh at [Elizabethtown, Kentucky]," wrote a Montgomery County cavalryman, and "Struck by Sabre three times at Reedville Tenn." During a minor scrimmage early in the war, Pinkney Martin heard the sickening thud as a bullet struck his brother's head. The youth recovered, only to be killed months later in Virginia.[34]

Added to the initial pain of injury was the prolonged torture experienced by many soldiers, some of whom lay for extended periods on the abandoned battlefields before receiving medical attention. Shot at Petersburg shortly before Lee's surrender, William Hollow lay on the ground for three days without food or water. Several other Confederate veterans recalled their trials following the South's defeat at Perryville, Kentucky. Bleeding from his wounds, F. B. Gause suffered through a long night's rainstorm; Benjamin Hagnewood sought medical attention for days in vain; and George Parks's torn flesh became infested with maggots.[35]

Those who survived the battlefields encountered further horrors in the hospitals. There the wounded soldiers were surrounded by appalling filth, cared for by overburdened nurses and frequently incompetent physicians; they usually had to endure their pain without the comfort of narcotics and other basic medications. Survivors never forgot the smell of rotting flesh and the screams of men in agony. "My experience in [the] hospital," declared David Bodenhamer, "was severe, bitter and sorely distressing beyond the power of words to tell." Joseph Hoover remembered that delirious patients "curse[d] the Doctors for all they were worth"; and over fifty years after the Civil War, Joel Ruffin could still affirm with anger that "nine tenths of the Doctors ought to have been hung."[36]

Because of their family connections, injured patricians occasionally received special considerations that ameliorated their sufferings. William Pollard, who estimated the worth of his father's estate at fifty thousand dollars, was severely wounded in the chest at Missionary Ridge. During his evacuation south, he was sought out by former Tennessee governor Neill S. Brown, who presented him with a bottle of apple brandy to ease his pain. "I will always believe," Pollard testified, that "this brandy with God's help, saved my life." The wealthy Hampton Cheney underwent a similar experience. Crushed by his dead horse during a scrimmage near Marietta, Georgia, he was packed into a freight car loaded with amputees. For hours, a battle-deranged soldier terrorized these sufferers, threatening to fall on top of his companions and crush the life out of them. "We were locked up . . . with this wild lunatic on the rampage," Cheney remembered, "and [we were] as helpless as infants." Once the train arrived in Atlanta, the young aristocrat's circumstances quickly improved. A longtime friend, who happened to be in charge of local transportation, separated Cheney from the masses and provided him with a comfortable private room. There he recuperated in relative luxury.[37]

The consequences of a severe wound varied according to the victim's social status. Most members of the poor and yeoman classes returned to farming and other manual occupations after the war, and their physical handicaps proved to be a great burden. Crippled aristocrats, by contrast, usually had the education, the financial means, and the family associations to enter professions where their injuries made little difference. Among the poor and the yeomen, J. M. Rich, Hiram Hawk, and Joseph Fox all returned to tilling their crops deprived of the use of one arm. Fox, who suffered an amputation, explained that he farmed "as best I could with my Left hand." For Liberty Duncan, the war provided a bitter irony. "I lost a leg," he pointed out, and therefore "I had to give up farming and I learned the shoe trade."[38]

Despite the shared pain of wounds and the permanent afflictions of amputation and paralysis, the wealthy fared better than their compatriots in the postbellum era. A hand wound at Shiloh did little more than waste Herman Doak's childhood violin and piano lessons. Upon his return from the war, he studied law, secured an appointment as clerk of the district court in Nashville, and held that post for thirty-five years. Elijah Knight's experience was similar. Despite being a semi-invalid, he entered the medical profession and in time took up politics in his home community. While serving as a trustee for Smith County, he engaged in several business enterprises and ultimately was elected to the Tennessee House of Representatives. Late in life, he wrote with satisfaction: "I am now retired from all business, and cares of life, patiently awaiting the call of the father of life [in] whome I have implicit trust."[39]

Called upon by their leaders to risk death and injury, the Confederate soldiers developed strong opinions about their commanders. They respected—and sometimes adored—those officers who demonstrated personal bravery, confidence in their men, and concern for their troops. Officers who proved incompetent, or who were high-handed with their soldiers, or who failed to demonstrate courage, were quickly condemned. The aristocratic tenor of southern society endowed some individuals with positive leadership traits but created in others an irritating arrogance. Successful Confederate officers tempered their natural disposition to leadership with a common touch. Those who possessed only the arrogance of command were despised.

In their questionnaires, the veterans frequently mentioned four famous generals—Joseph E. Johnston, Nathan Bedford Forrest, Braxton Bragg, and John B. Hood. The first two not only displayed tactical brilliance but also demonstrated concern and compassion for their men. Their soldiers responded with deep respect. In contrast to Johnston and Forrest, both Bragg and Hood held themselves aloof from the masses. Unapproachable in their aristocratic hauteur, the latter two never developed an empathy with their followers. As one yeoman reflected: "We . . . feared Gen Bragg and almost *Worshipped* Joseph E. Johnston."[40]

Tennessee soldiers appreciated Johnston's intelligent protection of their lives. They had faith that he would not waste his men in hopeless charges or lead them into death in a vain quest for honor. "We had the utmost confiedence in him," H. C. Gwyn wrote, "we knew we had a Gen that would take care of his men." J. H. Ewing thought he was "as great a man as ever lived"; Richard Colville praised "noble hearted Genl Johnston"; and Thomas Walthall claimed he was "a grand and nobl[e] Gen . . . who loved his men and his men loved him." Theodore Harris of Company C, Eighth Tennessee Infantry, proclaimed without shame: "we would have gone into hell if he had said the word go."[41]

If Johnston's troops remembered his humanity in broad terms, Forrest's men often recalled specific episodes. Of plebeian birth, crude and almost illiterate, Forrest was nonetheless a master of mass psychology. With an exquisite sense of timing, he could strike fear into his subordinates, or demonstrate extreme courage under fire, or show empathy toward those in pain. He was the embodiment of action. A. J. Williams proudly wrote: "I was with For[r]est so we moved lively"; and Robert Rogers explained with equal fervor that Forrest "was hunting yanks all the time and capturing and killing yanks . . . and I was in every little fight that [he] hauled up." Forrest exemplified courage. John Crofford claimed he was "one of the greates[t] Generals of all" because "he was always at the front when the battle was on"; and M. B. Dinwiddie simply pointed out: "he knew no fear."

Other aged veterans remembered that Forrest related well to the common soldier. On one occasion, recalled Christopher Robertson, the general came upon a cavalryman struggling with his horse, which was mired in quicksand. Glaring at several idle officers, Forrest shouted: "'git down thar you men and help git that horse out[,] git down thar.'" Everyone ran "into that water men and officers," Robertson wrote; "they were afraid not to." While on the desperate, freezing retreat from Nashville in December 1864, Jesse Green saw Forrest join with his men to pull reluctant mules across a creek— taking them "by the[ir] ears and tongue[s]"—and during the same withdrawal James Morey scribbled this poignant note in his diary: "Saw Gen. Forrest get off his horse and put a barefooted man on him." In his marginally literate style, Robert Street captured the adulation that many Confederates felt for this officer: "my commander war [was] jeneral N. B. forist one of the gratest men the Sun ever

Shined upon[.] he never war the man to fall back and Say go ahead men[.] it war follow me Boys[.] he war a kind harted christian jentle-man and god Saw fit to call him home and he air [is] there waitting and watching for his comand that he caried thrue the dark days from Sixty one to Sixty five and god being my helper I am to meat him Some Sweet day Some Sweet day."[42]

Like combatants in most wars, the Confederate soldiers not only wanted their sacrifices to result in victory, but they also hoped to be among the survivors, to be reunited with their families, and to rees-tablish a calm civilian life. For all but the most fanatical, the abstract concept of honor was far less important than simple survival. That was threatened by the murderous incompetence of Braxton Bragg and the haughty bravado of John B. Hood, both of whom were re-sponsible for an appalling waste of lives. Tennessee soldiers devel-oped an intense distaste for both commanders.

During his command of the Army of Tennessee, Bragg demon-strated an uncanny ability to seize defeat out of victory. In one cam-paign after another, hard-fighting Confederates were ordered to withdraw when their enemies should have been put to flight instead. Perryville, Murfreesboro, and Chattanooga stood as monuments to Bragg's ineptitude. Theodore Harris recalled the horrible carnage inflicted on his regiment at Murfreesboro. It was decimated in a charge against northern cannons. "We captured the battery," he wrote, but "of course Bragg lost. Nothing more could be expected of Mr. Know all." Henry Dunavant grumbled that "we were humiliated by Gen. Bragg['s] retreating," and a Fayette County veteran com-plained: "He was a very sorry Gen. [We] did not have any confidence in him."[43]

Tennessee veterans also held John B. Hood in deep contempt. Hood's patrician upbringing led him to view the Civil War as a cru-sade for southern honor. His notion of chivalry demanded that brave soldiers prove their valor on the attack. Hood, a handsome Texan who stood over six feet two inches tall, demonstrated his personal courage at Gettysburg, where he lost the use of an arm, and again at Chickamauga, where he had a leg amputated. Despite his physical impairments, Hood became even more aggressive. By the summer of 1864, President Jefferson Davis had come to admire this fighting aristocrat; at the same time he had begun to chafe at Joseph E. Johnston's slow and careful retreat from Chattanooga toward At-lanta. On 16 July, the southern chief executive removed Johnston from command of the Army of Tennessee and replaced him with Hood. For two brutal weeks, Hood threw his troops against William

T. Sherman's well-equipped army. Confederate casualties were staggering. By the end of July, Sherman controlled Atlanta; shortly thereafter he began his famous, unopposed march across Georgia to the sea. Hood aimed northward in a desperate thrust into Tennessee. There his once-powerful army was first shattered at Franklin, then endured some of the war's bitterest winter weather, and finally disintegrated in a two-day engagement at Nashville. By late December 1864, the Army of Tennessee had virtually ceased to exist. Thinking back on those tragic events, one West Tennessee veteran harshly criticized: "Jeff Davis acted the fool and removed Joseph E. Johnston and put Gen. Hood in com[m]and, which quickly demoralized the whole Army. . . . All the men . . . Hood failed to see Slaughtered at the Battle of Atlanta on the 22nd of July 1864 he got rid of at the Battle of Franklin Tenn in his . . . attempt to immortalize himself."[44]

Those Tennesseans who survived the dreadful Franklin bloodletting never forgave Hood. The Texas aristocrat had berated his soldiers at Atlanta, claiming they lacked fortitude and demanding that they demonstrate greater courage in future struggles. The march into Tennessee further enraged him. A series of poorly given or misunderstood orders allowed John Schofield's smaller Union army to escape capture, confirming Hood's negative image of his soldiers. In the late afternoon of 30 November, he arranged his command before Schofield's strongly entrenched forces at Franklin. Although prudence indicated that the Confederates should flank the Union army, he ordered a frontal assault without artillery support. In the next few hours, more Confederates died than in any other single southern charge. Under the cover of darkness, Schofield—his army intact—retreated toward Nashville. Years later Hood praised the heroes that fell "upon the field of Franklin." These men, he wrote, "had been gloriously led by their officers . . . dying as the brave should prefer to die, in the intense and exalted excitement of battle."[45]

While in Hood's mind southern honor had been redeemed at Franklin, his soldiers felt differently. William Reynolds witnessed the general's conference with his staff moments before the battle commenced and heard him dismiss Schofield's preparations as little more than "temporary brestworks." Reynolds was shocked. As he explained in his questionnaire: "We could see with the naked eye the first line we would come to was [made of] logs, the next . . . about one hundred yards beyond [consisted of] well excavated ditches [with] head logs and small trees . . . in front for intanglement. The last line was only twelve or twenty feet behind this . . . well supplyed with men. And across the river in the rear of their line of battle was a considerable hill" thick with cannon. "No commander except a crazy man would have had the least thought of making a charge," Reynolds cursed. "General Hood might have been excused for this bloody massacre had he not seen the enemies entire situation." H. C. Gwyn claimed that Franklin "was one of the worst mistakes a Gen ever made"; James Caldwell concurred that "at Franklin . . . Hood made a mistake"; and Richard Colville asserted: "Hood . . . lost one of the grandest armies that ever Marshelled."[46] Few common soldiers, most of whom had suffered injuries and lost friends in the battle, were able to share Hood's sense of honor restored.

As the Confederate armies suffered repeated defeats, Tennesseans of all social classes—the poor, the yeomen, and the wealthy—faced the grim reality of capture and prison camp. Incarcerated soldiers endured months of inactivity and inadequate food, housing, and clothing. Herded together in overcrowded camps, the prisoners were surrounded by disease, threatened by guards, and despised by the civilians who resided nearby. In the words of one West Tennessee veteran, the whole experience was "the hardest service ever rendered by a soldier."[47]

The need for an extensive system of prisoner-of-war camps developed by mid-1863, when the custom of exchanging captured troops collapsed. Before Lincoln's emancipation of the slaves, Union and Confederate commanders simply traded their prisoners on a basis of one for one and rank for rank. Once the Union armies enrolled black volunteers, however, the southern government refused to exchange captured blacks. Lincoln and his secretary of war saw a white-only quid pro quo as a shameful dishonor; by June 1863, they had ordered an end to prisoner trades. Despite this order, in July Union Generals Grant and Banks paroled thirty-six thousand southern troops who had surrendered at Vicksburg and Port Hudson. Desperate for troops, the Confederate War Department ignored these men's pledges not to fight, and many were reimpressed into their regiments in time to ensure a Confederate victory at Chickamauga. Confronted with southern intransigence on the issue of black soldier exchanges and aware of the probability that paroled Confederates would quickly return to combat, the Washington government expanded its prisoner-of-war facilities. By late fall 1863, thousands of Confederate officers were interned at Johnson Island in Ohio, and tens of thousands of enlisted men were imprisoned at such locations as Camps Douglas, Butler, and Rock Island in Illinois, Camp Morton in Indiana, Camp Chase in Ohio, Elmira in New York, Fort Delaware in Delaware, and Point Lookout in Maryland.[48]

By any standard, Civil War prisons—northern and southern—were sites of profound suffering. In addition to their physical discomforts, helpless internees experienced extreme psychological difficulties. "You may imagine the awful torture we endured," explained Joseph Riley, the "monotony of prison life [with] Nothing to read, no news from the outside, [and] the . . . realization of knowing that you . . . could not help yourself."[49] Union soldiers imprisoned at Belle Island in Richmond, Virginia, and at Andersonville in Georgia endured the same deprivations as their Confederate counterparts. In September 1863, Joseph Hoover escorted several hundred federal troops to the Belle Island stockade. Although he acknowledged that Union prisoners experienced both overcrowding and malnutrition, he also recalled his wish that "every Yanke on Gods Green Earth [was] right there on that Island where we could make them Sue for Peace." Ironically, within a few weeks after that expressed desire, Hoover found himself on his way north to the Rock Island prison.[50]

Hoover was among the Confederates trapped when Braxton Bragg's army retreated from Chattanooga in November. Happy to have survived, these unfortunate southern youths could not have anticipated the horror that awaited them. Roughly a month after capture, the prisoners reached Rock Island during a harsh December blizzard. Most of the Confederates wore little more than their lightweight uniforms, and many were virtually barefooted. Joseph Riley recorded that he was clad in only a "hickory shirt[,] a pair of cotton pantaloons and shoes without socks." He, along with others who were more pitifully clothed, entered the prison in the late afternoon and remained out of doors during long hours of bureaucratic record taking. "We . . . kept busy pounding ourselves, walking, [and] running . . . to keep from freezing," the aged veteran wrote. Every so often, one of his comrades dozed off and quietly died. Realizing the danger, Riley and others grabbed their lethargic comrades, shook them, "and use[d] whatever means at hand to arouse [their] lagging spirits and dormant circulation[s]."[51] One year later, Robert Holman surrendered at Nashville and shortly thereafter disembarked from the prison train at Camp Douglas near Chicago. Lacking shoes, he and his fellow sufferers stood for hours in twelve inches of snow. While Holman was fortunate to survive the painful ordeal with his feet intact, others lost their toes to frostbite.[52]

Accustomed to relatively mild southern winters, Tennessee soldiers suffered intensely from the brutal northern weather. At Camp Morton, J. R. Cox wrote, he was not issued a blanket in spite of temperatures as cold as ten degrees below zero; John Hinkle complained that, at Camp Douglas, he had little more than a "piece of oil cloth for cover in very Severe winter weather"; at Rock Island, John Chisum "had to trot the Burricks day and night in cold spells to keep from freezing." Ford Adams and his comrades fought the intense chill at Camp Chase "by piling up to gether," and at Fort Delaware, Carter Upchurch often slept on the frozen ground "hungry and nearly naked." As far as James Gold was concerned, Confederate prisoners "suffered more from cold than anything else."[53]

Hunger also plagued the prisoners. They grumbled loudly about both the quantity and the quality of prison fare. At Camp Douglas, Thomas Hatchet testified, "we could eat in one meal all we got in 1 day." Sam Grubb described his daily ration at Point Lookout as six crackers, a pint of soup, and a small slice of bacon; and both William Hunter and Lucullus Atkins received a daily allowance of rice soup supplemented with small bits of meat. Joseph Hoover often consumed sticky, green beef, and on one occasion he ate a hunk of mule neck with its hair still attached.[54] By the end of the war, many Confederates showed the effects of chronic malnutrition. Joseph Wall left Rock Island weighing 102 pounds. William Morelock ended a two-year prison stay weighing 70 pounds, and A. M. Bruce went home from Fort Delaware with his hip bones protruding from his skin.[55]

Desperate, hungry Confederate prisoners frequently ate dogs and rats. Canine meat was preferable to rodents, but it was also more dangerous to procure. Although some dogs were strays, others were the personal pets of the prison guards. Killing the latter often resulted in rigorous punishments. Jeremiah McKenzie helped consume a Union officer's dog, which a friend had "choked, . . . cleaned, and cooked." Had they been caught, the two might have been in as much difficulty as George Payne, who was severely reprimanded for making a Christmas dinner out of a general's pet.[56] Rats were more abundant and far less likely to inspire the guards' affections. Samuel Frazier constructed a small crossbow for spearing the fat rodents, and Flavius Landers admitted that he "got so hungary" that he willingly ate rats or anything else he could get. Joseph Riley thoroughly enjoyed his nocturnal hunts. Each night he dispatched three or four of the beasts. Then, every few days, he invited his friends to taste such delicacies as "rat broiled, rat stew and once rat and dumplings." In spite of an otherwise miserable prison experience, Riley wrote: "These feasts are pleasant memories to me yet. They . . . broke the monotony of prison life, and to play host to a rat dinner [which relieved] your comrades of that awful torture of gnawing hunger, gave you the consciousness of having done well."[57]

Weakened by cold, hunger, and overcrowding, interned Confederates suffered from a variety of diseases. In all probability, there was little difference between the illnesses found in prisons and those rampant in army encampments. Disease was devastating in both. Thinking back on his month-long stay in the Rock Island "Pest Hospital," one Middle Tennessee veteran recalled: "About one million or more Cooties Chas[ed] Each other up and down my Spine and now an then Stop[ped] to dig into [my] Small Pocks Sores." Asa Johnson wrote that, among the residents in his Rock Island barracks, about 90 out of 120 men died, "most of them with small pox," and Rody Anthony claimed that at Fort Delaware he was roughly treated during his forty-day bout with the disease.[58]

Even in the pestilential prison camps, wealth and family influence often had their advantages. When Archelaus Hughes lay near death in the Camp Morton infirmary, his father, a former U.S. attorney in Columbia, Tennessee, secured a private audience with Abraham Lincoln. The president ordered the young man released as a political favor to Tennessee Military Governor Andrew Johnson. Returning to the comfort of his own home, Hughes remained confined to his bed for three months before recovering.[59]

Confederate prisoners developed intense hatreds for their guards. By necessity the camps maintained strict discipline, and on the slightest provocation, trigger-happy sentries fired their weapons into the encampments. William Mantlo never forgave the Union soldier who killed one of his best friends at Camp Butler, and Charles Blackwell claimed that at Camp Morton the guards "were afraid of us and . . . would shoot through the Prison." Reflecting on the harsh punishments meted out by Fort Delaware's commandant and two of his soldiers, R. W. Michie cursed: "I Dont Think Thar is any Place in Hell Hot anuf for Thos 3 men."[60]

Black guards were assigned to Point Lookout in Maryland. Southern whites, most of whom ascribed to the premise of black inferiority, found this humiliating. Marcus Toney accused the sentries of shooting "our men for the slightest infringement of the rules." J. C. McCarty believed that angry whites were ready to riot against this indignity, and David Grable remembered that, following Lincoln's assassination, blacks severely retaliated against the helpless Confederate prisoners. Of his Point Lookout experience, Andrew Jernigan simply stated, "guarded by negroes which I did not like."[61]

During the long months of inactivity and stressful conditions, youthful soldiers had the time to reflect upon their conditions and to assess their loyalties to the southern crusade. The most fanatical sought to escape and to return to the Confederate army. Others repented of their commitments to the rebellion, took an oath of loyalty to the Union, and in a few cases joined federal troops fighting Indians in the West. Still others, when released from their northern bondage, refused to fight again for the Confederacy.

Only a small number (6 percent) of respondents to the questionnaires attempted to escape from prison. Most were slaveowners. Of the fourteen individuals who tried to escape, six were from the planter and professional class and five were sons of slaveholding yeomen. Only two nonslaveowning yeomen and one poor man fled their stockades. These efforts were exceedingly dangerous. Following the failure of his second project to tunnel out of prison, Joseph Riley was sentenced to death, but he was later pardoned by the camp's commander. An impetuous young aristocrat, Thomas Humes, also suffered for his endeavors. Left unattended to clean a Rock Island captain's quarters, he consumed a flask of the officer's whiskey, replaced the amber liquid with his own urine, dressed in the Union officer's best uniform, and waltzed out the front gate saluting the guards. Unfortunately he was thoroughly inebriated. Quickly recaptured, Humes was first stripped, bound, and exposed to six hours of an August sun and then locked in solitary confinement for four weeks on a ration of bread and water. John Dance was more successful. He merely paid a guard twenty dollars for passage out of Camp Douglas. Three sons of slaveowners—Andrew Bradley, Swimpfield Eidson, and Henry Moore—bragged that they escaped from their prisons and returned to their regiments for the balance of the war.[62]

Rather than suffer the constant deprivations of confinement, J. W. Bradley, John Brawner, and Augustus Buffat pledged loyalty to the Union, left their encampments, and remained north of the Ohio River until the war's end. Throughout the last two years of the conflict, federal policy gave captured Confederates the option of taking a loyalty oath or enduring imprisonment. Thousands chose the former. As a southern zealot, William Moss was perplexed at his comrades' lack of resolve. Captured after the Confederate retreat from Kennesaw Mountain in June 1864, he and nearly a thousand others were briefly incarcerated at the Nashville, Tennessee, penitentiary. "There were 890 of us when we arrived," he wrote, but "I never saw any of the others again. . . . The guards told me I could go with the others by taking an oath of allegiance to the United States, as all the others agreed to do." Because he refused, he ended the war in a northern stockade. Francis Bunch and Edmond O'Neill were less committed. Both were captured at Nashville in December 1864, and both renounced the rebellion. "I had to take the oath or go to prison," explained O'Neill, "so I took the oath."[63]

In early 1864, the northern government offered interned Confederates the opportunity to volunteer either for the Union navy or for frontier service against the Indians. Disillusioned with the southern cause and facing a bleak prison future, many switched their allegiances. Unrepentant in his old age, Joseph Hoover held in contempt the two thousand or more who left Rock Island. Those "what remained," he boasted, "were pretty true Rebells." Joseph Riley echoed this sentiment. He averred that "the thought of taking the oath and escaping prison life by fighting Indians never entered my head or heart, and until my dying day, I shall have little respect for those who did." With pride he concluded: "I have left my children the legacy of being true to my Southland under the most trying ordeal."[64]

Although the planters, the yeomen, and the poor shared similar prison experiences, one important statistical difference existed among the classes. Of those released before the end of the war, the elites were far more likely to return to active service in the Confederate army. Beginning in January 1865, the northern and southern governments resumed their policy of exchanging soldiers. Many were severely ill or injured. Despite this, 64 percent of the planter and professional class again took up arms against the Union. This declined dramatically to only 17 percent of the slaveowning yeomen, 26 percent of the nonslaveowning yeomen, and 20 percent of the poor. With the conflict nearing its conclusion, only those with a powerful social and economic stake in the Old South culture remained committed (Appendix 2, table 25).

Disloyalty and desertion constantly plagued the Confederate war effort. Once young Tennesseans faced the sobering reality of death, mutilation, and imprisonment, their initial war euphoria quickly subsided. Only a few aged veterans openly discussed their own infidelities, but many others freely admitted that their fellow Southerners were less than faithful. Shortly after the battle of Missionary Ridge, William Fonville was "detailed . . . to go after deserters," and during the summer of 1864, George Taylor's cavalry unit roamed throughout West Tennessee driving "all the old Soldiers back into the army." That fall, Robert Floyd's company was sent "near memphis to catch

Deserters." M. B. Dinwiddie explained that the larger portion of his cavalry company was "killed or wounded," and also added that "quite a number deserted." His unit was so notoriously disloyal that Nathan Bedford Forrest ordered two of its men shot and a crude sign hung over their bodies. Its message spelled out in large, threatening letters: "The fare of a deserter."[65]

For the most part, soldiers who remained loyal to the Confederacy had little sympathy for those who switched allegiances. M. B. Dinwiddie recalled with anger that Rice Bostic, a member of his company, "deserted after Shilo [and] joined the enemy." William Tucker described the sad fate of Frank Putman, who left the Confederate ranks to fight for the Union. "He was captured by Oliver Frese's Company," Tucker wrote, "and hanged on [the] Side of [the] road between Hickman Ky and Dyersburg Tenn." When members of the Fourteenth Tennessee Cavalry surveyed the Union dead at Fort Pillow, they found several of their former comrades. Not every turncoat was killed. Late in life, Thomas Hightower still held in contempt Chester Alison of Jonesboro, Tennessee, who switched to the Union following Vicksburg. "Last I herd of him," Hightower explained, "he was drawing a big pension." The loyal Confederate added parenthetically: "I dont think he was very happy."[66]

When filling out their questionnaires, the Civil War veterans were reluctant to acknowledge their desertions. This was more than a simple matter of pride. By Tennessee law, Confederate pensions were awarded only to those who were honorably discharged, or who were prisoners of war, or who surrendered with their commands at the war's conclusion. Desirous of protecting their small monthly stipends, many veterans refused to discuss their discharges from the army. Others employed such vague euphemisms as "cut off from my company" or "at home getting horses and supplies," and still others lied. Among the last group, John Johnston of Wilson County claimed that, in January 1865, he received a medical furlough from the trenches at Petersburg. This was true. But he omitted from his account the fact that, within ten days of leaving the Army of Northern Virginia, he deserted to the Union forces and provided them with valuable information concerning the destitute condition of Lee's command.[67] A close survey of the Civil War Veterans Questionnaires suggests that each southern setback lessened the soldiers' resolves. Long before the actual end of the war, thousands of Tennesseans—especially the poor and the yeomen—had given up the cause.

Defeats at Fort Donelson in February 1862 and at Shiloh the following April provoked the initial defections among Tennessee troops. In both battles, the state's youth witnessed for the first time the cruel carnage of war, and for hundreds that was enough. Having surrendered at Fort Donelson, J. W. Bradley's regiment was interned for seven months in a northern stockade. During their stay, sixteen members of his company took an oath of allegiance to the Union and went home. R. C. Holmes recalled that, although most of his company escaped before Donelson fell, several—including their captain—refused to return to the Confederate army. This battle constituted Alfred Abernathy's sole campaign. Deliberately vague about his departure from the military, he simply stated, "I footed it home." Other Tennesseans were disillusioned at Shiloh. Shortly after that battle, many of their twelve-month enlistments expired. Most volunteered again, but many did not. On 14 April, William Lucy joined sixty other Tennesseans heading home from Corinth, Mississippi, and at about the same time James Gross started home to his family in Grundy County. "I intended to go back," he insisted, "but my mother pleaded so hard for me to S[t]ay I joined the hom gards and Stayed home."[68]

Repeated defeats west of the Appalachian Mountains in 1863 led to more defections. Vicksburg, Port Hudson, Knoxville, and Chattanooga were the sites of decisive Union victories. In the aftermath of each, disheartened Confederates left the army individually, or in small groups, and occasionally by the hundreds. Among those that quit during the disastrous month of July 1863, W. M. Willis walked over four hundred miles from Port Hudson to his home in Maury County, William Perkins fearfully avoided Confederate agents who were impressing paroled troops into Braxton Bragg's army, and G. W. Wall returned from Vicksburg to his Giles County farm "bare footed and almost naked."[69] Joseph Hoover believed that, at Chattanooga, hunger and command incompetence caused "the Army . . . to Dwindle by Desertions," and in his diary, James Marsh recorded the mixed results of a soldier plebiscite taken shortly after the retreat from Missionary Ridge: "Our regiment declared unanimously for the war. The vote of the rest of the brigades was taken. They were not very strong for the war." Following Longstreet's futile charge at Knoxville in November 1863, Joe Sullivan noted: "I came home with 75 of my comrades." After the same battle, George Byrne slipped through the Union lines and walked back to his family in Jackson County.[70]

During the first half of 1864, the morale of western Confederates improved under Joseph E. Johnston's skillful leadership. When Hood replaced Johnston and threw his numerically inferior army against Sherman, the southern spirit quickly declined. The twin tragedies of the Battle of Franklin, on November 30, and the Battle of Nashville, two weeks later, shattered the army. It ceased to be a cohesive fighting force.

Devoid of confidence in Hood and disillusioned with the war, southern troops hemorrhaged out of the army. Looking back at the Franklin-Nashville campaign, John Scruggs emphasized that those "soldiers who escaped death and wounds, or captivity, became so disheartened, and . . . so discouraged [that they] left the army in large numbers never to return." John Crawford recalled that "after the Hood campaign some of us returned to our commands (many did not)."[71] In some cases, officers disbanded their units and dismissed their men; in other cases, individuals begged for furloughs to recover from illness or to procure supplies or to aid their families; and in still other cases soldiers abandoned the army without permission.

Hood's failures dramatically weakened the resolve of the Confederate officer corps. After the Tennessee defeats, Captain Blackburn dispersed his cavalry command; Captain Elijah Cantrell led the men of Company D, Forty-eighth Tennessee Infantry, back to their families in Hickman County; and Captain Benjamin Coleman of Company F, Forty-second Tennessee Infantry, urged his barefooted, frostbitten troops to return to their Middle Tennessee farms. When W. H. Harris asked his colonel for a fresh mount to replace his worn-out cavalry horse, the officer replied that he should go home, as "the thing was over." J. P. Dillehay's colonel instructed him to go home and to stay when he got there. William Mays's engineering company was rebuilding a railroad trestle when news arrived of the Franklin slaughter. Infuriated, his captain threw his hammer into the river, cursed, and then shouted: "Boys take care of yourselves[.] I'm going home."[72]

Desperate, disenchanted soldiers sought furloughs as an honorable exit from Hood's army. James S. Jackson and John A. Pearce received twenty-day leaves of absence and failed to return. M. B. Tomlinson viewed the rapid demise of Hood's army as the result of a liberal policy that granted soldiers permission to go home to get horses. Once there, he pointed out, many deserted. J. K. P. Heflin, a typical example, wrote: "I went home to get [a] fresh horse and clothes and my company got so far off I never went back."[73] Few old veterans were as candid as the impoverished William Mullins. "I had permission of my officers to come [home] but didnt return," he explained. "[I] came . . . through the snow . . . almost barefooted. I found my wife and children in a needy condition and I felt like I ought to stay and support them as the war was almost at a close." The state of Tennessee refused to grant Mullins a pension.[74]

Vast numbers of Hood's troops left of their own volition. Josia Reams, slightly wounded at Franklin, limped back to his native community in West Tennessee and within a short time was reunited with the discouraged remnant of his company. They sought out Union officials and surrendered. William Langley's horse gave out at Nashville, so he and the exhausted animal returned to his father's farm just north of Memphis. Barefooted and bleeding, the disheartened Russell Brown quit during the retreat from the Tennessee capital. After a painful week's march over frozen ground, he arrived at his Shelbyville home. There a Union sympathizer took pity on Brown and bought him "a Par of shoes." For Reams, Langley, Brown, and thousands of others, the southern crusade ended at Franklin and Nashville.[75]

If Hood's army quickly evaporated following the disastrous Tennessee campaign of November–December 1864, then Robert E. Lee's command slowly dissipated in the trenches before Petersburg, Virginia, during the Confederacy's final winter and spring. Having deserted along with his friend, Tilman Etheridge, John Johnston reported to Union officials that his regiment retained a mere sixty men—less than the size of a normal company—and that his brigade contained only about three hundred. He estimated that as many as two hundred individuals, faced with poor and irregular rations, crossed to the Union lines daily.[76] James Bradshaw remembered the demoralized state of the Army of Northern Virginia as the war neared its conclusion. "Our men lost heart," he reported, "and were going home every night." Although Bradshaw and his comrades were assigned to guard their own pickets to keep men from "going over to the Yankees," it did little good. "We all knew that when the campaigns opened in the spring, General Lee would be compelled to surrender," he explained, as "the men were very badly discouraged, low spirited; [and] they did not care to be killed for no purpose." At times entire companies quit. Bradshaw himself deserted at 9 A.M., 1 March 1865.[77]

By April 1865, the Confederate armies were severely depleted. Soldiers were absent without leave, languishing in prisons, recovering from wounds, and avoiding further combat with or without permission. A sharp class distinction was noticeable among Confederate soldiers in the final days of the war. Among the respondents to the questionnaires, only about 50 percent of the poor, the nonslaveowning yeomen, and the slaveowning yeomen surrendered with an active command. Still fanatically committed in the war's last days, 70 percent of the elite remained faithful to the Confederate cause (Appendix 2, table 26).

The collapse of the Confederacy was inevitable. Its demise was not only a miscarriage of military strategy but also a failure of culture. The South's upper classes assumed that the poor and the yeomen would obediently follow their leadership in a bloody contest with the North. Initially they were correct. But the realities of death, mutilation, and deprivation caused individual Southerners to assess their stake in the conflict. In the end, large numbers of small farmers and poor whites determined that the perpetuation of slavery was not worth their continued sacrifices. From the scattered and pitifully weakened armies, from the prisons, and from their woodland hiding places, young men matured by battle prepared to return home and reconstruct their lives. In this quest, Tennessee's patricians—despite the loss of their slaves—possessed the advantages of wealth and family connections. In due time they would regain their dominance over society, and a fundamental continuity of class and culture would bridge the Old South and the New.

Reflecting back on their times, however, most aged Confederate veterans saw the Civil War as the central event of their lives. They understood its grim realities and hoped to impart their hard-learned lessons to succeeding generations. "There was too much blood and suffering connected with that far-a-way time for me to remember it with pleasure," wrote Edwin Gardner in 1922. "If anyone is enough interested in this questionnaire to read it I would like for them to know my real Sentiments on the Subject. . . . I utterly abhor the idea of war." The impoverished William Beard echoed that view. "[I] lost [a] Brother in [the] Civil War[,] Samuel Beard[, and] Lost [a] Son in [the] World War[,] Tonie Beard[.] Now I dont want any more war."[78]

CHAPTER SIX

★ ★

EVERYTHING GONE BUT THE DIRT

In April and May 1865, the remnants of once-proud Confederate armies capitulated. Lee, Johnston, and Forrest yielded to the inevitable, surrendered their commands, and dispersed their troops. It was a defeat of culture and of spirit. Southern elites had discovered that the lower classes lacked their own fanatical commitment to a social system based on aristocratic dominance. The pitiful realities of amputated arms and legs, dead friends and relatives, and impoverished wives and children had convinced the poor and the yeomen to trade an idealistic defense of the South for their own self-interest. Many southern soldiers were emotionally shattered by defeat. "One of the sad[d]est events of my life," reflected Henry Hogan, "was the 29th of April, 1865 . . . when i stacked my gun in surrender to W[illiam] T. Sherman." He added that "strong men wept like children." Thomas Walthall wrote: "I cried I could not help it."[1]

Southern society was in shambles. Its young men were dead or scattered in broken commands, prisons, and various isolated locations far from the main battlefronts. Slavery had been abolished. Many farms had been ruined—crops destroyed, fences burned, animals killed. Edward Lee returned to his farm to find "everything gone but the dirt."[2] Throughout the spring of 1865, Confederate veterans drifted homeward. In the weeks, months, and years ahead, they faced the grim reconstruction of their lives and of their society.

The culture of the New South eventually reflected its antebellum antecedent. The elites had received serious blows to their affluence—through the loss of their slaves—and to their prestige, but they still possessed the advantages of superior educations, significant wealth, large property holdings, and a tradition of community domination. They emerged as the South's postwar political and professional leaders.

The rebuilding of the Tennessee class structure lay in the future. In the spring of 1865 most Civil War veterans had but one concern. As William Hazelwood and several friends headed toward Tennessee, they passed a squad of Union soldiers. One Northerner shouted in derision: "'Where are you going boys?'" "'Home,'" was the simple reply. Almost instantly a Union soldier responded: "'I would to God we were going there too.'"[3]

Slightly more than half of the Tennessee veterans surrendered with an active command. By far the largest number of these were serving under Johnston in North Carolina and under Forrest in Alabama. A large number also were with with Lee's command in Virginia, with Jefferson Davis's escort in Georgia, and with Richard Taylor's tiny army in Corinth, Mississippi (Appendix 2, table 27). The remainder were scattered in isolated companies and posts throughout the South.

As these men contemplated their defeat, many were struck by how few remained of those who had jubilantly gone to war four years earlier. Calvin Myers sadly recalled that, of the 107 men that he recruited in 1861, "only about 20 got home after the war was over." Frank Gilliland remembered that Company H, Eighth Tennessee Infantry, left Overton County with 85 men in 1861; only 17 surrendered in 1865. William Pullen, William Barnes, W. H. Epps, and Elijah Hassell were discharged from Johnston's command at Greensboro, North Carolina. "We had about one hundred when we left Waverly [Tennessee] on the 6th day of May 1861," Pullen wrote, but "at the Surrender there was only five or six of us." Barnes was the only member of his company to sign the final roll. Epps was the only remaining private in his company, and Hassell was the only man left out of 110 volunteers who enlisted in Company B, Fiftieth Tennessee Infantry, at the beginning of the conflict. Calvin Myers reflected that their comrades "were killed [or] died of sickness . . . all through the southern States."[4]

With the exception of a small number of zealots—almost all of whom were from the planter and professional class—most Tennesseans were willing to acknowledge defeat and return home. This rapid demilitarization of the southern forces posed both logistical and security problems. Union troops remained under the discipline of their officers and would eventually be discharged through systematic procedures. Confederate soldiers were governed by an entirely different set of circumstances. Because southern officers no longer had any legal status, their ability to maintain order quickly dissipated. Yet the men under their commands needed transportation home, and they also had to be fed and sheltered. At the same time, Union officials did not relish the idea of undisciplined, armed mobs roaming the countryside. But in the last desperate months of combat, little thought had been given to these problems. As a result, while some southern troops returned home in reasonable order, others faced severe trials from hunger, confusion, and sometimes violence.

Tennesseans serving under Johnston and Forrest encountered typical difficulties in returning home. Forrest surrendered deep in Alabama, and his troops, most of whom were cavalry, were simply dismissed and told to make their way as best they could to Tennessee. Johnston's men, who were mostly in the infantry, faced more complicated problems. Many of them had to walk across the Appalachian Mountains before securing rail transportation near Greeneville, Tennessee. Throughout this march, they had to be kept together in order to be fed, to keep them from ravaging the countryside, and in some instances to protect them from the Unionist majority that populated the region.

Forrest's command structure broke up almost immediately upon his formal surrender. Most of his troops separated into small groups of ten, twenty, or more individuals and then began the sad trek back to their communities. Andrew McEwen rode with "a squad of 25" until he reached his family in Lincoln County; Charles Jackson returned to Fayette County with six or seven others; and Robert Rogers recorded that "about 12 of us boys came home together." The defeated veterans faced a bleak trip. They traveled across a devastated land, largely devoid of adequate sustenance for either soldier or civilian. In a typical statement, James Dickinson wrote: "It was rough [we had] no feed for horses and nothing to eat only what we could beg."[5]

Southerners who had served under Johnston retained their command discipline after the surrender, as federal officials appointed Confederate officers to supervise the Tennessee soldiers' homeward journey. The men were issued rations, provided with baggage wagons, and allowed to retain one-fifth of their rifles. The last proved necessary. As a weary contingent of several hundred returning soldiers neared Asheville, North Carolina, they confronted a regiment of belligerent mountain Unionists under the command of Colonel George W. Kirk. This federal officer feared that even vanquished Confederates constituted a threat to the loyal mountaineers. When he ordered the Tennesseans to surrender their remaining arms, the officers responded by aligning their men in battle formation. Violence seemed imminent. Sensing the resolve of his enemies and wishing to avoid unnecessary bloodshed, Kirk relented. Although the Tennessee troops remained largely unmolested from this point on, the incident proved to be a harbinger of Unionist distrust of former Confederates.[6]

Homeward-bound veterans, already defeated on the battlefield, suffered the additional humiliations of taunts from black soldiers, the confiscation of horses and weapons, and the ugly threats of revenge-minded Unionists. Four years of war had shattered the fabric of society. Not only had blacks apparently been freed from their submissive status, but white community trust seemed diminished. Eventually both the status of blacks and white community relations reverted almost to their antebellum norms. But in the immediate aftermath of the war, most veterans were troubled by what they saw. Few were optimistic about their futures.

A special frustration for some former Confederates was the confrontation with black troops. To men raised in a culture based on the superiority of one race to another, the sight of blacks wearing federal uniforms was a strong reminder of the magnitude of southern defeat. White veterans recalled the experience with some bitterness. Racial tensions were especially high in three locations: in Greeneville, where Johnston's troops assembled for rail transportation to Middle and West Tennessee; in Chattanooga, where Confederates returning from Georgia and the deep South were guarded by black regiments; and in Nashville, which, as the state capital, seemed to symbolize the extent of social disruption brought by the war.

Hampton Cheney pictured his stay in Greeneville as "two days and nights of hell," during which the "negro troops . . . taunted us [concerning] our loss of 'Southern rights' . . . and several bloody collisons were narrowly averted." Chafing at the ridicule heaped upon his companions by black soldiers, Henry Hogan condescendingly observed: "They yelled like Hyenas." Thomas Walthall wrote, "we was humiliated," and John Reagan stressed, "we had to endure it." In Chattanooga Lee Sadler, George Donnell, and John Fergus were harassed by black troops. Sadler remembered the humiliation of marching through the city with black guards. Donnell complained that "a Co [of] negroes took my horse from me and talked very rough and command[ed] us," and Fergus recalled that a near riot resulted when black troops charged toward Confederate prisoners shouting that "old Jeff Davis was a d—— S—— B——." The state capital was particularly inhospitable to former Confederates. "[When] I got to Nashville," wrote James Hendricks, "the Legislature was . . . denouncing 'Rebels.' . . . Negroes tried to push me from the side walk into the street, but I threw one of them into the gutter."[7] After four bitter years of struggle, southern whites were ill prepared to accept significant changes in race relations.

Confederates crossing through East Tennessee were further debased by having their weapons and horses stripped from them. Grant, Sherman, and other Union commanders had allowed the southern troops to retain their animals and their arms as private property. The action was magnanimous. These items had a definite utilitarian value, but they were also of tremendous symbolic importance. The privilege of retaining weapons and horses left Southerners with a small sense of salvaged honor. But East Tennessee Unionists viewed the situation as potentially disastrous. Thousands of Confederates—armed and mobile—had begun marches into or across East Tennessee to their home communities. The residents of Tennessee's eastern valleys and mountains—the one major section of the Confederacy with a Unionist majority—had suffered four cruel years of occupation and savage guerrilla warfare. Loyal mountaineers cringed at the bloody prospects represented by this migration of defeated but still armed and bitter former rebels.

Union commanders halted returning Confederates at three points along the East Tennessee and Virginia Railroad—at Strawberry Plains, Sweetwater, and Chattanooga—confiscated their weapons and horses, and then herded them aboard freight trains destined for the state's middle and western sections. Southern veterans deeply resented this. E. K. Cook, who surrendered with Jefferson Davis's escort near Washington, Georgia, was initially allowed to retain his horse, his pistol, and his equipment. Despite this, he remembered, "when we got to Chattanooga . . . our [surrender] Terms were ignored[.] we were insulted until we resented it, and were strip[p]ed of every thing, Then sent to Nashville on Stock Cars." At Strawberry Plains, just east of Knoxville, David England recalled how pro-Union "extremes[ts] seamed . . . disposed to a buse us and throw up [to us] our southern rites."

In this environment of animosity and mutual distrust, a few Confederates defiantly frustrated the Union efforts. Warned by a "Miss Bogus" that federal troops at Sweetwater were confiscating Confederate property, Edward Woodward, Zachary Crouch, and other veterans from the Fourth Tennessee Cavalry swam the Tennessee River in order to by-pass the blue-clad troops. When ordered to turn in their arms at Strawberry Plains, John Frierson, Thomas Williams, and other recalcitrant rebels threw their pistols into the Holston River.[8]

Bushwhackers—some pro-Unionist, others little more than outlaws—posed an ugly menace to the young veterans. Throughout rural Tennessee, a collapsed civil authority offered little protection to individuals on their isolated farms. Bushwhackers roamed freely, intimidating southern veterans, stealing their property, and killing the unwary. After federal troops confiscated his horse at Jonesboro, Tennessee, Daniel Long walked in fear the last sixty miles to his Grainger County community. "[I] Traveled by night," he wrote, "and tried to find [a] friend to hide with in day." He finally reached the safety of home "with sholeless shoes and blistered feet, tired, but happy." R. P. Lanius, James J. White, and William Kirkham were less fortunate. A few miles outside of Knoxville, several women instructed Lanius and his companions to go to a nearby cabin for food. There, he recorded, "men . . . with . . . guns [took] the horses and left us a foot." Just four miles from his home near Dresden, White "was arrested by three Bush Whackers," who stole his horse, bridle, and spurs; Kirkham's horse was taken from him "by stragglers or bushwackers who claimed to be in the Union army."

Some encounters proved fatal. "In Nashville about May 1, 1865," George Lewis remembered with bitterness, "two Union bushwackers followed [my father] out and killed him because he would not give them a thousand dollars." Shortly after the close of the war, Isaac Bartlett parted from an army comrade and never again heard from or about him. "Bushwackers," he speculated, "may have killed him."[9]

Some Confederates had more positive experiences on their homeward journeys. Wealth, social standing, and family connections often enabled young patricians to travel apart from the masses; along the way they were frequently hosted by upper-class families. The aristocratic William Johnston, who journeyed from southern Alabama to Madison County, Tennessee, testified: "[I] came through Mississippi horseback—Always welcome and entertained everywhere." The night before Josiah House finally arrived at his father's Gibson County plantation, he and three friends accepted an evening's lodging in a "nice looking house across from [a large farm]." There the owner's daughter amused them by singing choruses of "Yankee Doodle." Pressley Conner, designated an "invalid officer" after a wound at Chickamauga, spent the last months of the war at a remote Confederate outpost at Opelika, Alabama. "When the surrender came," he reminisced, "I escorted a very charming young lady . . . back to her home at Eufalla." This patrician remained thankful for such associations "with refined and hospitable people, [who] kept our minds and lives pure." Hampton Cheney remembered a May afternoon spent with the local gentry in Asheville, North Carolina, sipping juleps and lamenting the collapse of the late Confederacy; Herman Doak paused in Nashville to watch the classic play "She Stoops to Conquer," but found the audience contaminated by too many " 'damnyankees' soldiers." When Thomas Webb reached his native Memphis, he rode straight to the southwest corner of Court Square to purchase two drinks that were, he reflected, "the best I ever had."[10]

A few fanatical aristocrats refused to accept defeat and fled westward to continue the struggle. For Charles Samuel, the war concluded on 15 May 1865, when he was captured trying to "cross the Mississippi [River] to Texas." Victor Locke left Lee's army at Appomattox, Virginia, skirmished with free blacks in Louisiana, and finally accepted the reality of defeat in Texas. For a brief time, he hired out as a cowboy, but soon opened a "Mercantile Business" in the Indian Territory. Eventually he married a Choctaw woman and served as superintendent of public instruction for the tribe. Rather than surrender to General William T. Sherman, the hot-blooded John Wilson fled from Johnston's army and headed for the western territories. He got as far as Alabama, where, as he explained, "a citizen friend of mine told me I was making a fool of myself [and urged] me to go home."[11]

Most young veterans were happy that the carnage had ended. They made their painful treks back to the family farm and quickly sought to restore their prewar routines. As James Lasley and several friends neared their Gibson County residences, they were detained by a Union regiment. "The Colonel," he wrote, "looked at our Payrole [and then] told us you have made damned good Soldiers[.] go home and make damn good citizens. . . . we did."[12]

Confederates released from northern prisons confronted fewer hazards on the road home than did those who surrendered with an active command. Anticipating an end to the war, the federal bureaucracy established systematic procedures for repatriating the former rebels. Prisoners were simply required to swear an oath of loyalty to the Union in exchange for their freedom and, in some cases, for transportation home. Although most Southerners were released by the end of June, J. H. Jewell of Rhea County was an exception. Because he stubbornly refused to sign the oath, he remained incarcerated at Elmira, New York, until 27 August 1865.[13]

Most prisoners accepted government-provided transportation. The vast majority came home on crowded passenger and freight trains, a few rode chartered steamboats, and still fewer sailed on coastal ships. For the most part, these journeys were uneventful. William Durrett, a typical case, was released on 18 June 1865, left Johnson Island, and headed toward his Sumner County farm. The Union Army, he recorded, "gave me transportation and [I] came via Cincinnati by train home. [It] was pleasant and [I] was not molested during my trip." W. T. Askew agreed that he "was Treated fine along the road," but Jessie Broadaway complained that during his train ride through the North he "Nearly starved."[14]

A few veterans, having survived both combat and prison camp, lost their lives in tragic end-of-war accidents. Both Samuel Adkisson and Samuel Clemmons lived through train derailments in which several of their comrades were killed. From Point Lookout, Maryland, Jack Busly was transported to New York City, where he boarded a vessel destined for Mobile, Alabama. The "Ship was blown away," he explained, "No one drowned but several died after."[15] The war must have been particularly bitter for those who lost their sons and husbands after the conflict had ended.

As the young Confederates traveled home from prison, some met with kindness in the North, while others encountered hostility. The wife of a Rock Island physician provided food for hungry Confederates waiting to board south-bound steamboats. William Baldridge remembered a kind Ohio citizen who donated two days' rations for those discharged from Johnson Island, and both Samuel Frazier and Benjamin Hagnewood appreciated the hospitality shown to lonely, destitute southern soldiers by the "fair women" of Louisville, Kentucky.[16] In contrast to these incidents, R. A. Bryant and John Hickman felt the sting of northern enmity. En route home aboard an Ohio River steamer, Bryant witnessed the nasty contrast between beneficence and brutality. "The good women of Cincinnati," he testified, "brought us something to eat . . . and were preparing to spread it out[,] when a Yanke Capt Came a board[,] kicke[d] the baskets in the river[,] cussed the women and left us hungry." Hickman wrote that "when we reached Louisville, Ky. we were arrested—carried to Yankee Headquarters, and the brass buttons . . . cut from our uniforms."[17]

Despite the relative ease with which most Confederate prisoners of war returned to their communities, they tended in later years to be more antagonistic toward the North than other former Confederates. Long months—and in some cases years—of imprisonment left a legacy of distrust and hatred. In his old age, Joseph Riley delighted in recounting to his large family of nephews and nieces his many hardships and adventures in Rock Island Prison. He always concluded with the observation: "On April 7th, 1865 I landed at my home in Obion County. . . . I went to work, kept my mouth shut and have not taken the 'Damn Nasty Oath' yet."[18]

Whether fighting with an active command, languishing in prison, or hiding in the woods, Confederate soldiers longed to rejoin their families. At the war's conclusion, the opportunity came, but the homes they returned to had been profoundly affected by the conflict. Most families had lost one or more members, and thousands of surviving soldiers had suffered permanently debilitating injuries or illnesses. Slavery had been abolished, causing a great change in the economic order. In addition, many communities remained violently divided between those who had favored secession and those who had remained loyal to the Union. Edward Gannaway aptly illustrated the feelings of many of his contemporaries. "I left a wife and four children with my father," he recounted, "and never [saw] them the last two years but they ocupied my thoghts almost incessantly. . . . It was dark when I got home. . . . [The] joyful scene [that] followed [I] could not describe . . . if I had roome."[19]

When James Holder arrived home, he found that "some of my family did not know me"; James Logan arrived "so dirty and ragged" that his mother did not recognize him until he spoke; and Acey Green declared: "I rode on a grey mule and was certainly proud to see my old father and mother." Wounded in the right lung just before Johnston's surrender, William Lillard came back to his father's Rutherford County plantation to discover that his parents had presumed him dead. The following day, his ebullient mother prepared a dinner for sixty-five friends, and the youthful Lillard savored the first real coffee he had tasted in years. Frustration marred James Anthony's homecoming. He completed the long journey to his farm near Tullahoma only to find his family quarantined with smallpox. Reluctantly he bedded down under a shade tree for a week, but he recalled how thankful he was just to see and talk to his mother.[20]

Despite these heartwarming reunions, returning veterans were frequently confronted with news of the death of friends or family. War-related deaths had widespread emotional and social consequences for the South. They engendered a generation of bitterness and left a legacy of hardship to the surviving families. Several respondents to the questionnaires lost their fathers during the conflict. James

Haymes's father fell during the siege of Island Number 10 on the Mississippi River, John Crawford's father succumbed to disease at Camp Morton prison, and bushwhackers murdered Elijah Wolfe's father.[21] Even more Southerners lost brothers and friends. Ford Adams wrote, "my brother G. W. Adams and a dear friend Cymes Sugg were killed at Missionary Ridge." Three of Berenes Carter's four brothers died in combat—one at Murfreesboro, another at Atlanta, and the third at Franklin. James Bass recorded that he lost two brothers in battle and a third who died of his wounds after the war. Elijah Knight's older brother was mortally wounded at Gaines Mill, and a younger sibling failed to return from Rock Island Prison. A. W. Applewhich lost a brother at Perryville, another at Chattanooga, and a brother-in-law at Gettysburg. Despite desperate family pleas, John Dunavant's youngest brother insisted on fighting for the Confederacy. He fell at the "battle of shylo [Shiloh]," the veteran wrote, "and his bones . . . bleached on the battle field."[22]

Some men anticipated a joyous return to their families only to find tragedy when they got there. "[I] had no home," stated Robert Kittrell. "[My] Wife and three children [were] dead." When Robert Moss arrived at his farm near Donelson, he learned that his mother had passed away two years earlier; James Haymes found that his mother had died during the first year of the war, and as a result the "family . . . scattered." The war decimated Josia Reams's McNairy County family. "My father and stepmother . . . died," he testified. "My only brother was killed . . . and a half brother on the Union side . . . died. So our home was broken up and I was peniless." More than fifty years later, the old Confederate suffered from yet another war. Of two grandsons who fought in World War I, one was buried in France.[23]

War left a harvest of hardship. The returning veterans often found themselves saddled with the care of a deceased relative's dependents. For five years after the Confederate surrender, Joseph Wilson struggled to care for his father and mother, and to aid his late brother's wife and her children. In a similar case, Constantine Nance found his parents dead and dedicated himself to the care of his six younger sisters.[24] Such selfless efforts were repeated throughout Tennessee and across the South.

About 4 percent of veterans were left more a burden than a benefit to their families (Appendix 2, table 28). Found among all the social classes, these individuals required weeks, months, and, in some cases, years of nursing to overcome the results of wounds and diseases. In 1922 G. R. Boles proclaimed: "i am to Day Suffering from

Disease i contacted in prison," and Franklin Wilson complained that "at this time being 80 years old [I] can hardly endure the pains I have [from] my . . . wound at Atlanta." Chronic diarrhea incapacitated Theodoric Lipscomb for twelve months following the Confederacy's collapse. W. H. Lamastus hobbled on crutches for three months after his discharge, and William Baker used crutches for several years. Tom Childress left one of the more pathetic accounts. "I got hit with a bum shell in the ware," he said, "and it caused me to go blind. . . . I have not never ben able to work since I have ben back [and] all I have to live on is the little salary I get [from the state]. . . . I have suffered a lot."[25]

The Confederate veterans faced not only the disruption of their families, but they also had to adjust to a major reordering of social relations in their communities. Blacks had been freed from their bondage, and in many neighborhoods—especially those of East Tennessee—private wars continued among local whites long after the formal end of hostilities. Violence characterized the time.

The abolition of slavery provoked turbulence and instability. Although the destruction of the South's peculiar institution must have distressed many Southerners, the Civil War Veterans Questionnaires failed to solicit information concerning this major event. Nonetheless a few aged veterans provided small insights into the impact of emancipation on their lives. Some defended slavery, painting a romanticized image of faithful antebellum servants in contrast to what they perceived as the degraded moral state of postwar blacks. Reflecting on racial tensions in the 1920s, Henry Tally proclaimed that the white "people of the south and [the] negro would settle the race queston if left alone to them[selves]." Invoking a past that had never existed, he declared that he would "allways respect the old antebellum negro[es] [for] the way they conducted themselves . . . during the war." Hampton Cheney was convinced that before the conflict, blacks remained docile and loyal because "they knew they would be well cared for . . . in sickness, [and] in health, and when old age come . . . that same care . . . would still be given [with] perhaps added tenderness." Charles Rice of Henning confidently proclaimed that "under the old regime [the Negro's] close contact with the southern white gave him a moral training which was the wonder of the world." As a result, he stated, "our refined women [were able] to remain at home during the war . . . surrounded by a throng of blacks without a thought of fear."[26]

The behavior of freed blacks, however, belied the image of faithful and contented slaves, as other veterans attested. H. A. Humphreys arrived at his parents' Henry County plantation to find the "Negros all free and gone." The eight former slaves of Lewis Howse's father remained on the family farm long enough to complete the spring planting but left soon after. Lee Billingsley reached his mother's Bledsoe County estate to find "the fences had all been burned [and] the negros all gone except two." Returning to his parents' Henry County plantation, M. B. Dinwiddie discovered that a few of his father's old servants remained, but "the bulk of the younger ones" departed. He immediately commenced the reconstruction of the farm with hired help, which he found to be "much better labor than slaves, more satisfactory, in every way."[27] Former slaveowners, no longer responsible for housing, feeding, and caring for black dependents, quickly realized that the new free labor could easily be exploited.

To oppose the new status of blacks and the politics of Republican Reconstruction, an unknown number of veterans joined the Ku Klux Klan. Only six respondents—five of whom were from the planter and professional class—openly acknowledged their involvements, and they were reluctant to provide significant details. Thomas Blackwell of Lauderdale County and W. H. Kearney of Madison County simply mentioned their affiliations with the Klan; Robert Brunson of Giles County proudly noted that he still owned his original robe. Robert Morris of Davidson County declared: "I could tell you much of the history of [the Reconstruction] period in Tennessee as I was a member of the Ku Klux Klan but I desist." In Marcus Toney's obituary, which was attached to his questionnaire, a journalist for the *Nashville Banner* reported that Toney was "a member of the original Ku Klux Klan and on occasion would recall some of the stirring events of that period."

Only Amos Jones of Madison County elaborated on his experiences in the Klan. Two years after the fall of the Confederacy, he left his father's home in Jackson, Tennessee, and moved just south of Corinth, Mississippi; there he opened a girl's academy and began to ride with the Klan. Although vague about his escapades, he indicated that his activities were clearly beyond the law. In the spring of 1869, the local sheriff, a close personal friend, warned Jones that federal agents had sworn out a warrant for his arrest. He immediately dismissed his school, ordered his wife to pack their belongings, and fled northward to Tennessee on the next train. When Jones arrived in Jackson, his father, who was president of a Methodist female college, provided refuge for the fugitive Klansman and appointed him to the position of "Professor of Ancient Languages and Mathematics."[28]

East Tennessee Confederates were much more willing to discuss the persecutions they suffered from the vengeful Unionist majority in the region. Wartime bitterness remained long after the southern armies surrendered. Many former rebels were threatened, others were beaten or killed, and still others were forced into exile. "Our chances among so many Union men were pretty bad," reported a Polk Countian. "It mattered not how honest or upright a Confederate was[,] he had no favors from the other side."[29] Whatever community harmony had existed before 1861 was thoroughly shattered by four years of intense strife. W. C. Carden was forgiven by his Unionist grandfather, who then welcomed the young man home to Bradley County. But the neighbors were less gracious. "The boys of the community threatened [to] run us off," Carden wrote, "but Grand-father sent them word back that the war was over and . . . if they came they would get a warm reception. *They never came.*" J. B. King was also harassed in McMinn County. During the spring and summer of 1865, he frequently conducted farm-related business in the county seat of Athens. There veterans from both sides intermingled, but ever so often, he recalled, "some Federal would mount a stump . . . and yell . . . that he would give every Rebel 5 minutes to get out of town." King emphasized: "That always proved to be ample time for we sure did get."[30]

Carden, King, and thousands of their Confederate peers had good reason to be apprehensive. Floggings and assassinations were frequent. In Washington County, Franklin Leonard reported, "Federal soldiers and bushwackers were making raids on Rebels whipping and killing them to such an extent that it was very unsafe to remain here." Both William Kirkham of Grainger County and James Harris of Blount County felt the full impact of postwar hatreds. Along with his close friend John Long, Kirk was overwhelmed by ten bushwhackers, who beat them "with large switches." Harris recalled that such Union veterans organized themselves as "Night Riders" to intimidate Confederate soldiers and to chase southern preachers out of the county. One evening, he testified, "Fourteen of these surrounded me . . . and with a pistol at my breast I was given 34 liks with a two-handed brush." On 15 July 1865, William E. McElwee witnessed a particularly ugly incident. While visiting in the spacious Morristown home of J. M. Mims, he saw a Unionist mob rush the house intent upon lynching his host's brother, a Confederate captain. The would-be victim escaped when J. M. Mims single-handedly charged the rabble, leveling several of them with a large club. The consequences proved fatal. Seized by the mob, Mims was impaled on his own fence and then shot to death.[31]

Fear of such actions caused many former Confederates to flee from East Tennessee. A. M. Bruce remained in Virginia for a year before returning to his Campbell County farm. "I was a little afraid," he wrote, "that it might not be right healthy up here in this mountain country." M. D. L. Taylor left Blount County to teach school in Illinois, and Henry Parrott stayed in Scott County, Virginia, "until things got quiet in East Tenn." George McMahan fled to northern Alabama to avoid violence in Sevier County. Abraham Gredig abandoned his hardware business in Knoxville and sought refuge in Atlanta, and Augustus Gotham moved to Texas because, as he observed, "the people who had been in the union army were so bitter that I had to leave home." Many never returned. As one of the permanent emigrés explained: "Bushwackers were so bad [in Hawkins County] I could not stay . . . for [more than] a few meals[.] so [I] went to Lee Co. Va. [and] Never lived in Tenn a day after the war."[32]

A few wealthy exiles sought asylums that offered advanced educational opportunities. When James McColgan heard that a Jackson County grand jury planned to indict local Confederates for wartime horse stealing, he fled to Louisiana and entered the New Orleans Medical College, from which he graduated a year later. James Morey left the hostile environment of Greeneville, Tennessee, to seek safe haven among New England relatives. There he enrolled in a Boston business college and later became a partner in the family wholesale ceramics enterprise. William Taylor quickly found that "disbanded federal soldiers" made Jefferson County "unsafe for ex confederates." He spent a year at Kentucky University and then studied for three years at Virginia's Washington and Lee University. Nathaniel Harris's experience demonstrated the importance of family connections among southern elites. Born into a family that was well connected to secessionist politicians, Harris was forced from his home in Jonesboro in 1865 and sought sanctuary in Georgia. After a few weeks, he borrowed enough money from former Confederate Vice President Alexander Stephens to enter the University of Georgia's law school.[33]

The ability of affluent Tennesseans to turn adversity to advantage illustrated a phenomenon common throughout the South. Veterans from across the social strata—from plebeians to patricians—returned to a devastated land filled with bitterness and turmoil. Nonetheless the sons of planters and professionals possessed attributes of wealth, education, and family associations that enabled them to reestablish their dominance in society.

Most Confederate veterans, rich and poor, were wearied by four years of hardships and longed only to return to the normal routines of their civilian lives. In the months immediately after the war, their activities clearly indicated that the antebellum class structure would be a continuing feature of the New South.

A few individuals from poor or modest backgrounds were able to move up the social scale, with aid from wealthy patrons. Allen Gibbs of Rhea County, whose father was a nonslaveowning yeoman, was given credit by a local judge in order to purchase half interest in a general store. "I made good," he wrote with pride, and "was able to bye a small farm." Years later, unfortunately, he "Trusted a friend and lost all." A. T. Bransford returned to Smith County and enrolled at a local academy, which prepared him to become a teacher. With gratitude he noted: "My education was paid for by my wealthy friends of my home neighborhood." These circumstances were unusual. More common was the frustrating experience of indigent Samuel Ray. "My father arranged for me to go to school for a short time," he related, but "[I] gave that up on account of the lack of funds to buy clothes and pay tuition."[34]

Statistics gathered from the Civil War Veterans Questionnaires demonstrate significant social-class trends. The majority of former Confederates returned to farm occupations, but the wealthy were less likely (56 percent) to till the soil than the slaveowning yeomen (71 percent), the nonslaveowning yeomen (74 percent), and the poor (77 percent).* The sons of planters and professionals entered manual occupations only about half as often as the sons of the poor and the yeomen. By contrast 18 percent of the wealthy moved into professions, three times more than the slaveowning yeomen (6 percent), nine times more than the nonslaveowning yeomen (2 percent), and eighteen times more than the poor (1 percent). During the first months following the Civil War, 9 percent of the sons of planters and professionals and 2 percent of the slaveowning yeomen's sons received college training. Few nonslaveowners could afford this luxury (Appendix 2, table 28). These activities not only paralleled the soldiers' antebellum lifestyles, but they also assured that the New South would develop a social system that was not radically different from the Old.

Although the overwhelming majority of veterans returned to agricultural pursuits, there were important differences in their social and

---

*The terms slaveowning yeoman and nonslaveowning yeoman have been retained to indicate the veterans' antebellum origins.

economic levels. As might be expected, the poor worked wherever they could as hired hands or renters, the yeomen cultivated their modest holdings, and the wealthy dedicated themselves to rebuilding their estates. All these men wanted mainly to forget war and to create normal, stable family situations. As the son of one former small slave-owner in Middle Tennessee declared: "[I went to] Farming and raising children."[35]

The poor, who had little before the conflict, came home to almost nothing. Owning no land and having almost no access to economic or social advancement, they grasped whatever meager opportunities were at hand. Andrew Beaner leased a small farm, but accomplished little with it. In 1922 he pointed out that he had "been a renter ever since I [came to] White County." Frank Duckworth migrated to Texas but failed to make his fortune there. He picked cotton for two years, drove cattle for three years, and then became a lifelong "common laborer." In Sullivan County, George Payne hired out his labor for eight dollars per month; in Perry County, Ezkiel Inman did the same for ten dollars per month; and in Stewart County, George Horn-berger sold his labor "for $15 per Mo. and board." These former Confederates were born poor in the Old South, and they continued to eke out a marginal existence in postwar Tennessee. The indigent Elijah Barnes declared that at the war's end, he immediately commenced "digging in the ground to try to make a living."[36]

The yeomen equated cultivation with stability. Subdued by the rigors of war, they gladly exchanged their rifles and bayonets for plows. When Robert Holman arrived at his Robertson County home, he borrowed a good suit to attend Sunday services; the next day, he remembered, "I stepped down into the furrow, and went to work as if nothing had happen." William Roach "arrived home Friday afternoon the 19th of May 1865 and Monday morning hitched a mule to a plow," while Thomas Wood "commenced plowing a day or two after I returned home." Robert Mosley visited friends for three days and then joined his father in the fields, and John Prather proudly stated: "I Went between the plow Handles In three days after I got Home [and have] bin Farming Every year since that time."[37]

Those affluent Tennesseans that returned to the farm came back to an environment far more comfortable than that of the other social classes. Although their fathers had suffered significant losses in slaves and destroyed buildings, most retained sizable landholdings and their considerable advantage in the economic system. The sons quickly dedicated themselves to the restoration of their family fortunes. "I took up my work on the farm," wrote a Middle Tennessean whose father had owned thirty slaves, "helping readjust matters which had been neglected during [the] troublous war time." Charles Rice's family lost their one hundred slaves but still owned 1,500 acres in Lauderdale County. The young Rice immediately set out to manage his father's farm. In the same county, Lauchlan Donaldson oversaw his father's estate and studied law, and Joshua Mewborn of Fayette County gave up his ambition of a professional career in order to rebuild his father's 2,100-acre plantation. Mewborn bragged: "I became a farmer and a good one too." Alexander McKay proved that his social class had retained much of its wealth. "[I] farmed a while," he noted, "[and] then took up the race horse business."[38]

Several of the more affluent families held on to widely scattered estates. Having surrendered with Forrest in Alabama, Benjamin Hawkins headed straight for his uncle and guardian's Mississippi plantation on the Tallahatchie River. He supervised this estate for a year before returning to his Memphis home. Despite the loss of a leg, A. W. Applewhich was sent to oversee his father's Mississippi farms, and David Watkins of Maury County reported that he was soon employed "building up our desolated farms." Newton Cannon emphasized the responsibility felt by these youthful veterans. "[I] helped my father to get things in the best shape possible on his two farms in Tennessee," he recalled, "and then went to Mississippi to do what I could with his deserted farm in the delta or swamp[.] that was before I was twenty one years old."[39]

Aristocratic Tennesseans may have been severely damaged by the Civil War, but they demonstrated a tremendous economic resilience. In the Old South, land and slaves were the foundations of massive fortunes. Not only did the elites retain their significant acreage in the postbellum years, but at the same time, most blacks were soon reduced to peonage, which gave the former planters and their sons the benefits of black labor without the responsibilities associated with caring for slaves.

In the months following the Civil War, more than one out of four veterans from the planter and professional class either entered a profession or studied at a college in preparation for a profession. George Lewis of Wilson County, Carrick Heiskell of Knox County, and James Womach of Warren County pursued law practices. Several became merchants, including John Kirby and Aratus Cornelius of Shelby County, John Dance of Gibson County, and Milton Head of Sumner County. Others found journalism enticing. Gideon Baskett edited the *Murfreesboro News*; Charles Hubner was appointed the associate editor of the *Selma Times* (Alabama). Samuel Sparks became a printer for the *Memphis Appeal* and years later founded the *Fayette County Falcon*. William Carnes took charge of the newly created *Memphis Commercial*'s business department.

The possession of significant capital and ready credit enabled a few affluent veterans to speculate on cotton. At the close of the war, William Timberlake of Henderson County began "speculating in Farms[,] mules and cotton." Both William Sebring and Thomas Webb worked out of Memphis. Sebring purchased and ran a wholesale "Grocery and cotton House" until he moved to Florida in 1871, and Webb and his father "bought and sold cotton until we could get possession of our property from the Federals." Later the younger Webb read law. Thomas Williams had a similar experience. "In the fall of 1865," he explained, "I was employed to go to Alabama on business connected with collecting Cotton bought by some Maury County citizens. On my return home in 1866, I entered the mercantile business."[40]

Beginning in the fall of 1865, many of Tennessee's aristocratic veterans attended college classes. Robert Herbert of Williamson County helped his two brothers work their family's farm until September, when he left to study medicine at the University of Nashville. This institution was by far the most popular among Tennessee patricians seeking careers in the healing arts. Those wishing to practice law often gravitated to Lebanon's Cumberland University. Others left the state in their quest for knowledge. John Johnson and Lycurgus Taylor entered Virginia's Emory and Henry College, James Carringer studied at the University of Virginia, James Jones went to the University of Mississippi, and Lemuel Tyree eventually graduated from Princeton. Upper-class Tennesseans had a strong appreciation for the value of an education. As John Johnson reflected: "The things that I have studied in my lifetime—for personal satisfaction only—are too numerous to mention here."[41]

The Civil War experience had formed a common bond among all members of Tennessee's Confederate generation. But as soon as Lee, Johnston, Forrest, and other southern commanders surrendered, most veterans returned to their homes and assumed approximately the same social status that they had before the war. The aged men who filled out the Civil War Veterans Questionnaires between 1915 and 1922 were still youths in 1865. Although most of their lives remained before them, however, their social values were well entrenched. In the decades following the war, these individuals became Old South men in a New South world.

CHAPTER SEVEN

OLD SOUTH MEN, NEW SOUTH WORLD

Well into the twentieth century, the aristocratic William P. Timberlake and the impoverished W. M. Willis embodied opposing characteristics of the Old South. Timberlake, born into one of Henderson County's most prominent families, resided in a community named after one of his ancestors. His father owned a 2,200-acre plantation worked by thirty slaves, and young William received an excellent academy education, polished by two years at Tennessee's Union University in Murfreesboro and graduation from the University of North Carolina at Chapel Hill. In 1865 he returned from Nathan Bedford Forrest's command with the rank of captain and immediately began a long, satisfying career as a land and cotton speculator and gentleman farmer. He settled in Jackson, Tennessee, purchased a sizable estate northwest of the city, and continued the patrician traditions of his parents.[1]

In 1927 an admiring journalist portrayed Timberlake as imbued with the aura of the old regime. Noting that the aged Confederate personally supervised his crops on even the hottest summer's day, the reporter was impressed that he rode out to his farm in a slow, comfortable carriage rather than in a speedy, modern automobile. His approving observation that "every Saturday [Timberlake] continued his custom of seeing the farm negroes downtown and taking care of their needs" is reminiscent of the paternalistic attitudes of slave-owners.[2]

From the other end of the white social scale, W. M. Willis of Maury County summarized his postwar experience in a single compact sentence. "I worked at Ashton's mill for a time, farmed, and belonged to

the Campbellite Church . . . about 70 years, and never held an office."[3] In common with most of Tennessee's Confederate generation,
Timberlake and Willis's lives followed patterns set in their antebellum
adolescences.

Most Civil War soldiers were mere youths when they volunteered,
but they came home battle-hardened adults. For the vast majority,
the future was determined by social class, educational attainment,
wealth, and family influence (or lack of it). A few impoverished veterans overcame tremendous odds to accomplish modest success, but
most individuals discovered that poverty bred poverty and wealth
reproduced wealth. In the postbellum decades social-class relations
closely mirrored those of the Old South.

After the war, the vast majority of Tennessee veterans returned to
their home counties and remained there. Seventy-eight percent of all
nonslaveowners' sons—poor and yeomen—and 74 percent of slaveowning yeomens' sons failed to move far from their birthplaces, although only about 61 percent of the patricians remained rooted to
their original communities (Appendix 2, table 29). Wealth, education, and family support gave the latter opportunities not available to
lesser whites.

Many of the old Confederates proudly stressed their loyalties to
their home neighborhoods. "[I] settled on my Father's place," wrote
Arthur Davis, "and [am] still living there." Moses Garton of Dickson
County emphasized that he had always "lived near where I was
born," and George Hodge of Maury County noted that "I have lived
not more than a mile from where I was born." Halyard Wilhite of
White County declared: "I am now living on the old farm owned by
my father. . . . I expect to die where I was born." Although most of
these men led somewhat sedate lives, Francis Arnold displayed re-
freshing vitality. "[I] have lived on the farm I am on now since 1861,"
he testified. Then the ninety-two-year-old veteran bragged: "[I] have
been married three times and might just marry again."[4]

Wealth gave some Tennesseans an opportunity to migrate. Forty
percent of the affluent made significant geographic moves as compared to slightly more than 20 percent of the other social classes. A
majority of nonslaveowners' sons who moved away from the home-
place remained in Tennessee, but a slight majority of the emigrating
slaveowning yeomen's sons and a notable majority of the wealthy left
the state (Appendix 2, table 29). No significant class differences appeared in the regional destinations of the emigrés. Eighty-two percent of the poor and 88 percent of the nonslaveowning yeomen's

sons who left Tennessee settled either in the South or the West. Only the wealthy (3 percent) moved to the hotbed of Yankeedom, the Northeast (Appendix 2, table 30).

The former soldiers had notably varied incentives for moving. Necessity forced the poor to leave. They typically gave, as the reason for pulling up stakes, the hope of greater economic opportunity. By contrast, planters' sons were already financially comfortable, and they often expressed their ambition in terms of personal growth and fulfillment rather than economic success. Far more often than the yeomen and the poor, they moved for the sake of their professional lives or to gain an education. Among those who gave their motives for moving, 84 percent of the poor set out in a simple quest for economic opportunity, compared with 76 percent of the nonslaveowning yeomen's sons, 65 percent of the slaveowning yeomen's sons, and 52 percent of the planters and professionals' sons. On the other hand, 33 percent of the wealthy moved in pursuit of a profession, while only 8 percent of nonslaveowning yeomen's sons and 3 percent of the poor did so (Appendix 2, table 31). These responses clearly indicated that a change in geographic location rarely modified a veteran's social status.

Most indigent Tennesseans who moved about continued a marginal life of poverty. David Odle explained that, after the Civil War, he returned to his native White County for about five years, "working here and there for a living." Hoping for economic improvement, he went to Wayne County to labor in an iron foundry; then, after five years, he moved on to Perry County. Destitute after two years of sharecropping, he returned to Wayne County, only to drift back into sharecropping. Although Odle was eventually able to purchase a small farm, he recorded that, for him, survival was an intense struggle and that in old age he was almost entirely reliant upon his meager Confederate pension.[5] W. A. Duncan, Timothy Leigon, Alax Underhill, and Richard Rigsby shared similar experiences. Throughout his postbellum life, Duncan rented or sharecropped in Tennessee, Arkansas, and Texas; Legion failed at silver mining in the West and then spent his adulthood leading "a roving life." Underhill labored in different places, making buckets, iron rails, and boxes; and Rigsby wandered from sharecropping to clearing new ground, to drilling water wells.[6]

Although migration rarely led to financial success for the impoverished, William Moss, Ephriam Randle, and John Garren were exceptions. In a southern version of the Horatio Alger myth, Moss hauled wood for several months following his release from an Ohio prisoner-of-war camp. With his savings, he purchased a small mercantile business near his Williamson County home. He sold this shortly before his marriage in 1868, moved to Madison County, and opened a grocery in the tiny community of Denmark, near Jackson. Active in Republican politics, Moss served as Jackson's postmaster, first under President Benjamin Harris and again under President William McKinley. Randle and Garren's achievements were more modest. In 1870 Randle left Henry County, Tennessee, for Bastrop County, Texas. Over the years, he purchased small parcels of land on credit. By the end of his life, he had accumulated a comfortable four-hundred-acre farm. Garren escaped poverty in East Tennessee to set up a blacksmith shop in a small Indian Territory community. A well-respected citizen, he counted among his honors an appointment as postmaster in 1894.[7]

The sons of some yeomen—slave- and nonslaveowning—migrated, but they generally maintained lifestyles similar to those they left behind. Thomas Bryan left his father's Coffee County farm in 1868 or 1869, settled in California for twenty years, and then returned to his Tennessee home. James L. Cooper forsook farming to work as a carpenter in various Tennessee and Texas counties, and George A. Rice owned, at different times, small farms in the Tennessee counties of Decatur, Haywood, and Dyer. In old age, both Cooper and Rice lived contentedly with their own children. Cooper quietly tended his garden and fed chickens, and Rice observed with satisfaction that he had "always had good neighbors[,] plenty of friends, and no enemies."[8]

Wealthy Tennesseans moved in pursuit of larger goals than those of other whites. Like other social classes, affluent veterans followed careers and engaged in social activities that reflected their antebellum upbringings. Having learned dentistry from his father in McMinn County, Daniel Buckner later set up a thriving practice in Franklin County. James Coffin, the son of a Rogersville, Tennessee, bank president, emulated his father when he moved to Batesville, Arkansas, and became one of the state's outstanding financiers. John Crawford of Rhea County settled in Texas, where his life followed the pattern set in antebellum Tennessee. In his youth, Crawford had been personally acquainted with such notable Tennesseans as future president Andrew Johnson and Governor Isham G. Harris. As an adult in the Lone Star State, he established a lucrative insurance enterprise and counted among his friends Texas governors James S. Hogg and Samuel Lanham.[9]

Unlike the poor and the yeomen, the sons of planters and professionals could move out from their homes confident that their fathers' wealth and family associations would protect them from failures. This was well illustrated in the oscillating career of Benjamin Rogers. In the spring of 1865, he hobbled to his Wilson County home crippled by a Union bullet. By fall, however, he was able to complete his education at Mt. Vernon Academy. With money borrowed from his father, he moved in 1871 to Phillips County, Arkansas, and rented a large cotton plantation. There, in his words, he lost his fortune because the "niggers [got] sick and the mules all came down with Pink Eye." With broken health and an empty pocketbook, Rogers retreated to Tennessee. His prospects improved when his father put him in charge of a general store at Leeville, and in 1884, his popularity led to a term in the Tennessee legislature. Following his wife's death, Rogers devoted his declining years to serving as a ruling elder of his local Cumberland Presbyterian congregation.[10]

Although a sizable minority of Tennessee's Confederate generation changed domiciles at some point in their adult lives, few found that geographic mobility led to significant social advancement. In all but the rarest of cases, only Tennessee patricians possessed the keys to social and economic accomplishment: wealth, education, and family connections.

Throughout the postbellum decades, Tennessee's classes were just as segregated from one another as they had been before the Civil War. Some interclass mingling occurred, but, as a rule, like associated with like. A vast social gulf separated janitor Edward Love, of the Sullivan County public schools, from wealthy cotton entrepreneur Charles G. Samuel, who often entertained prominent southern personalities—among them the former vice president of the Confederacy. As one veteran from a yeoman background observed: "i lived most of my life in [the] 22nd civeldistrict of Williamson Co. . . . i havent none [known] no grate men."[11]

The Civil War Veterans Questionnaires revealed divergent trends in the soldiers' lives after 1865. A majority of the poor and the yeomen remained in agricultural occupations, whereas Tennessee's patricians turned in large numbers to the professions. Seventy-six percent of the impoverished veterans and the same percent of nonslaveowning yeomen farmed—as hired hands, sharecroppers, or small landowners. The proportion declined to 68 percent of the slaveowning yeomen's sons and to only 45 percent of planters and professionals' sons. Forty-five percent of Tennessee's aristocrats employed their special educations and social backgrounds to pursue careers as attorneys, physicians, merchants and other professions. Nineteen percent of small slaveholders' sons entered a profession, but only 12 percent of the nonslaveowning yeomen's sons and 8 percent of the impoverished did so (Appendix 2, table 32).

Some members of each class entered the professions, but their social backgrounds strongly influenced their career choices. Law, medicine, journalism, and college teaching all required a high level of education. As a result, only one impoverished veteran became a physician, and none became attorneys, editors, or professors. The numbers were only slightly better for nonslaveowning yeomen's sons. None were journalists, two became lawyers, and one each practiced medicine or taught college. Slaveowners' sons did somewhat better. Among the slaveowning yeomen's sons, two were attorneys and eleven were physicians. The patrician class produced sixteen lawyers, ten doctors, five editors, and three college professors. Indigent veterans usually joined the lesser professions; they tended to become local magistrates (five), schoolteachers (four), or small-town merchants (four); three became ministers in denominations that did not require an educated clergy (Appendix 2, table 33). Physicians, attorneys, and merchants who responded to the questionnaires occasionally recalled a colleague who had risen from a lower class, but most of their fellow professionals had come from similar, affluent backgrounds.

Notable differences existed in the quality of the veterans' lifestyles. Many endured intense poverty, struggling to survive from season to season and from year to year; a few enjoyed the amenities of wealth and cultured society. The vast majority experienced the simple joys and tragedies of the common folk—life cycles marked by marriages, births, baptisms, and funerals. As the veterans related their personal histories, some voiced frustrations, others expressed contentment, and a few revealed great pride in their accomplishments. To a large extent, these emotions reflected their class standings.

Veterans from impoverished backgrounds emphasized that they lived "hard lives." Holston Roddy recorded that he barely subsisted on the Maury County farm that he had rented for fifty-three years. James Coakley wrote that after the Civil War he "rented all the time," and Alexander Teasley farmed "on shares as long as I was able to work—never owned any land." Under these circumstances, indigent former Confederates found life difficult. "I have lived from place to place trying to make a living," explained Albert Townsend, and "[I] did the best I could to raise a family." J. K. P. Thompson led "a hard life working on razin my family," and H. C. Furry wrote that "[I] have managed to live but sometimes [it] was hard." Alax Underhill nicely summarized the almost universal experience of his social class: "I have did nothing but hard Work all my life."[12]

The sons of yeomen often concluded their questionnaires with expressions of satisfaction with their lifetime achievements. Whether they tilled their own small farms or practiced such crafts as blacksmithing or carpentry, they labored diligently for themselves and their families. "I came home [after] the war to my wife and 2 children," wrote Ozias Denton, "went to work[,] have ben a church member nearly 52 years [and] have tried to live a moral good life as well as I know how." In the same spirit, S. H. Clayton stated: "I have had a very pleasant time Since the war Farming." James McKnight counted himself among the more contented. Living in Jefferson County, he took pleasure daily in the "beautiful scerenry all around" his small farm. Reflecting on the inevitable future, he found comfort that there was "a nice cemetary on the place."[13]

Tennessee's patricians expressed profound satisfaction with their attainments. Many of them made notable achievements in finance and politics. David Watkins, whose father had owned between fifty and seventy-five slaves and two thousand Maury County acres, succinctly capsuled his postwar experiences: "I have been a successful farmer and stock trader [and] a member of Zion Presbyterian Church."[14] Most other affluents expressed their achievements at greater length.

Some of the wealthy pictured themselves as having risen from rags to riches. Their testimonies provided the evidence for those future scholars who pictured the New South—and postbellum America as a whole—as fertile ground for social and economic mobility. Invited to deliver the Walter Lynwood Fleming Lectures in Southern History for 1948, Frank L. Owsley proclaimed to the faculty and students of Louisiana State University that "in the lower South and in Tennessee and Kentucky . . . the bulk of lawyers, physicians, preachers, editors, teachers, businessmen, and political leaders below the national level were members of families who were poor or only comfortably well off." He assured his audience that a "young man of ability, energy, and determination—barring unusually bad luck—could scarcely fail of considerable success in any of the professions."[15]

Civil War veteran William Reynolds would have enthusiastically echoed Owsley's optimistic pronouncements. A well-esteemed physician with a thriving practice in Hopkinsville, Kentucky, he closed an eleven-page autobiography with this assessment of his humble Montgomery County, Tennessee, origins: "As my parents were poor, and my education limited and having no relatives holding positions in higher circles of life, I was always too timid . . . to meet and associate with great men. So I have been content to associate, and feel equal to the best people of this community."[16] Despite his claims of an unpretentious background, Reynolds's questionnaire revealed an affluent family. His father, the superintendent of a sizable iron foundry, owned ten slaves, five hundred valuable acres, a seven-room house, and an estate valued at between eighteen and twenty thousand dollars. Encouraged by his brother-in-law, William Reynolds concluded his education with a degree from Vanderbilt University's medical department.[17] Although late-nineteenth-century Americans gave lip service to the Horatio Alger myth, financial success was actually attained primarily by those who began with economic or social advantages.

Marcus Toney and Charles Samuel illustrated the connection between wealth, education, and family background and postbellum accomplishment. Raised at Edgefield, a Davidson County plantation worked by his father's thirty-five slaves, Toney grew up in luxury. After a fine academy education, he received two years' instruction at the Virginia Military Institute. The youthful Toney, who had prominent relatives in both Tennessee and Virginia, developed social skills and the personal contacts needed to achieve notable success. After the Civil War, he became an important official at the Nashville office of the New York Central Railroad and counted among his friends the exceptionally wealthy capitalist, William Vanderbilt. Following Toney's death in 1929, a eulogy in the *Nashville Banner* praised him as "an authority on . . . the development of the city's industries and educational institutions."[18]

Like Toney, Charles Samuel was the product of a rich environment. His father was president of Forrest Hill Academy in Athens, Tennessee. The school provided the young Samuel with an excellent grounding in the classics, and it also brought him into contact with numerous future southern leaders. Samuel attained the rank of colonel in the Confederate army; after the war, he practiced law in Rome, Georgia, and served several years on the city council. Late in the century, he returned to Athens, Tennessee. There he encouraged his numerous acquaintances among northeastern and southern investors to exploit East Tennessee's considerable timber, coal, and iron resources. Samuel retired in the early 1920s to his comfortable estate named "Sunshine Hill," overlooking the placid Hiwassee River, and devoted his energies to writing religious tracts. The most popular of these, "A Sinner's Friend," sold more than four thousand copies.[19]

In the decades following the Civil War, the poor, the plain folk and the planters moved in vastly different circles. Impoverished Tennesseans struggled for simple survival, and the plain folk were largely relegated to the limited occupations of farming and artisanship. New

South patricians continued their fathers' domination of the region's economy and politics.

From the impoverished to the wealthy, all Confederate veterans were slightly more active in politics than their fathers, but major class differences still existed. Ten percent of those from economically deficient backgrounds held civic offices. The proportion climbed to 19 percent of the nonslaveowning yeoman class, 23 percent of the slaveowning yeoman class, and 29 percent of the planters and professionals (Appendix 2, table 34). In some communities, an individual's ambition and inherent abilities might overcome inadequacies in education and family position. More often than not, however, aristocrats retained key positions in politics.

Most indigent Tennesseans, as well as many yeomen, were not sufficiently literate to fulfill civic responsibilities. "My parents wasent able to give me any scooling," complained Jacob Slinger of McMinn County, "and I couldent hold any office." George Willing and Thomas Booker supported this view. Willing emphasized that he never attained an elected position because he "had no education," and Booker stressed: "I have . . . never had no education to hold no office of any kind."[20]

Some veterans, whose war injuries limited their physical abilities, turned to politics for a livelihood. James M. Rogers, a Dickson County yeoman, lost both an arm and a leg at Murfreesboro. After the Civil War, he moved to Montgomery County, and in 1870 he was elected county magistrate, a post he retained until 1894. Another native of Dickson County, the impoverished Samuel Reynolds, relied on community sympathy to secure remunerative public employment. "After the war was over," he wrote in his questionnaire, "i was not able to work much[.] in the 10th district the people Elicted me as consable. i served six years then i was appointed Sherif[.] then after i got Sum beter i was Elicted tax Sesser. i Served 4 years [until] i got So Porley i could not at tend the office. . . . i have not bin able to do no work in a long time."[21]

Most officeholding veterans served in local positions. County magistrates, sheriffs and constables, and justices of the peace were usually far more important to an isolated rural people than those individuals who held state or national posts. The sons of nonslaveowners frequently served in postbellum governments, although they usually found that their more affluent contemporaries dominated community politics.

Wealthy veterans boasted of their long tenures in public office.

Napoleon Johnson of Maury County proudly noted: "I [was] Elected a Justice of the Peace in 1870 and [have] been continued in office up to the Present time . . . which will be 54 years." In Davidson County, Stephen Hows secured a position on the county court. Over the next half century, he served on the court eighteen years, as the county tax assessor for twenty years, and as a member of the school board for fifteen years. William Pollard pointed out that he was a member of the Davidson County court for sixteen years; James Nesbitt explained that he was an active participant on the Montgomery County court for twenty-four years. L. H. Russe served "two or three times as Alderman, and for six years . . . Secretary and Treasurer of Shelbyville Tenn." The aristocratic Walter Lenoir understated his years of community service. "In 1867 [I] came to Humbolt Tenn," he wrote, and "was mayor and councilman occasionally."[22]

State and national offices were almost entirely the domain of the elite. One percent of the impoverished, less than 1 percent of the nonslaveowning yeomen's sons, and 2 percent of the slaveowning yeomen's sons achieved high offices, while 6 percent of the planters and professionals' sons were elevated to notable positions (Appendix 2, table 34). Charles Rice was a county magistrate for forty years and then served two terms in the Tennessee legislature. William B. Bates served the state both as governor and U.S. senator, and Nathaniel Harris moved to Georgia, where his long political career included a term as governor. The haughty Herman Doak, proud of his sinecure as clerk of the U.S. district court at Nashville, boasted that he held the post "for thirty-five years—to the great disgust of many good folks—who wanted the job."[23]

Some aristocratic veterans held no office but came from politically active families. Before the Civil War, James Warner's father served two terms in the Tennessee general assembly. Following the conflict, his brother—Richard Warner, Jr.—was elected first to the constitutional convention of 1870 and later to two terms in the U.S. Congress.[24] In postbellum politics, the sons of patricians had many advantages over lesser whites. Wealth, education, and family associations opened the paths to social control. Within a decade after the capitulation of the Confederate armies, Tennessee's aristocratic families had regained their traditional dominance over their society.

A continuity in lifestyles spanned the Old South to the New. Tennessee's Confederate generation imitated the social patterns set by its fathers. Although they lived in the same communities, the impoverished, the yeomen, and the elites were largely segregated from one another, each group pursuing its own particular goals with little interaction. Unfortunately the Tennessee Civil War Veterans Questionnaires solicited only the sketchiest of biographical information on the soldiers' lives after 1865 and failed to ask pertinent questions concerning social-class relations. Both Gustavus W. Dyer and John Trotwood Moore assumed that a felicitous white solidarity characterized postbellum society. But at least one veteran, Robert Z. Taylor of Gibson County, could attest that the potential for class violence lurked within the state's social strata.

In October 1908, Taylor became one of the victims of the nightriders of Reelfoot Lake. Beginning in April of that year, approximately two hundred farmers and lake fishermen conducted a campaign of terror against local merchants and land speculators. Yeomen in Obion County resorted to violence to prevent the West Tennessee Land Company from monopolizing fishing rights to the lake. For generations area residents had eked out meager livings by harvesting Reelfoot's abundant acquatic resources. These people deeply resented the West Tennessee Land Company's efforts to restrict access to the lake and assess a royalty for each fish caught. They were further appalled by the rumor that the company intended to drain the shallow lake and convert it into a gigantic cotton plantation. As an attorney, speculator, and agent for the company, Tayor became a natural target for the nightriders.[25]

Born in 1846 to considerable wealth, Taylor was insensitive to the needs and aspirations of the impoverished and the yeomen. His father, a planter and land speculator, had owned a nine-room mansion, fifteen or twenty slaves, and at least one thousand acres in Tennessee and three thousand acres in Indiana. Taylor characterized his father as doing "but little manuel labor." He "traded largely in lands and mules," the son explained, "and this required . . . all his time." Before the Civil War, the young Taylor occasionally worked on the farm but spent ten months out of twelve in the classroom, and he studied briefly at Andrews College, a small Methodist institution in nearby Trenton, Tennessee. In 1864 Taylor joined Nathan Bedford Forrest's cavalry. He never attained officer's rank, although in later years he answered to the honorific title of "colonel." At the conflict's end, he returned home, reentered college, and in 1868 received his attorney's licence. Taylor then pursued a long, profitable career as a Trenton lawyer and land agent.[26]

In 1907 Taylor and a younger associate, Quentin Rankin (aged thirty-nine), became two of the principal organizers of the West Tennessee Land Company. Over the next several months, they procured most of the acreage surrounding Reelfoot Lake. To further that end, they met on 19 October 1908 with a local property owner in the tiny fishing community of Walnut Log. Their decision to remain at the local sporting lodge until the following day proved fatal.[27]

As midnight approached, nightriders appeared and ripped Taylor and Rankin from their beds. The two attorneys were dragged to the lake's edge, a rope appeared, and within moments Rankin dangled from a limb. As the angry farmers and fishermen riddled the writhing lawyer with shotgun blasts, their other captive broke loose and dived into the murky lake. Their vision obscured by darkness, the nightriders sprayed the water with gunfire. Assuming that the hated land agent had drowned, they dispersed and returned to their homes.[28]

Taylor was not dead. The tough old Confederate veteran hid beneath a hollow log until nearly dawn. For several days thereafter, he wandered around the lake's shore—suffering from frequent hallucinations—until he eventually stumbled into a friendly cabin.[29]

This bloody event attracted national attention. The nightriders were arrested and tried for murder, and in the many interviews inspired by the drama, the normally inarticulate yeomen had ample opportunity to express their grievances. Their tales attested to a class conflict that went beyond the local incident of the moment. Tom Johnson explained to a journalist for *Current Literature* his view of the lake's supernatural origins and his class's claim to its resources:

> It's like this heah, stranger. God, He put them red hills up theah. An' He put some of us po' folks that He didn't have room foh no wheah else, up theah, too. An' then He saw that we couldn't make a livin' farmin', so He ordered an earthquake an' the earthquake left a big hole. Next He filled the hole with watah an' put fish in it. Then He knew we could make a livin' between farmin' and fishin'. But along comes these rich men who don't have to make no livin', and they tell us that we must not fish in the lake any mo', cause they owns the lake an' the fish God put theah foh us. It jus' naturally ain't right, stranger, it ain't no justice.[30]

The state arrested fifty-four suspects, tried eight, and sentenced two to extensive prison terms and six to hanging. No one was ever executed. Over the next half decade appeals and legal technicalities led to a call for retrials. Given the emotional atmosphere extant in northwest Tennessee, the state quietly dropped its prosecutions.[31]

The nightriders of Reelfoot Lake exemplified the frustrated response of some yeomen to aggressive aristocrats. Pushed beyond what they considered reasonable bounds, the small farmers and others resorted to brute force. Deprived of adequate education, lacking an understanding of legal procedures, and often denied fair access to courts of law, Tennessee yeomen turned to violence as the one avenue of persuasion open to them.

Tennessee patricians created the documents by which historians have traditionally assessed the state's past. They published contemporary articles portraying their view of southern society; they presented the memorial addresses that glorified the Confederate crusade; and they printed local histories and personal memoirs that preserved their interpretations of the state of class relations.

These postbellum aristocrats had a vested interest in describing a society characterized by white solidarity. Faced with criticism from northern intellectuals and social commentators and fearing unrest from the lower classes, southern elites of the New South created an intellectual paradigm that justified their control of politics, wealth, and the avenues of social advancement. From their perspective, their social class had enriched the South. Their enlightened leadership made possible an orderly community in which each group—the free blacks, the small farmers, and the elites—remained in its proper place. To be sure, social inequalities existed. But the elites believed that their spirit of paternalism would enable the Negro race to achieve its "limited potential" unburdened by competition with "superior" Caucasians, and they assumed that their practice of *noblesse oblige* gave certain deserving yeomen the opportunity to advance into a better social class.

The two men responsible for developing and distributing the Tennessee Civil War Veterans Questionnaires—Gustavus W. Dyer and John Trotwood Moore—were members of the New South elite. They possessed the assumptions of white consensus common to others in their social class. But, ironically, their questionnaires gave a normally inarticulate class of Tennesseans an excellent mode of expression. By surveying a broad spectrum of the Confederate generation, Dyer and Moore made possible an examination of society beneath the upper crust.

As a whole, these hoary veterans emphasized that the South was more a land of social seams than a region of social seamlessness. A continuity of class structure spanned the decades from the Old to the New South. From birth to death, individuals in these classes were aware of their social status and most remained "in their place."

THE TENNESSEE CIVIL WAR
VETERANS QUESTIONNAIRES

A. THE DYER COVER LETTER AND QUESTIONNAIRE

Department of Archives and History,
State of Tennessee, Nashville

G. W. Dyer, Director

My dear Sir: March 15, 1915

You will find inclosed a series of questions relating to important phases of Southern history. As a student and teacher of history, I am convinced after much critical study and much original research, that the leading history of the United States grossly misrepresents conditions in the old South. This is doubtless more due to ignorance than to prejudice. The true history of the South is yet to be written.

As Director of the Department of Archives and History, I am trying to collect and preserve all the material possible, bearing on the Civil War period. By answering these questions, you will make a real contribution to the land you love, and to the cause for which you have made many sacrifices.

In answering the questions, I am anxious for you to make your answers as full as possible. Be sure to number the pages of the paper on which you write the answers to the questions that have to be answered at length.

In giving account of your War experience, tell everything of interest that happened in your own way, just as you would relate stories to friends in conversation. Don't be afraid of writing too much; the more you write the better.

Mail us your answers as soon as you complete them.

Yours very sincerely

G. W. Dyer

Director

The chief purpose of the following questions is to bring out facts that will be of service in writing a true history of the Old South. Such a history has not yet been written. By answering these questions you will make a valuable contribution to the history of your State.

In case the space following any question is not sufficient for your answer, you may write your answer on a separate piece of paper. But when this is done, be sure to put the number of the question on the paper on which the answer is written, and number the pages of the paper on which you write your answer.

Read all the questions before you answer any of them. After answering the questions here given, if you desire to make additional statements, I would be glad for you to add just as much as you desire.

1. State your full name and present postoffice address.

2. State your age now.

3. In what State and county were you born?

4. In what State and county were you living when you enlisted in the service of the Confederacy?

5. What was your occupation before the war?

6. What was the occupation of your father?

7. If you owned land or other property at the opening of the war, state what kind of property you owned, and state the value of your property as near as you can.

8. Did you or your parents own slaves? If so, how many?

9. If your parents owned land, state about how many acres.

10. State as near as you can the value of all the property owned by your parents, including land, when the war opened.

11. What kind of a house did your parents occupy? State whether it was a log house or frame house or built of other material, and state the number of rooms it had.

12. As a boy and young man, state what kind of work you did. If you worked on a farm, state to what extent you plowed, worked with a hoe and did other kinds of similar work. (Certain historians claim that white men wouldn't do work of this sort before the war.)

13. State clearly what kind of work your father did, and what the duties of your mother were. State all the kinds of work done in the house as well as you can remember—that is, cooking, spinning, weaving, etc.

14. Did your parents keep any servants? If so, how many?

15. How was honest toil—as plowing, hauling and other sorts of honest work of this class—regarded in your community? Was such work considered respectable and honorable?

16. Did the white men in your community generally engage in such work?

17. To what extent were there white men in your community leading lives of idleness and having others to work for them?

18. Did the men who owned slaves mingle freely with those who did not own slaves, or did slaveholders in any way show by their actions that they felt themselves better than respectable, honorable men who did not own slaves?

19. At the churches, at the schools, at public gatherings in general, did slaveholders and non-slaveholders mingle on a footing of equality?

20. Was there a friendly feeling between slaveholders and non-slaveholders in your community, or were they antagonistic to each other?

21. In a political contest in which one candidate owned slaves and the other did not, did the fact that one candidate owned slaves help him any in winning the contest?

22. Were the opportunities good in your community for a poor young man, honest and industrious, to save up enough to buy a small farm or go in business for himself?

23. Were poor, honest, industrious young men, who were ambitious to make something of themselves, encouraged or discouraged by slaveholders?

24. What kind of school or schools did you attend?

25. About how long did you go to school altogether?

26. How far was it to the nearest school?

27. What school or schools were in operation in your neighborhood?

28. Was the school in your community private or public?

29. About how many months in the year did it run?

30. Did the boys and girls in your community attend school pretty regularly?

31. Was the teacher of the school you attended a man or a woman?

32. In what year and month and at what place did you enlist in the service of the Confederacy?

33. State the name of your regiment, and state the names of as many members of your company as you remember.

34. After enlistment, where was your company sent first?

35. How long after your enlistment before your company engaged in battle?

36. What was the first battle you engaged in?

37. State in your own way your experience in the war from this time on to the close. State where you went after the first battle—what you did, what other battles you engaged in, how long they lasted, what the results were; state how you lived in camp, how you were clothed, how you slept, what you had to eat, how you were exposed to cold, hunger and disease. If you were in hospital or in prison, state your experience here.

38. When and where were you discharged?

39. Tell something of your trip home.

40. What kind of work did you take up when your came back home?

41. Give a sketch of your life since the close of the Civil War, stating what kind of business you have engaged in, where you have lived, your church relations, etc. If you have held any office or offices, state what it was. You may state here any other facts connected with your life and experience which have not been brought out by the questions.

B. THE MOORE COVER LETTER, QUESTIONNAIRE (VERSIONS 1 AND 2), AND FOLLOW-UP LETTER

State of Tennessee
Department of Library, Archives and History
Nashville   John Trotwood Moore, Director

My Dear Sir:

The General Assembly has directed this department to collect and preserve first-hand information of all persons and events that have a part in the making of Tennessee history. Such a task would be impossible without the full cooperation of those who participated in the actual service during the Civil War. You can render your state no better service now, and leave to your posterity no more valued heritage than a full account of your war experiences.

I am enclosing a list of questions which will give us many of the more important facts. Should the space not admit of full answers, please number the questions you wish to enlarge upon and write additional information on separate sheets of paper. I am enclosing a self-addressed, stamped envelope in which you will return your questions just as soon as you can find time to answer them.

Without the information I am asking you to assist in furnishing, the old Volunteer State can never properly record the deeds and heroism of her sons, and I feel sure that you will aid us in our earnest endeavor to collect and preserve a record of our soldiers in the Civil War.

Please let me hear from you as soon as you can supply the desired information.

I am, Very truly yours,
John Trotwood Moore,
Director

Moore questionnaire #1

State of Tennessee
Tennessee Historical Committee   John Trotwood Moore, Director
Department of Libraries, Archives and History

Note.—Should this Questionnaire fall into the hands of one who is not a Veteran of the Civil War, or who did not live during those days, you will confer a favor on this Department by giving it to some Soldier who has not received a copy, or return to us.

The chief purpose of the following questions is to bring out facts that will be of service in writing a true history of the Old South. Such a history has not yet been written. By answering these questions you will make a valuable contribution to the history of your State.

In case the space following any question is not sufficient for your answer, you may write your answer on a separate piece of paper. But when this is done, *be sure* to put the number of the question on the paper on which the answer is written, and number the pages of the paper on which you write your answer.

Read all the questions before you answer any of them. After answering the questions here given, if you desire to make additional statements, I would be glad for you to add just as much as you desire.

1. State your full name and present postoffice address.

2. State your age now.

3. In what State and county were you born?

4. Were you a Confederate or Federal soldier?

5. Name of your Company?   (B) Number of Regiment

6. What was the occupation of your father?

7. Give full name of your father. __ Born at __ in the County of __ State of __ He lived at __

Give also any particulars concerning him, as official position, war services, etc., books written by, etc.

8. Maiden name in full your mother.
She was the daughter of (Full Name)   and his wife (Full Name)
Who lived at

9. Remarks on Ancestry. Give here any and all facts possible in reference to your parents, grandparents, great-grandparents, etc., not included in the foregoing as were they lived, offices held, Revolutionery or other war service; what country the family came from to America; first settled, county and State; *always* giving *full* names (if possible), and *never* referring to an ancester simply as such without giving the name. It is desirable to include every fact possible, and to that end the full and exact record from old Bibles should be appended on seperate sheets of this size, thus preserving the facts from loss.

10. If you owned land or other property at the opening of the war, state what kind of property you owned, and state the value of your property as near as you can.

11. Did you or your parents own slaves? If so, how many?

12. If your parents owned land, state about how many acres.

13. State as near as you can the value of all the property owned by your parents, including land, when the war opened.

14. What kind of a house did your parents occupy? State whether it was a log house or frame house or built of other material, and state the number of rooms it had.

15. As a boy and young man, state what kind of work you did. If you worked on a farm, state to what extent you plowed, worked with a hoe and did other kinds of similar work. (Certain historians claim that white men would not do work of this sort before the war.)

16. State clearly what kind of work your father did, and what the duties of your mother were. State all the kinds of work done in the house as well as you can remember—that is cooking, spinning, weaving, etc.

17. Did your parents keep any servants? If so, how many?

18. How was honest toil—as plowing, hauling and other sorts of honest work of this class—regarded in your community? Was such work considered respectable and honorable?

19. Did the white men in your community generally engage in such work?

20. To what extent were there white men in your community leading lives of idleness and having others do their work for them?

21. Did the men who owned slaves mingle freely with those who did not own slaves, or did slaveholders in any way show by their actions that they felt themselves better than respectable, honorable men who did not own slaves?

22. At the churches, at the schools, at public gatherings in general, did slave-holders and non-slave-holders mingle on a footing of equality?

23. Was there a friendly feeling between slave-holders and non-slave-holders in your community, or were they antagonistic to each other?

24. In a political contest in which one candidate owned slaves and the other did not, did the fact that one candidate owned slaves help him any in winning the contest?

25. Were the opportunities good in your community for a poor young man, honest and industrious, to save up enough to buy a small farm or go in business for himself?

26. Were poor, honest, industrious young men, who were ambitious to make something of themselves, encouraged or discouraged by slaveholders?

27. What kind of school or schools did you attend?

28. About how long did you go to school altogether?

29. How far was it to the nearest school?

30. What school or schools were in operation in your neighborhood?

31. Was the school in your community private or public?

32. About how many months in the year did it run?

33. Did the boys and girls in your community attend school pretty regularly?

34. Was the teacher of the school you attended a man or a woman?

35. In what year and month and at what place did you enlist in the service of the Confederacy or of the Federal Government?

36. After enlistment, where was your Company sent first?

37. How long after enlistment before your Company engaged in battle?

38. What was the first battle you engaged in?

39. State in your own way your experience in the War from this time on to its close. State where you went after the first battle—what you did, what other battles you engaged in, how long they lasted, what the results were; state how you lived in camp, how you were clothed, how you slept, what you had to eat, how you were exposed to cold, hunger and disease. If you were in hospital or in prison, state your experience there.

40. When and where were you discharged?

41. Tell something of your trip home.

42. What kind of work did you take up when you came back home?

43. Give a sketch of your life since the close of Civil War, stating what kind of business you have engaged in, where you have lived, your church relations, etc. If you have held any office or offices, state what it was. You may state here any other facts connected with your life and experience which has not been brought out by the questions.

44. On a separate sheet give the names of some of the great men you have known or met in your time, and tell some of the circumstances of the meeting or incidents in their lives. Also add any further personal reminiscences. (Use all the space you want).

45. Give the names of all the members of your Company you can remember. (If you know where the Roster is to had, please make special note of this.)

46. Give here the NAME and POST OFFICE ADDRESS of living Veterans of the Civil War, whether members of your Company or not; whether Tennesseans or from other States:

Name	Post Office	State

Moore questionnaire #2

The chief purpose of the following questions is to bring out facts that will be of service in writing a true history of the Old South. Such a history has not yet been written. By answering these questions you will make a valuable contribution to the history of your state.

In case the space following any question is not sufficient for your answer, you may write your answer on a separate piece of paper. But when this is done, *be sure* to put the number of the question on the paper on which the answer is written, and number the pages of the paper on which you write your answer.

Read all the questions before you answer any of them. After answering the questions here given, if you desire to make additional statements, I would be glad for you to add just as much as you desire.

1. State your full name and present postoffice address.
2. State your age now.
3. In what State and county were you born?
4. In what State and county were you living when you enlisted in the service of the Confederacy, or of the Federal Government?
5. What was your occupation before the war?
6. What was the occupation of your father?
7. If you owned land or other property at the opening of the war, state what kind of property you owned, and state the value of your property as near as you can.

8. Did you or your parents own slaves? If so, how many?

9. If your parents owned land, state about how many acres.

10. State as near as you can the value of all the property owned by your parents, including land, when the war opened.

11. What kind of a house did your parents occupy? State whether it was a log house or frame house or built of other material, and state the number of rooms it had.

12. As a boy and young man, state what kind of work you did. If you worked on a farm, state to what extent you plowed, worked with a hoe and did other kinds of similar work. (Certain historians claim that white men wouldn't do work of this sort before the war.)

13. State clearly what kind of work your father did, and what the duties of your mother were. State all the kinds of work done in the house as well as you can remember—that is, cooking, spinning, weaving, etc.

14. Did your parents keep any servants? If so, how many?

15. How was honest toil—as plowing, hauling and other sorts of honest work of this class—regarded in your community? Was such work considered respectable and honorable?

16. Did the white men in your community generally engage in such work?

17. To what extent were there white men in your community leading lives of idleness and having others do their work for them?

18. Did the men who owned slaves mingle freely with those who did not own slaves, or did slaveholders in any way show by their actions that they felt themselves better than respectable, honorable men who did not own slaves?

19. At the churches, at the schools, at public gatherings in general, did slave-holders and non-slaveholders mingle on a footing of equality?

20. Was there a friendly feeling between slaveholders and non-slaveholders in your community, or were they antagonistic to each other?

21. In a political contest in which one candidate owned slaves and the other did not, did the fact that one candidate owned slaves help him any in winning the contest?

22. Were the opportunities good in your community for a poor young man, honest and industrious, to save up enough to buy a small farm or go in business for himself?

23. Were poor, honest, industrious young men, who were ambitious to make something of themselves, encouraged or discouraged by slaveholders?

24. What kind of school or schools did you attend?

25. About how long did you go to school altogether?

26. How far was it to the nearest school?

27. What school or schools were in operation in your neighborhood?

28. Was the school in your community private or public?

29. About how many months in the year did it run?

30. Did the boys and girls in your community attend school pretty regularly?

31. Was the teacher of the school you attended a man or a woman?

32. In what year and month and at what place did you enlist in the service of the Confederacy or of the Federal Government?

33. State the name of your regiment, and state the names of as many members of your company as you remember.

34. After enlistment, where was your company sent first?

35. How long after your enlistment before your company engaged in battle?

36. What was the first battle you engaged in?

37. State in your own way your experience in the war from this time on to the close. State where you went after the first battle—what you did, what other battles you engaged in, how long they lasted, what the results were; state how you lived in camp, how you were clothed, how you slept, what you had to eat, how you were exposed to cold, hunger and disease. If you were in hospital or in prison, state your experience here.

38. When and where were you discharged?

39. Tell something of your trip home.

40. What kind of work did you take up when you came back home?

41. Give a sketch of your life since the close of the Civil War, stating what kind of business you have engaged in, where you have lived, your church relations, etc. If you have held any office or offices, state what it was. You may state here any other facts connected with your life and experience which has not been brought out by the questions.

42. Give full name of your father __ born at __ in the county of __ state of __

He lived at __

Give also any particulars concerning him, as official position, war services, etc., books written by, etc.

43. Maiden name in full of your mother __ She was the daughter of __ and his wife __ who lived at __

44. Remarks on Ancestry. Give here any and all facts possible in reference to your parents, grandparents, great-grandparents, etc., not included in the foregoing, as where they lived, offices held, Revolutionary or other war service; what country the family came from to America; where first settled, county and state; *always* giving *full* names (if possible) and *never* referring to an ancestor simply as such without giving the name. It is desirable to include every fact possible, and to that end the full and exact record from old Bibles should be appended on separate sheets of this size, thus preserving the facts from loss.

Moore follow-up letter

Tennessee Historical Commission
State Capitol, Nashville, Tennessee   John Trotwood Moore, Chairman

My Dear Sir:

Since the inauguration of the sending our of inquiries to the survivors of the Civil War, the replies have given us so many historical facts not before acquired, that we feel it would be unjust to posterity to allow the opportunity to pass without getting in touch with every surviving participant in the Civil War and obtaining his experience and reminiscences. Will you not, on the lines below please send me the name and address of every Confederate and Federal soldier of your acquaintance, regardless of where he enlisted or now lives?

Very truly yours,
John Trotwood Moore
Chairman

Name   Address

_____   _____

_____   _____

_____   _____

_____   _____

STATISTICAL TABLES BASED ON THE QUESTIONNAIRES

Unless otherwise indicated, all tables are based upon information gleaned from the Tennessee Civil War Veterans Questionnaires. This study focused upon the 1,250 Tennessee Confederate veterans who resided in the state prior to 1861. With the exception of Table 1, the actual number of responses will be slightly less than that number. Numbers appearing in parentheses below the class groupings in some tables denote the number of respondents who supplied information on that particular question.

Table 1. Respondents by Class and Region

		Yeoman		
	Poor	Nonslave-owning	Slave-owning	Elite
East Tennessee	97	156	121	75
Middle Tennessee	89	91	149	122
Northwest/Southcentral Tennessee	41	72	78	42
Southwest Tennessee	16	17	37	47
Total	243	336	385	286

Table 2. Respondents by Age

Age	Number	Age	Number
67 to 73	45	80 to 81	216
74 to 78	472	82 to 85	255
79	140	86 or over	101

Note: The median age of respondents was 79; the age of 14 respondents could not be determined. Seven of the respondents were deceased by the time of the survey, and their questionnaires were completed by relatives.

Table 3. Median Wealth of Respondents' Fathers

	Number[a]	Median Wealth
Poor		
Farm tenants	141	$ 160
Blacksmiths	16	0
Carpenters	12	300
Yeoman		
Farmers (nonslaveowning)	242	1,000
Farmers (slaveowning)	312	4,000
Blacksmiths	29	2,000
Carpenters	31	4,000
Elite		
Merchants	42	20,000
Physicians	22	20,000
Attorneys	8	30,000
Planters	101	40,000

[a]These figures are based only on estimates provided by those veterans giving information.

Table 4. Fathers' House Type

		Yeoman		
	Poor (225)	Nonslave-owning (332)	Slave-owning (378)	Elite (225)
Log	92.0%	78.3%	54.5%	22.2%
Log weatherboarded	.4	5.4	11.1	12.7
Log, frame	.9	4.8	11.9	10.2
Frame	6.2	10.8	20.4	40.0
Brick	.4	.8	2.1	14.9
Total	99.9	100.1	100.0	100.0

Table 5. Rooms in Fathers' Houses

| | | Yeoman | | |
	Poor	Nonslave-owning	Slave-owning	Elite
		Log		
	(182)	(240)	(184)	(57)
One room	35	14	3	1
Two rooms	80	70	30	4
Three rooms	43	74	36	4
Four rooms	19	53	52	18
Five rooms	4	10	26	8
Six rooms	1	13	24	14
Seven or more rooms	0	6	13	8
Median rooms	2	3	4	5
		Frame		
	(12)	(34)	(71)	(99)
One room	0	0	0	0
Two rooms	2	4	3	1
Three rooms	2	2	7	1
Four rooms	3	10	17	5
Five rooms	2	8	7	8
Six rooms	3	8	19	29
Seven or more rooms	0	2	18	55
Median rooms	4	5	6	7+

Table 6. Slaves Owned By Planters and Selected Professionals

	Merchants (51)	Attorneys (10)	Physicians (25)	Planters (103)
No slaves	6	1	1	0
One to nine slaves	25	2	10	0
Ten to nineteen slaves	9	3	7	0
Twenty to twenty-nine slaves	10	1	5	42
Thirty to forty-nine slaves	0	1	2	30
Fifty or more slaves	1	2	0	31
Median	6	10	10	30

Table 7. Domestic Condition of Respondents' Mothers

		Yeoman		
	Poor (233)	Nonslave-owning (321)	Slave-owning (372)	Elite (273)
Performed own work	92.7%	87.9%	30.1%	7.7%
Hired out to others	4.3	1.9	.8	.4
Hired help	3.0	10.3	2.4	2.2
Supervised slaves	.0	.0	66.7	89.7
Total	100.0	100.1	100.0	100.0

Table 8. Per Capita Expenditures for Tennessee Schools, 1860

	Students	Expenditures	Per capita average
Common schools	115,765	$233,333.34	$ 2.02
Academies	9,667	$250,712.69	$25.93
Total	125,432	$484,046.03	

Source: 1860 Tennessee Census, Social Statistics, microfilm, University of Tennessee Library, Knoxville.

Note: The printed volumes of the 1860 census failed to include statistics on local education. The reason becomes clear after an examination of the manuscript census reports. County marshalls were inconsistent in their terminology and in the type of information they supplied. In compiling statistics from the census, I counted as common schools all references to "common schools," "public schools," "free schools," and "subscription schools"; I counted as academies all references to "academies," "high schools," and "seminaries"; and I excluded from my figures those institutions listed as "colleges." Some counties failed to supply information on expenditures and others used terminology that was impossible to classify. Only partial information on expenditures was available from the counties of Dickson, Lawrence, Stewart, Shelby, Greene, Washington, Jefferson, Johnson, Rhea, Roane, and Sumner; no information was used from the counties of Henderson, Henry, Humphreys, Perry, Fayette, Haywood, Tipton, Cannon, Knox, Van Buren, Robertson, Davidson, and Williamson.

Table 9. Types of Schools Attended by Respondents

		Yeoman		
	Poor (235)	Nonslave- owning (312)	Slave- owning (377)	Elite (276)
Poor quality				
No school	2.6%	1.6%	.3%	.0%
Public school	48.5	48.1	37.4	12.0
Subscription school	34.5	35.6	32.4	26.1
Public or subscription school	4.7	5.4	6.4	3.3
Good quality				
Public supplemented by subscription school	.9	2.2	5.8	7.2
Academy	8.9	7.1	17.8	49.6
Tutor	.0	.0	.0	1.8
Total	100.1	100.0	100.1	100.0

Table 10. Median Years of School Attendance

| | | Yeoman | | |
	Poor	Nonslave-owning	Slave-owning	Elite
Public school	3	4	4	4
Subscription school	3	3	5	10
Academy	2	5	5	9

Table 11. Distribution of Students at Academies and Common Schools by Region

| | Academies | | Common schools | |
	Number	%	Number	%
East Tennessee	4,331	6	73,252	94
Middle Tennessee	3,192	21	11,890	79
Northwest/Southcentral Tennessee	1,756	5	32,721	95
Southwest Tennessee	1,511	32	3,240	68
Total	10,790	8	121,103	92

Source: 1860 Tennessee Census, Social Statistics, microfilm, University of Tennessee Library, Knoxville.

Note: The above information was based on statistics gathered only from those counties for which common school and academy attendance could be compared. The following counties were excluded: Henry, Humphreys, Perry, Shelby, Tipton, Jefferson, Johnson, Knox, Rhea, Roane, Van Buren, and Davidson.

Table 12. Types of Schools Attended by Region

		Yeoman		
	Poor	Nonslave-owning	Slave-owning	Elite
		East Tennessee		
	(93)	(139)	(117)	(71)
Poor quality				
No school	2.2%	2.2%	.0%	.0%
Public school	58.1	57.7	51.3	25.4
Subscription school	25.8	28.8	20.5	21.2
Public or subscription school	5.4	5.6	9.4	8.5
Good quality				
Public supplemented by subscription school	1.1	2.2	3.4	8.5
Academy	7.5	3.6	15.4	33.8
Tutor	.0	.0	.0	2.8
Total	100.1	100.1	100.0	100.2
		Middle Tennessee		
	(85)	(88)	(146)	(118)
Poor quality				
No school	1.2%	1.1%	.7%	.0%
Public school	44.7	39.7	34.2	9.3
Subscription school	36.5	34.1	32.2	22.9
Public or subscription school	4.7	9.1	6.2	.8
Good quality				
Public supplemented by subscription school	1.2	2.3	8.2	8.5
Academy	11.7	13.6	18.5	56.8
Tutor	.0	.0	.0	1.7
Total	100.0	99.9	100.0	100.0

Table 12 *continued*

	Poor	Yeoman Nonslave-owning	Yeoman Slave-owning	Elite
	Northwest/Southcentral Tennessee			
	(41)	(69)	(77)	(41)
Poor quality				
No school	4.9%	.0%	.0%	.0%
Public school	46.3	42.0	35.1	9.8
Subscription school	43.9	49.3	41.6	43.9
Public or subscription school	4.9	5.8	5.2	4.9
Good quality				
Public supplemented by subscription school	.0	2.8	6.5	4.9
Academy	.0	.0	11.7	34.1
Tutor	.0	.0	.0	2.4
Total	100.0	99.9	100.1	100.0
	Southwest Tennessee			
	(16)	(16)	(37)	(46)
Poor quality				
No school	6.3%	6.3%	.0%	.0%
Public school	18.8	18.8	10.8	.0
Subscription school	50.0	43.8	51.4	26.1
Public or subscription school	.0	.0	.0	.0
Good quality				
Public supplemented by subscription school	.0	.0	2.7	4.3
Academy	25.0	31.2	35.1	69.6
Tutor	.0	.0	.0	.0
Total	100.1	100.1	100.0	100.0

Table 13. College Attendance of Respondents

		Yeoman		
	Poor (235)	Nonslave-owning (247)	Slave-owning (283)	Elite (235)
Attended college	.0%	1.6%	7.4%	29.4%
Did not attend college	100.0	98.4	92.6	70.6
Total	100.0	100.0	100.0	100.0

Table 14. Period of Attendance of College Students

	Number	%
Attended before Civil War	49	53.3
Attended after Civil War	33	35.9
Attended both before and after Civil War	10	10.9
Total	92	100.1

Table 15. Effect of Army Service on College Studies

	Attended before army service (50)	Attended after army service (40)
Liberal arts studies	72.0%	35.0%
Professional studies	28.0	65.0
Total	100.0	100.0

Table 16. Respondents' Awareness of Class Conflict

		Yeoman			
	Poor (234)	Nonslave- owning (323)	Slave- owning (377)	Elite (278)	All Classes (1,212)
Not aware of conflict	59.4%	70.3%	78.8%	77.7%	72.5%
Aware of some conflict	19.2	17.6	14.9	17.3	17.0
Aware of significant conflict	21.4	12.1	6.4	5.0	10.5
Total	100.0	100.0	100.1	100.0	100.0

Table 17. Awareness of Class Conflict by Region

| | | Yeoman | | |
	Poor	Nonslave-owning	Slave-owning	Elite
		East Tennessee		
	(91)	(149)	(118)	(74)
Not aware of conflict	74.7%	72.5%	79.7%	75.6%
Aware of some conflict	13.2	13.4	11.9	17.6
Aware of significant conflict	12.1	14.1	8.5	6.8
Total	100.0	100.0	100.0	100.0
		Middle Tennessee		
	(86)	(89)	(145)	(117)
Not aware of conflict	53.5%	68.5%	75.9%	74.4%
Aware of some conflict	22.1	24.8	18.6	21.4
Aware of significant conflict	24.4	6.7	5.4	4.3
Total	100.0	100.0	99.9	100.1
		Northwest/Southcentral Tennessee		
	(41)	(68)	(76)	(41)
Not aware of conflict	43.9%	69.1%	88.2%	90.2%
Aware of some conflict	29.3	14.7	10.5	4.9
Aware of significant conflict	26.8	16.2	1.3	4.9
Total	100.0	100.0	100.0	100.0
		Southwest Tennessee		
	(16)	(15)	(37)	(46)
Not aware of conflict	43.8%	66.7%	67.6%	78.3%
Aware of some conflict	12.5	26.7	18.9	17.4
Aware of significant conflict	43.8	6.7	13.5	4.3
Total	100.1	100.1	100.0	100.0

Table 18. Respondents' Perception of Work Done by Slaveowners and
Nonslaveowners

| | | Yeoman | | | |
	Poor (235)	Nonslave-owning (328)	Slave-owning (376)	Elite (273)	All Classes (1,212)
Everyone worked	74.5%	83.2%	85.9%	75.5%	80.6%
Slaveowners labored with their slaves	5.5	7.0	4.5	5.5	5.6
Slaveowners contributed other than manual labor	.9	.9	1.6	5.1	2.1
Slaveowners were idle	19.1	8.8	8.0	13.9	11.7
Total	100.0	99.9	100.0	100.0	100.0

Table 19. Respondents' Perceptions of Economic Opportunity

| | | Yeoman | | |
	Poor (234)	Nonslave-owning (322)	Slave-owning (369)	Elite (275)
Economic opportunity available	62.0%	81.7%	87.8%	93.1%
Economic opportunity not available	38.0	18.3	12.2	6.9
Total	100.0	100.0	100.0	100.0

Table 20. Respondents' Perceptions of Political Advantage of Slaveownership

| | | Yeoman | | |
	Poor (209)	Nonslave-owning (299)	Slave-owning (355)	Elite (261)
Slaveownership was political advantage	23.9%	11.7%	11.0%	5.7%
Slaveownership was not political advantage	76.1	88.3	89.0	94.3
Total	100.0	100.0	100.0	100.0

Table 21. Political Activities of Respondents' Fathers

| | | Yeoman | | |
	Poor (239)	Nonslave-owning (331)	Slave-owning (383)	Elite (278)
No political activity	95.8%	89.4%	83.0%	76.9%
Local politics	3.8	10.6	15.9	18.7
State politics	.4	.0	1.1	4.3
Total	100.0	100.0	100.0	99.9

Table 22. Army Service of Respondents

| | | Yeoman | | |
	Poor (235)	Nonslave-owning (330)	Slave-owning (380)	Elite (277)
Infantry	69.8%	66.4%	65.0%	56.3%
Artillery	4.3	2.1	2.6	2.2
Cavalry	26.0	31.5	32.4	41.5
Total	100.1	100.0	100.0	100.0

Table 23. Army Rank of Respondents

		Yeoman		
	Poor (146)	Nonslave- owning (190)	Slave- owning (246)	Elite (188)
Private	85.6%	80.5%	69.1%	66.5%
Corporal	4.8	7.4	4.9	5.3
Sergeant	6.2	6.8	14.2	9.0
Lieutenant	2.1	5.3	8.1	9.0
Captain	1.4	.0	2.4	8.0
Major	.0	.0	.4	.5
Colonel	.0	.0	.8	.5
General	.0	.0	.0	1.1
Total	100.1	100.0	99.9	99.9

Note: The Civil War Veterans Questionnaires failed to ask the subjects' ranks. This was determined by locating the soldiers in Tennessee Civil War Centennial Committee, *Tennesseans in the Civil War: A Military History of Confederate and Union Units with Available Rosters of Personnel* (2 pts., Nashville, 1964), pt. 2.

Table 24. Respondents Wounded during Army Service

		Yeoman		
	Poor (243)	Nonslave- owning (338)	Slave- owning (386)	Elite (286)
Wounded	20.6%	24.4%	23.8%	21.3%
Not wounded	79.4	75.6	76.2	78.7
Total	100.0	100.0	100.0	100.0

Table 25. Disposition of Soldiers Released from Northern Prisons, January–March, 1865

		Yeoman		
	Poor (15)	Nonslave-owning (19)	Slave-owning (23)	Elite (14)
Returned to active service	20.0%	26.3%	17.4%	64.3%
Entered parole camp	33.3	36.9	43.5	7.1
Went on furlough	46.7	36.9	39.1	28.6
Total	100.0	100.1	100.0	100.0

Table 26. Respondents Ending War with Active Command

		Yeoman		
	Poor (220)	Nonslave-owning (297)	Slave-owning (353)	Elite (260)
With active command	48.2%	52.9%	50.4%	69.6%
Not with active command	51.8	47.1	49.6	30.4
Total	100.0	100.0	100.0	100.0

Table 27. Distribution of Respondents by Active Command at War's End

		Yeoman			
	Poor (110)	Nonslave-owning (167)	Slave-owning (187)	Elite (183)	All Classes (647)
Joseph E. Johnston	33.6%	41.3%	32.6%	31.7%	34.7%
Robert E. Lee	9.1	4.8	5.3	6.6	6.2
Nathan B. Forrest	24.5	18.0	28.3	36.6	27.4
Jefferson Davis	2.7	5.4	7.0	6.6	5.7
Richard Taylor	.9	3.0	2.1	1.6	2.0
Other commands	29.1	27.5	24.6	16.9	24.0
Total	99.9	100.0	99.9	100.0	100.0

Table 28. Immediate Postbellum Activity of Respondents

		Yeoman		
	Poor (239)	Nonslave-owning (322)	Slave-owning (374)	Elite (270)
Farming	77.0%	74.2%	71.1%	55.9%
Nonfarming, nonprofessional	14.2	14.9	13.1	7.4
Professional	.8	2.2	5.6	17.8
Attending college	.0	.3	2.4	9.3
Attending other school	2.5	2.8	2.7	3.3
Exiled[a]	.0	1.9	1.1	.7
Recovering from wounds	5.4	3.7	4.0	5.5
Total	99.9	100.0	100.0	99.9

[a]Other veterans fled Tennessee, fearing violence. These individuals gave no other indication of their immediate postbellum activities.

Table 29. Postbellum Geographic Mobility

		Yeoman		
	Poor (238)	Nonslave-owning (325)	Slave-owning (378)	Elite (281)
Remained in home county	77.7%	78.2%	74.1%	60.9%
Moved within Tennessee	12.6	12.6	12.4	15.3
Moved out of Tennessee	2.5	1.8	3.7	8.9
Moved out of Tennessee but later returned	7.1	7.4	9.8	14.9
Total	99.9	100.0	100.0	100.0

Table 30. Destination of Respondents Leaving Home Counties

| | | Yeoman | | |
	Poor (52)	Nonslave-owning (67)	Slave-owning (99)	Elite (108)
Within Tennessee	57.7%	61.1%	47.5%	39.8%
South	15.4	13.4	21.2	24.1
West	19.2	20.9	24.2	27.8
Midwest	7.7	4.5	6.1	3.7
Northeast	.0	.0	.0	2.8
Outside the United States	.0	.0	1.0	1.9
Total	100.0	99.9	100.0	100.1

Note: The South is defined as all the seceding states east of the Mississippi River and also Kentucky, Delaware, and Maryland; the West as all states west of the Mississippi River except Missouri, Iowa, Minnesota, and Wisconsin; the Midwest as Ohio, Indiana, Illinois, Michigan, Wisconsin, Minnesota, Iowa, and Missouri; and the Northeast as Pennsylvania, New Jersey, New York, and the New England states.

Table 31. Respondents' Reasons for Moving

| | | Yeoman | | |
	Poor (38)	Nonslave-owning (51)	Slave-owning (71)	Elite (86)
Economic opportunity	84.2%	76.5%	64.8%	52.3%
Profession	2.6	7.8	16.9	32.6
Education	2.6	.0	5.6	9.3
Fear	10.5	15.7	12.7	5.8
Total	99.9	100.0	100.0	100.0

Table 32. Postbellum Careers of Respondents

| | | Yeoman | | |
	Poor (233)	Nonslave-owning (322)	Slave-owning (372)	Elite (268)
Farmers	76.0%	76.4%	68.3%	45.1%
Nonfarm/nonprofessionals	15.8	11.5	12.4	9.7
Professionals	8.2	12.1	19.4	45.1
Total	100.0	100.0	100.1	99.9

Table 33. Number of Respondents in Postbellum Professions

| | | Yeoman | | |
	Poor	Nonslave-owning	Slave-owning	Elite
Merchants	4	20	32	52
Attorneys	0	2	2	16
Physicians	1	1	11	10
Ministers	3	7	9	4
Teachers	4	2	6	5
Clerks	2	1	1	6
Magistrates[a]	5	1	2	6
Professors	0	1	0	3
Carriage manufacturers	0	3	2	3
Hotel owners	0	1	1	1
Surveyors	0	0	2	1
Newspaper editors	0	0	0	5
Druggists	0	0	0	4
Bankers	0	0	0	2
Insurance agents	0	0	0	1
Cotton brokers	0	0	0	1
State legislators[a]	0	0	0	1
Total	19	39	68	121

[a]Several other veterans served in public offices, but these individuals gave no indication of their specific postbellum careers.

Table 34. Respondents Holding Public Office

		Yeoman		
	Poor (233)	Nonslave-owning (323)	Slave-owning (373)	Elite (271)
Held no office	89.7%	81.1%	76.9%	70.8%
Held local office	9.4	18.6	20.9	23.6
Held state office	.9	.3	2.1	4.4
Held national office	.0	.0	.0	1.1
Total	100.0	100.0	99.9	99.9

NOTES

PREFACE

1. Vance, *The Negro Agricultural Worker*; Couch, *Culture in the South*; Raper, *Preface to Peasantry*.
2. Davis et al., *Deep South*, 276–77.
3. Frank L. Owsley to Robert Penn Warren, 12 Apr., 26 Apr. 1937, *Southern Review* Papers, Yale University Library, New Haven, Conn.; Owsley, *Plain Folk of the Old South*; Coles, "Some Notes on Slaveownership and Land-ownership in Louisiana," 381–94; Mooney, *Slavery in Tennessee*; Clark, *The Tennessee Yeomen*; Weaver, *Mississippi Farmers*.
4. Bailey, "Caste and the Classroom in Antebellum Tennessee," 39–54; Bailey, "The Poor, Plain Folk, and Planters," 5–24; Bailey, "Tennessee's Antebellum Society," 260–73; Bailey, "Class and Tennessee's Confederate Generation," 31–60.

CHAPTER 1

1. John Johnston, The Civil War Veterans Questionnaires. Each questionnaire was stored in a folder that often included newspaper clippings, letters, and internal memoranda from library officials. Hereafter the questionnaires will be referred to as CWVQ.
2. Ibid.
3. Some confusion exists as to the actual number of questionnaires in the collection. In his biography of John Trotwood Moore, Claud B. Green wrote that 5,000 veterans responded; however, he was misled by an article that appeared in the *Knoxville Sentinel* on 6 October 1926. The actual number is 1,648. This latter figure does not include two forms filled out by former slaves and two that were returned blank. The following endorsement appeared on one of the blank questionnaires: "W. D. Burnley is not able to ans. no questions for He Has Been Sick and under the Dr. Be impossible for Him to ans eny questions and we as his Friends Dont Expect Him to Be able eny more. and If you could but See him you would not Expect ans from Him." Green, *John Trotwood Moore*, 101–2; *Knoxville Sentinel*, 6 Oct. 1926; W. D. Burnley, CWVQ.

4. Benjamin Alexander Hagnewood, Henry Clay Dunavant, CWVQ. *See also* John Benton Allen, Carroll Henderson Clark, James W. Harmon, James Madison Harris, William Sidney Hartsfield, Charles Edward Jackson, James Monroe Jones, George W. Kibert, William R. H. Matthews, James William Trusty, CWVQ.

5. William E. Orr, Isaac Griffith, CWVQ. *See also* Lee T. Billingsley, Samuel Henry Darnell, Hamilton Mortimer Hennessee, Julius C. Martin, CWVQ.

6. Tilly, "Aspects of Social and Economic Life," 101–5.

7. Ash, "Middle Tennessee Society in Transition," 19; Ash, "Civil War," 1–19.

8. Samuel N. Reynolds, CWVQ; *see also* W. H. Lamastus, Francis Marion McClure, Joseph H. Stamper, CWVQ.

9. Robert L. Jones, John L. McMurty, B. F. Neville, Joseph P. J. Hoover, CWVQ.

10. Clipping [*Vanderbilt Alumnus?*], Jan.–Feb. 1928, Dyer folder; Sensing, "Dr. Gus Dyer Dies at 81," 2; Dyer, *Library of American Lives*; *Nashville Banner*, 1 Mar. 1948, 1, 2, 4; *Nashville Tennessean*, 1 Mar. 1948, 1, 6, 8; Weaver interview. The Weavers met in one of Owsley's seminars, married, and later taught at Vanderbilt University.

11. *Nashville Banner*, 1 Mar. 1948, 1, 2; *Nashville Tennessean*, 1 Mar. 1948, 1, 8; news release, 23 May 1923, Dyer folder.

12. Dyer, *Democracy in the South.*

13. Phillips, review of *Democracy in the South.*

14. Dyer, *Democracy in the South*, 86–90.

15. Phillips, *Life and Labor in the Old South*, 438n; Cash, *The Mind of the South*, 6; Green, "Democracy in the Old South," 19n.

16. Dyer, "Social Tendencies in the South," x, 657–61.

17. Dyer, "My Experiences on the Stump," 113–15; "Faculty Notes," 137; Newspaper clipping, 29 Jan. 1932, Dyer folder.

18. Gustavus W. Dyer to dear Sir, 15 Mar. 1915, in Robert Josephus Dew file, CWVQ.

19. Green, *John Trotwood Moore*, 99–111.

20. John Trotwood Moore to Charles H. Myers (16 Sept. 1919, 31 Oct. 1922), to J. B. Stanley (27 Sept. 1921), to Ben P. Hunt (4 Oct. 1921), to A. W. Thomson (25 Jan. 1922), to J. B. Brown (11 Apr. 1922), to Mrs. Dorsey M. Kelly (14 Mar. 1923), Moore Papers.

21. Green, *John Trotwood Moore*, 99–111.

22. John Trotwood Moore to John C. Bauer (4 Dec. 1919), to Mrs. Cammie G. Henry (27 Sept. 1921), Moore Papers.

23. Moore, "The Tennessee State Library in the Capitol," 15–18; Weaver interview; Robert E. Corlew, letter to author, 6 July 1983.

24. John Trotwood Moore to James Joe Smith, CWVQ; John Trotwood Moore to New Cannon, CWVQ; John Trotwood Moore to Richard Fallin, CWVQ; *Confederate Veteran* 30 (Mar. 1922): 82, 84; *Confederate Veteran* 30 (Apr. 1922): 122.

25. William D. Harkleroad, Richard C. Howell, James Monroe Jones, CWVQ; Adine Marshall to John Trotwood Moore, 20 May 1922, in Joseph Kennedy Marshall folder, CWVQ.

26. Phillips, "The Central Theme of Southern History," 30–43.

27. Woodward, *The Strange Career of Jim Crow*; Newby, *Jim Crow's Defense*; Meier, *Negro Thought in America*; Daniel, *The Shadow of Slavery*.

28. Helper, *The Impending Crisis of the South*; Brutus, "An Address to the Citizens of South Carolina," pamphlet (ca. 1850), South Caroliniana Collection, University of South Carolina, Columbia, S.C.; Roark, *Masters Without Slaves*, 21, 54–67.

29. Roark, *Masters Without Slaves*, 66; Escott, *After Secession*, 94–103.

30. Kraus, *The Writing of American History*, 190.

31. Rhodes, *History of the United States from the Compromise of 1850* 1:344.

32. Holst, *Constitutional and Political History of the United States* 1:388; Schouler, *History of the United States under the Constitution* 2:231–33, 4:30–31; McMaster, *A History of the People of the United States* 2:12–15.

33. Referring to the actions of northern politicians during Reconstruction, Dunning wrote in 1907: "Few episodes of recorded history more urgently invite thorough analysis and extended reflection than the struggle through which the southern whites, subjugated by adversaries of their own race, thwarted the scheme which threatened permanent subjection to another race" (Dunning, *Reconstruction, Political and Economic*, 1). Among Dunning's students, Ulrich B. Phillips was exceptional because of his interest in southern social and economic history.

34. Dyer, *Democracy in the South*, 7–19.

35. Weaver interview.

36. *Dictionary of American Biography*, s.v. "Owsley, Frank Lawrence"; Shapiro, "Frank L. Owsley," 75–94; *I'll Take My Stand*, ix; Frank L. Owsley, "The Irrepressible Conflict," in *I'll Take My Stand*, 66–68; O'Brien, *Idea of the American South*, 162–84; Andrew Lytle, Foreword to *The South*, edited by Harriet C. Owsley, ix–xiv; Weaver interview.

37. O'Brien, *Idea of the American South*, 178–82.

38. Frank L. Owsley to Charles A. Beard, 12 Oct. 1940, Owsley Papers; Frank L. Owsley to Red [Robert Penn Warren], 25 Mar. 1937, *Southern Review* Papers; Clark, "The Agricultural Population in Tennessee"; Mooney, "Slavery in Tennessee"; Weaver, "The Agricultural Population of Mississippi"; Coles, "A History of the Administration of Federal Land Policies"; Clark, *The Tennessee Yeomen*; Mooney, *Slavery in Tennessee*; Weaver, *Mississippi Farmers*; Coles, "Some Notes on Slaveownership," 381–94.

39. Owsley, *Plain Folk*, 133.

40. Shugg, *Origins of Class Struggle in Louisiana*, 156.

41. Owsley, review of *Origins of Class Struggle*.

42. Owsley, *Plain Folk*, 133.

43. Linden, "Economic Democracy in the Slave South"; Linden, review of *Mississippi Farmers*; William C. Binkley to Wendell H. Stephenson, 16 June

1945, Stephenson Papers. I wish to thank Jackie Goggin at the Library of Congress in Washington, D.C., for sharing her knowledge of this letter and others from the Stephenson collection.

44. Frank L. Owsley, letter to editor, *American Historical Review* 52 (July 1947): 846; Harry Cole to Frank L. Owsley, 9 June 1945, Owsley Papers (this letter is extracted in part in Binkley to Stephenson, cited in note 43 above); Weaver interview.

45. Linden interview.

46. Bradford, "What We Can Know for Certain," 665; Wilson, Introduction to *Recovering Southern History*, iv.

47. McWhiney, "Historians as Southerners," 22–23. Much of this same material appeared in McWhiney, Introduction to *Plain Folk*, vii–xvii.

48. Eaton, *The Growth of Southern Civilization*, 156.

49. Foner, "The Causes of the American Civil War," 210; Genovese, "Yeomen Farmers in a Slaveholders' Democracy," 341–42.

50. Genovese, *Roll, Jordan, Roll*; Blassingame, *The Slave Community*; Escott, *Slavery Remembered*; Litwack, *Been in the Storm So Long*. For a critical analysis of the value of the slave narratives, see John W. Blassingame, "Status and Social Structure in the Slave Community: Evidence from New Sources," in Owens, *Perspectives and Irony in American Slavery*, 137–52; Kenneth M. Stampp, "Slavery—the Historian's Burden," in Owens, *Perspectives and Irony in American Slavery*, 166–68.

51. Clark, *Tennessee Yeomen*, xxii, 10–19.

CHAPTER 2

1. Meriwether Donaldson, John W. Wade, Isaac N. Rainey, Lewis F. Gulley, C. W. Hicks, CWVQ.

2. Francis Marion Arnold, William Thomas Mays, William Wryley Archer, CWVQ. *See also* William D. Beard, John W. Garren, T. J. Kersey, William H. Patterson, Ephriam O. Randle, CWVQ.

3. J. R. Miles, James K. P. Agnew, William D. Beard, John T. Clayton, William S. Phillips, Francis M. Tripp, CWVQ.

4. Wesley M. Sheets, CWVQ.

5. As examples see Leander K. Baker, Ridley S. Brown, John D. Bryant, Moses Garton, William J. Kirkham, William R. Perkins, CWVQ.

6. John H. Bittick, Thomas H. Hightower, CWVQ. *See also* C. W. Hicks, George W. Martin, Pinckney T. Martin, George A. Rice, CWVQ.

7. For examples see Samuel Adkisson, Jesse C. Brown, Russell L. Brown, Jesse B. Caudle, William J. Gregory, Andy W. Guffe, Thomas Hatchett, Hugh L. Hope, James Alexander Moore, Reuben Thomas Moore, George F. Wray, CWVQ.

8. J. P. Wilson, CWVQ.

9. Joseph K. Marshall, CWVQ. *See also* James H. Bandy, J. W. Barnes, John

W. Bell, Samuel B. Clemmons, Sumner F. Cocke, Thomas Higgason, Andrew J. McNeill, J. H. Peyton, CWVQ.

10. John W. Osborne, Thomas B. Neil, Christopher W. Robertson, Evander Lytle, John R. McClelland, CWVQ. *See also* Lee T. Billingsley, Newton Cannon, Elijah H. Knight, Robert A. Parker, Benjamin D. Rogers, David F. Watkins, CWVQ.

11. John B. Masterson, CWVQ. *See also* Raleigh P. Dodson, George W. Gordon, Samuel T. Hardison, Creed Haskins, William G. Hight, James Koger, J. H. Peyton, David C. Scales, CWVQ.

12. John N. Johnson, Thomas C. Hindman, Marcus B. Toney, Thomas C. Webb, CWVQ.

13. William W. Carnes, William and Hewitt Witherspoon, John A. Pickard, James G. Sims, Gideon H. Baskett, CWVQ.

14. Robert Lankey, Daniel Webster, James B. West, CWVQ.

15. Owsley and Owsley, "The Economic Structure of Rural Tennessee," 175. The Owsleys focused their attention on the landed majority and were apparently unimpressed with the fact that a large landless population represented a significant maldistribution of wealth. Other social historians have examined various regions of the South and noted the concentration of both real and personal property into the hands of the few.

Across the larger region, the Owsleys—as well as more recent scholars—estimate that, as a rule in the antebellum era, between 20 and 50 percent of a community's households did not own real estate, and in some areas these figures were dramatically higher. Sampling one thousand Middle Tennessee families in the 1860 census, Steven Ash confirmed the Owsleys' figures. He observed that 43 percent of his subjects owned no land. In some areas of the South, the dispossessed constituted a majority of the population. Harry Coles, a graduate student of Owsley, pointed out that on the eve of the Civil War landless households were in the majority in the Louisiana parishes of Ascension (51 percent), Calcasieu (57 percent), Catahoula (63 percent), Claiborne (50 percent), Livingston (74 percent), Sabine (70 percent), and Washington (60 percent). Grady McWhiney reported that, in Alabama, 58 percent of Covington County's household heads in 1850 were tenants, and Donald Dodd's study of impoverished Winston County during the Civil War revealed that 60 percent of the Confederate sympathizers and 73 percent of the Union supporters owned no land. In other regions, Paul Escott discovered that 30 percent of North Carolina's white families were landless in 1860, and Randolph B. Campbell and Richard Lowe reported the same condition for 33 percent of all Texas families. In both states, numerous landowners possessed only small farms. Escott's close examination of several North Carolina counties revealed that families with less than fifty acres constituted 30 percent of Randolph County households, 42 percent of Caldwell County households, and 52 percent of New Hanover County households. In their Texas sample, Campbell and Lowe estimated that 6 percent of the wealthiest families controlled 60 percent of all real estate and that 37 percent of the landed population resided on holdings valued under $250. In his detailed study of Harrison County, Texas, Campbell wrote: "While property ownership was widespread, property itself was concentrated in the hands of a relatively small minority of households. Put another way, most families in Harrison County owned some property, but a few owned a great deal more than others."

Wealth figures for 1860 suggest the economic power of southern elites. In Middle Tennessee, Ash estimated that the top 10 percent of the region's households owned 52 percent of all real estate; in the planter-dominated Marengo County, Alabama, Jonathan Wiener found that the top 10 percent of the families controlled 55 percent of the total wealth (real and personal property) and that the bottom 50 percent held only 6 percent of the wealth; in the nonplanter regions of Georgia, Steven Hahn found that the top 20 percent of Jackson County inhabitants possessed 61 percent of real estate wealth, and the top 20 percent of Carroll County inhabitants possessed 68 percent of real estate wealth; and in Edgefield County, South Carolina, Vernon Burton noted that the most affluent 10 percent of the population held 73 percent of personal property and 57 percent of the county's total wealth. Studying the South's cotton economy, Gavin Wright divided the region by soil types. Looking at the brown loam and alluvial (delta) soil regions that covered the western thirds of Tennessee and Mississippi, Wright estimated that the top 10 percent of brown loam landowners possessed 45 percent of real estate holdings and that the top 10 percent of alluvial land owners possessed 52 percent of the landed wealth. By contrast, the poorest 50 percent of the population owned respectively 12 and 7 percent of the real real estate wealth.

Although the above studies employed a variety of methodologies and investigated different community types, a pattern that encompasses the entire South has emerged. On the eve of the Civil War, a few Southerners were notably affluent, while the majority resided in their economic shadow.

Ash, "Civil War," 125, 128; Coles, "Some Notes on Slaveownership," 385; McWhiney, "Revolution in Nineteenth-Century Alabama Agriculture," 19; Dodd, "Unionism in Confederate Alabama," 98; Escott, *Many Excellent People,* 9–10; Campbell and Lowe, *Wealth and Power in Antebellum Texas,* 38, 39; Campbell, *A Southern Community in Crisis,* 29; Wiener, *Social Origins of the New South,* 15; Hahn, *The Roots of Southern Populism,* 24; Burton, *In My Father's House are Many Mansions,* 41; Wright, *Political Economy of the Cotton South,* 30. I appreciate Paul Escott and Vernon Burton for providing me with advance copies of their works.

16. J. J. McCoy, Isaac W. Grimes, Jesse Collins, J. H. Feathers, James C. Hodge, CWVQ.
17. Robert R. Bayless, CWVQ. *See also* William D. Beard, James C. Hodge, Henry H. Patterson, William S. Phillips, James V. Walker, CWVQ.

18. George V. Payne, Samuel N. Reynolds, J. T. Killen, CWVQ. *See also* William T. Fields, H. C. Furry, William J. McClarrin, Samuel N. Reynolds, Milton N. Rowell, John Scruggs, Thomas W. Walthall, CWVQ.

19. Julius C. Martin, CWVQ.

20. William D. Beard, George V. Payne, A. J. Ferrell, CWVQ. *See also* John T. Clayton, John T. Duke, William T. Eskew, Robert P. Lackey, William A. Vardell, John L. Young, CWVQ.

21. James Walker, Constantine Nance, Flavius S. Lander, CWVQ.

22. James F. Anthony, Ambrose Bennett, Julius C. Martin, Joe Sullivan, George W. Willing, CWVQ.

23. James F. Anthony, CWVQ.

24. Tom Childress, Theodoric E. Lipscomb, Edward S. Payne, CWVQ.

25. Jeptha M. Fuston, CWVQ.

26. For descriptions of the hog culture in Tennessee, see the memoirs of Tom Bryan, Bryan Papers; McDonald and McWhiney, "The Antebellum Southern Herdsman."

27. Burnett, "Hog Raising and Hog Driving"; Burnett, "The Hog Drivers' Play-Song." For a small collection of letters dealing with the business negotiations of the Tennessee hog drivers, see the Prior family papers.

28. Thomas H. Hightower, R. T. M. Jones, CWVQ. For a description of shoemaking, see Edward M. Gardner memoir.

29. Isaac Griffith, CWVQ; Tom Bryan memoirs.

30. David Bodenhamer, W. F. Blevins, William D. Harkleroad, George W. Samuels, CWVQ.

31. F. M. Copeland, James Aiken, John M. Barron, Joe Rich, CWVQ.

32. Demarus P. Cunningham, James Dickinson, J. W. Bradley, Elijah T. Hassell, William H. Key, James S. Pearce, George W. Sanford, CWVQ.

33. William P. Baker, George W. Barrow, John Scruggs, CWVQ; Tom Bryan memoirs; Edward M. Gardner memoir.

34. John B. Masterson, Thomas Yancey, James G. Sims, CWVQ.

35. William A. Johnston, Joshua W. Mewborn, Andrew B. Webster, Louis Bledsoe, CWVQ. *See also* Robert Austin, George B. Baskerville, Samuel Bennett, Lee T. Billingsley, George E. Donnell, Robert Z. Taylor, James W. Williams, CWVQ.

36. Newton Cannon, F. A. Turner, Benjamin F. Hawkins, CWVQ. *See also* Robert Z. Taylor, William and Hewitt Witherspoon, CWVQ.

37. Joshua Mewborn, Lee T. Billingsley, Robert Rogers, CWVQ. *See also* Louis J. Bledsoe, George E. Donnell, Edwin M. Gardner, Creel Haskins, Carrick W. Heiskell, John P. Hickman, James K. P. Jackson, John Johnston, John A. Kirby, Walter T. Lenoir, Evander Lytle, Robert M. McAlister, James T. McColgan, John A. Reid, William G. Taylor, John W. Wade, Andrew B. Webster, A. J. Williams, James W. Williams, CWVQ.

38. James H. McClister, CWVQ. For examples of other nonwealthy persons who expressed resentment at the affluent class's leisure ethic, see Thomas Booker, John D. Bryant, James P. Caldwell, John T. Clayton, J. C. Davidson, Isaac B. Day, William E. Deason, James E. Dickinson,

William C. Dillihay, S. H. Freeze, Arin W. Goans, D. H. Hall, George E. Hornberger, Ezkiel Inman, T. J. Kersey, R. P. Lanius, Timothy W. Leigon, W. T. Martin, L. B. Odeneal, Samuel M. Ray, William H. Roach, Wesley M. Sheets, James W. Trusty, Charles P. Williams, CWVQ.

39. John B. Tate, CWVQ.

40. Robert K. Morris, CWVQ.

41. Gentry R. McGee, John A. Fite, CWVQ.

42. Lewis B. McFarland, CWVQ.

43. For example, one antebellum Tennessee almanac suggested, as a sure cure for whooping cough, rubbing a concoction of garlic and melted lard onto the soles of an afflicted child's feet. The results, it suggested, "have been astonishing." *Wilson's Tennessee Farmer's Almanac.*

44. Samuel F. Whitsitt, CWVQ. *See also* Lewis B. McFarland, Gentry R. McGee, Christopher W. Robertson, CWVQ. For discussions of slavery and medical care see Stampp, *The Peculiar Institution*, 307–21; Genovese, "Medical and Insurance Costs of Slaveholding"; Savitt, "The Special Problem of Slavery" (a typescript of this paper and others read at the symposium are available from the Center for the Study of Southern Culture, The University of Mississippi, University, Mississippi). Paul Escott makes the point that slaves preferred their own folk medicines over white-imposed health care (Escott, *Slavery Remembered*, 108–9).

45. A small but quality collection of antebellum country store account books is available at the Mississippi Valley Collection, Memphis State University Library, Memphis, Tennessee. The quotation was taken from the account book of C. Y. Gray's General Store, near Union City, Tennessee.

46. Edwin M. Gardner, CWVQ. *See also* Calvin B. Crook, John F. Mason, William G. Taylor, Joseph F. Watt, CWVQ.

47. Charles E. Jackson, CWVQ. *See also* Richard Beard, James P. Coffin, Amos B. Jones, CWVQ.

48. Thomas Porter, Lee T. Billingsley, Edward S. Bringhurst, James L. Nesbitt, Hervey Whitfield, CWVQ.

49. James A. Carringer, James H. McNeilly, James P. Warner, CWVQ.

50. James M. Jones, Arthur V. A. Deadrick, CWVQ.

51. Nathaniel E. Harris, John P. Hickman, CWVQ.

52. Harrison Farrell, CWVQ.

53. C. W. Hicks, Benjamin L. Swafford, CWVQ. For samplings of the work done by nonslaveowning wives, see McKager C. Alexander, Andrew J. Allen, Elijah C. Barnes, Isaac N. Broyles, James P. Byrne, James Coakley, William K. Cox, Lewis F. Gulley, James A. Holder, William O. Hollingsworth, Pleasant E. Hunter, Flavius S. Landers, J. J. McCoy, James M. McKnight, John R. Pinkleton, William P. Sims, William F. Smith, William A. Vardell, Joseph F. Wilson, CWVQ.

54. William C. Aydelott, Charlie F. Blackwell, John S. Welch, Samuel N. Reynolds, CWVQ. *See also* Robert P. Lackey, James M. Thurman, CWVQ.

55. Samuel W. Daimwood, William J. Kirkham, David Sullins, CWVQ.

56. Jeptha Fuston, William G. Allen, William H. Key, Sims Lata, William T. Mays, CWVQ.

57. Samuel J. Adams, James C. Shofner, Powhatan P. Pullen, Columbus C. London, CWVQ. For examples of the activities of the wives of slaveowning yeomen, see J. Press Abernathy, John B. Allen, Lucullus C. Atkins, W. H. Barrows, Lemuel J. Benne, A. M. Bruce, Thomas L. Bryan, James P. Coffin, Alexander G. Felts, Thomas G. Harris, John G. Herbert, B. P. Hooker, Josiah S. House, Robert L. Jones, R. P. Lanius, William J. Mantlo, Pinckney T. Martin, John H. O'Neal, John R. Reagan, Ephraim P. Riddle, Benjamin C. Seaborn, M. B. Tomlinson, J. P. Wilson, Jacob Young, CWVQ.

58. William Taylor, Isaac N. Rainey, Lee T. Billingsley, CWVQ. *See also* William W. Carnes, Lewis B. McFarland, Hervey Whitfield, Samuel P. Whitsitt, CWVQ.

59. John A. Fite, Hampton J. Cheney, James G. Sims, Thomas Yancey, Theodoric E. Lipscomb, CWVQ. *See also* Gideon H. Baskett, Richard Beard, Charles A. D. Faris, Thomas J. Firth, William F. Greaves, James M. Johnson, William G. Lillard, Evander Lytle, Cannon Newton, Charles S. O. Rice, Robert E. Rogers, F. A. Turner, David F. Watkins, Thomas S. Webb, CWVQ.

60. Gentry R. McGee, L. H. Russe, John T. Crawford, McCage M. Oglesby, CWVQ.

61. Marcus Vesley, James Thompson, James S. Tyner, CWVQ.

62. Andrew B. Webster, CWVQ.

63. George W. D. Porter, R. P. Lanius, Gilbert B. Harrell, Thomas Harrison Whitfield, James M. Rogers, Mark LaFayette Anderson, CWVQ. William Frazier, James C. Giles, Uriah M. Payne, George W. D. Porter, William C. Pullen, James L. Singleton, and James Stiles are among those who began plowing at age eight; Burl W. Flemming, Pinkney T. Martin, Linzey L. Thompson, and J. P. Wilson were set to the plow at age nine; J. K. P. Andrews, Thomas A. Barnett, J. V. Deck, and Robert C. Pafford testified that they commenced plowing at age ten; and Lee Sadler and William F. Sims began to plow at age eleven (CWVQ).

64. William G. Lillard, CWVQ. *See also* Andrew J. McNeill, CWVQ.

65. A. T. Bransford, John Hank, John T. C. Fergus, Timothy W. Leigon, William T. Eskew, CWVQ. *See also* Swimpfield Edison, William H. Patterson, George V. Payne, John S. Wilson, CWVQ.

66. C. W. Hicks, George W. Willing, CWVQ. For examples of nonslaveowning yeomen's sons and their work duties, see William L. Anders, Thomas W. Arnold, James H. Coop, Augustus H. Gothard, Robert S. Holman, William L. Morelock, Loranzo J. Sanders, Carter Upchurch, CWVQ.

67. William C. Needham, A. M. Bruce, CWVQ.

68. Josiah A. Hinkle, Baxter R. Hoover, Turner L. Johnson, CWVQ. For a sampling of slaveowners' sons working with the family's slaves, see J. W. Ashmore, William H. Blackburn, Tom Childress, Peter Donnell, John E.

Gold, J. F. Littleton, James H. Morton, John H. O'Neal, John M. Prewitt, Powhatan P. Pullen, John F. Sehon, James C. Shofner, Thomas B. Utley, F. S. Williams, J. G. Williamson, CWVQ.

69. Ridley S. Brown, CWVQ.

70. Elijah H. Knight, Augustine T. Atkins, Robert Z. Taylor, CWVQ.

71. William G. Lillard, McGage M. Oglesby, Rober L. Morris, CWVQ.

72. James M. Morey, William L. Anthony, Charles Mison, F. A. Turner, Herman M. Doak, Louis J. Bledsoe, CWVQ. *See also* George B. Baskerville, Lee T. Billingsley, Hampton J. Cheney, Thomas J. Firth, James M. Johnson, John Johnston, Robert M. McAlister, Walcham S. Roberts, Marcus B. Toney, James S. West, Thomas H. Williams, CWVQ.

73. James C. Hodge, CWVQ. *See also* Timothy W. Leigon, W. T. Martin, George V. Payne, CWVQ.

74. Lee T. Billingsley, Colman David Smith, Benjamin F. Hawkins, Preston Y. Hill, CWVQ.

75. William D. Beard, CWVQ.

76. Hampton J. Cheney, CWVQ. *See also* Edwin S. Payne, Charles S. O. Rice, Henry J. Rogers, CWVQ.

77. Hampton J. Cheney, CWVQ.

78. Elijah Hassell, W. A. Rushing, CWVQ.

79. A. J. Childers, CWVQ.

80. Leuel Beene, Jeremiah McKenzie, John Mitchell, Ephraim Riddle, CWVQ.

81. George W. Brown, William Herbison, Flavius S. Landers, J. P. Funk, CWVQ.

82. Colman Davis Smith, CWVQ.

83. Peter Collman (Union), CWVQ.

CHAPTER 3

1. William C. Dillihay, CWVQ.

2. James K. Clifton, CWVQ.

3. Owsley, *Plain Folk*, 148–49; Clark, *The Tennessee Yeomen*, 107.

4. Samuel Bowles, "Unequal Education and the Reproduction of the Social Division of Labor," in Carnoy, *Schooling in a Corporate Society*, 45–47.

5. Napoleon B. Abbott, E. C. Alexander, George W. Alexander, John B. Allen, Thomas A. Barnett, Isaac A. Bartlett, Lemuel J. Beene, Jesse C. Brown, J. B. Harrell, John H. Hunt, William H. Luckey, Marquis L. Morrison, John A. Pearce, CWVQ.

6. Gilbert Harrell, James M. Frazer, Reuben T. Moore, CWVQ.

7. William T. Durrett, William J. Gregory, James R. Spurlock, CWVQ.

8. Robert S. Holman, Patton T. Mitchell, William J. Tucker, Carter Upchurch, CWVQ.

9. James J. Carroll, Arthur Davis, Francis A. McKnight, CWVQ. *See also*

Leander K. Baker, William D. Beard, Carroll H. Clark, John T. Clayton, J. C. Davidson, William E. Deason, Robert J. Dew, William S. Hartsfield, James A. Holder, Josiah S. House, William M. Hunter, J. W. Jones, Andrew J. Killebrew, J. F. Littleton, Andrew M. McKnight, Julius C. Martin, William R. Perkins, William S. Rogers, John Smith, William F. Smith, Joseph H. Stamper, John P. Stribling, Jasper N. White, Halyard Wilhite, F. S. Williams, Elijah H. Wolfe, Thomas W. Wood, CWVQ.

10. William H. Blackburn, L. B. Cooper, Thomas N. Driver, Zachary T. Dyer, John E. Gold, William J. McLarrin, L. B. Odeneal, John Vincent, CWVQ.

11. James F. Anthony, James W. Trusty, N. B. Nesbitt, James S. Tyner, Andrew J. McNeill, CWVQ.

12. Isaac Gore, Samuel E. Matthews, Robert Austin, Sam H. Ralls, William J. Briggs, CWVQ.

13. James F. Anthony, Felix G. Bilbrey, John D. Bryant, Isaac Griffith, W. H. Harris, Pleasant E. Hunter, Andrew J. Killebrew, Fesington C. Lowry, John W. Rymer, James A. Vernon, CWVQ.

14. David S. England, Joe Sullivan, Wiley B. Daniel, CWVQ.

15. One of the best descriptions of this method of teaching was found in the questionnaire filled out by M. B. Dinwiddie, CWVQ. Julius C. Martin, Juilus A. Vernon, James Aiken, CWVQ.

16. George F. Wray, CWVQ.

17. James B. Thomason, William S. Phillips, Turner L. Johnson, Jacob E. Slinger, Hiram Riemes Brown, CWVQ.

18. John T. Crawford, William F. Greaves, Berenes Carter, Meriwether Donaldson, John H. Wharton, James M. Morey, CWVQ. *See also* George B. Baskerville, Richard Beard, Newton Cannon, CWVQ.

19. Charles G. Samuel, CWVQ.

20. Joshua W. Mewborn, M. B. Tomlinson, Charles E. Jackson, William C. Needham, CWVQ.

21. McCage M. Oglesby, CWVQ.

22. Marcus V. Crump, D. T. Patton, Henry J. Rogers, James B. Thompson, Lawrence Turner, Samuel P. Whitsitt, Thomas H. Williams, CWVQ. Some of these institutions possessed more pretension than substance. As one veteran explained: "In Obion County there were round log school houses . . . [and] one frame school house in Troy which by courtesy was called an Acadamy" (John Cavanaugh, CWVQ).

23. Hampton J. Chiney, William M. Pollard, CWVQ.

24. John S. Welch, James M. Wiser, CWVQ. *See also* John W. Carpenter, J. O. Johnson, Timothy Leigon, Samuel M. Ray, Wesley Welch, F. S. Williams, CWVQ.

25. John R. Dance, Herman M. Doak, CWVQ.

26. Eli L. Hinson, David S. Bodenhamer, CWVQ. *See also* Romulus Barbee, Russell L. Brown, John N. Epps, William Frazier, J. P. Funk, Samuel T. Hardison, William J. Mantlo, Laurence L. Milan, James L. Nesbitt, Calvin J. Orr, John A. Pickard, CWVQ.

27. D. P. Chambers, CWVQ. *See also* James B. Anderson, John S. Prather, Powhatan P. Pullen, David C. Scales, John W. Shaw, James N. Shivers, Alexander Teasley, John C. Wallace, Jackson R. Watson, CWVQ.

28. William W. Eads, CWVQ.

29. Thomas S. Webb, CWVQ. *See also* George B. Bakerville, Richard Beard, James C. Coffin, Herman M. Doak, John A. Fite, William H. Halbert, Elbert C. Reeves, Charles S. Rice, James G. Sims, William P. Sims, Samuel G. Sparks, Marcus B. Toney, CWVQ.

30. Herman M. Doak, CWVQ.

31. John K. Roberts, Edwin Gardner, CWVQ.

32. William Orr, Flavius S. Landers, James M. Sain, CWVQ. *See also* James A. Anderson, James B. Anderson, William L. Anthony, Henry C. Arrington, Thomas Booker, Russell L. Brown, John D. Bryan, Willie R. Bryant, E. J. Bynum, James P. Caldwell, James J. Carroll, George C. Camp, Richard W. Colville, J. P. Dillehay, Peter Donnell, William T. Durrett, William T. Fields, Edward N. Gannaway, William T. Gregory, Gilbert B. Harrell, John G. Herbert, David Jennae, William C. Jenkins, Thweatt H. McCartney, Jr., William R. Perkins, Milton W. Prewitt, Josia M. Reams, Benjamin C. Seaborn, Johnson R. Spurlock, John H. Travis, Carter Upchurch, George F. Wray, CWVQ.

33. Newton Cannon, James H. McNeily, William P. Timberlake, CWVQ. *See also* Henry A. Barrett, Samuel L. Barron, Richard Beard, Thomas W. M. Courtney, John H. Frierson, William H. Halbert, Henry C. Haynes, Robert N. Herbert, Preston Y. Hill, Lewis B. McFarland, James H. Morton, John C. New, George W. Nowlin, Deering Roberts, James J. Smith, Robert Z. Taylor, William G. Taylor, Harvey Whitfield, CWVQ.

34. Dero F. Mills, James T. McColgan, Zach Thompson, CWVQ. *See also* George B. Baskerville, Marcus V. Crump, William A. Johnston, William G. Lillard, Walcham S. Roberts, G. B. Sale, James A. Vincent, John W. Wade, CWVQ.

35. McCage M. Oglesby, George B. Baskerville, Robert E. Rogers, CWVQ. *See also* Thomas J. Aldrich, Theodore F. Harris, Robert Z. Taylor, James A. Vincent, CWVQ.

36. Marcus B. Toney, CWVQ.

37. James M. Cole, John W. Foster, William T. Eskew, Elijah C. Barnes, Burl W. Flemming, CWVQ. *See also* Mark L. Anderson, John T. Clayton, Thompson S. Glenn, James C. Hodge, Asa Johnson, Napoleon B. Johnson, David W. Martin, W. A. O'Dell, George W. Willing, CWVQ.

38. James C. Giles, CWVQ.

39. John F. Cole, CWVQ.

40. John M. Patrick, CWVQ. *See also* Jesse Collins, Henry C. Naylor, J. T. Roberts, CWVQ.

41. Robert L. Morris, James Shivers, CWVQ.

42. William T. Barnes, John T. Fergus, William W. Eads, CWVQ. *See also* James K. Clifton, James A. Gross, James C. Hodge, William J. Jones, Jacob E. Slinger, J. P. Wilson, CWVQ.

43. John S. Welch, CWVQ.
44. Daniel W. Long, CWVQ.
45. John W. Osborne, Isaac N. Rainey, Christopher W. Robertson, CWVQ. *See also* Joseph L. Cardwell, William H. Halbert, George S. Hodge, Robert E. Moss, Joshua W. Mewborn, John A. Pickard, Thomas H. Williams, CWVQ.
46. M. B. Dinwiddie, CWVQ.
47. G. W. Miller, CWVQ.

CHAPTER 4

1. John T. Clayton, William A. Johnston, CWVQ.
2. CWVQ.
3. David C. Scales, CWVQ.
4. Benjamin A. Hagnewood, J. G. Williamson, CWVQ.
5. CWVQ.
6. Temple, *Notable Men of Tennessee*, 44–45; Bryan, "The Civil War in East Tennessee," 22.
7. William Morelock, James T. McColgan, CWVQ.
8. William J. Jones, George W. Willing, Johnson R. Spurlock, James A. King, James Kinsley, James McClister, CWVQ.
9. John W. Wade, William Lillard, Henry Rogers, CWVQ. *See also* Louis J. Bledsoe, W. M. Courtney, John T. Duke, William T. Eskew, Lemuel H. Tyree, John Henry West, CWVQ.
10. E. C. Alexander, CWVQ.
11. John S. Welch, Francis M. McClure, Elijah T. Hassell, James C. Hodge, S. P. Larkins, CWVQ. *See also* John H. Browner, John Cavanaugh, J. C. Davidson, Meriwether Donaldson, John W. Foster, Creed Haskins, James A. Haymes, William J. Herbison, Ezekiel Inman, William T. Mays, J. R. Miles, Isham Qualls, Ephriam O. Randle, Samuel N. Reynolds, William H. Roach, John M. Smith, James W. Trusty, A. J. Williams, CWVQ.
12. John I. Bruce, Arthur Davis, R. L. Ivy, CWVQ. *See also* Charles E. Jackson, David W. Martin, Joshua W. Mewborn, William C. Needham, Samuel G. Patterson, Samuel M. Ray, Wesley M. Sheets, Lee F. Yancey, CWVQ.
13. William D. House, John S. Luna, John M. Patrick, Marcus B. Toney, C. W. Hicks, CWVQ.
14. Richard Beard, Robert E. Moss, Benjamin B. Batey, CWVQ.
15. Robert E. Rogers, Theodoric E. Lipscomb, William H. Patterson, CWVQ.
16. George W. Taylor, William A. Pursely, CWVQ. *See also* Robert L. Bowden, Josiah S. House, Nathan R. Martin, William S. Nolen, William A. Pursley, Vercume H. Ray, CWVQ.
17. William G. Allen, CWVQ. *See also* William E. Hazelwood, Samuel E. Matthews, Elvin K. Murdock, CWVQ.
18. Clark, *The Tennessee Yeomen*, 13–14. In her quotation of Allen's statement, Clark modified his grammar and corrected his spelling.

19. U.S. Bureau of the Census, *Eighth Census*, 466.
20. Tennessee M. Hooper, William K. Cox, Harvey L. Chase, William D. Harkleroad, Samuel Moulock, Isaac Griffith, F. G. Durham, James K. P. Agnew, John Leonard, CWVQ. *See also* James F. Anthony, Robert R. Bayless, William H. Blackburn, John T. Cole, Robert C. Crouch, Zachary T. Crouch, James A. Deloier, Liberty S. Duncan, George W. Durbin, Swimpfield Eidson, Wiley B. Ellis, George D. Fleming, Jeptha M. Fuston, Nathaniel Hicks, James H. Hinson, James A. Jackson, Thomas B. Kendrick, John W. Ketron, William D. Lady, John M. Leonard, James H. McClister, George W. McMahan, William T. Mays, John N. Meroney, John T. Nelson, George W. Park, Elbert C. Reeves, Jonathan K. Rogers, W. C. Shirley, L. L. Standefer, James P. Walker, Jackson R. Watson, James B. West, J. T. Williams, CWVQ.
21. Robert J. Dew, Marshall B. Jones, John H. Frierson, Joseph K. Marshall, Robert M. McAlister, Robert N. Herbert, CWVQ.
22. William G. Lillard, Robert N. Herbert, Thomas H. Williams, CWVQ.
23. Aratus T. Cornelius, John A. Reid, Harrison Randolph, John Lipscomb, M. B. Dinwiddie, CWVQ. *See also* Gideon H. Baskett, Robert B. Bates, David S. M. Bodenhamer, James W. Chisom, Pleasant E. Hunter, Amos B. Jones, Victor M. Locke, George W. Nowlin, John W. Shaw, Robert Z. Taylor, William P. Timberland, James W. Williams, CWVQ.
24. Hampton J. Cheney, Jeremiah McKenzie, Andrew K. Miller, CWVQ. *See also* William C. Boze, T. D. Coffey, Samuel B. Kyle, George W. D. Porter, F. A. Turner, John H. Wharton, CWVQ.
25. James M. Hill, Lee T. Billingsley, CWVQ.
26. John N. Johnson, Edward P. Martin, Lemuel H. Tyree, CWVQ. *See also* Stephen J. Brown, Hampton J. Cheney, Charles A. D. Faris, Edward P. Martin, Isaac N. Rainey, Henry J. Rogers, James G. Sims, CWVQ.
27. Robert H. Mosley, CWVQ.
28. Zachary T. Dyer, CWVQ.
29. Harrison W. Farrell, CWVQ. *See also* Robert R. Bayless, Samuel W. Daimwood, Edward S. Doe, James M. Glasgow, Green B. Grier, John P. Hickman, J. C. J. Kirby, R. P. Lanius, John A. Pearce, George W. D. Porter, Cyrus N. Simmons, James G. Sims, Benjamin L. Swafford, John H. Walthall, Thomas S. Webb, Charles P. Williams, CWVQ.
30. Marcus B. Toney, Creed Haskins, James M. Johnson, Robert M. McAlister, William F. Greaves, CWVQ. *See also* Lee T. Billingsley, R. S. Cowles, Charles A. D. Faris, Edwin M. Gardner, Benjamin F. Hawkins, Carrick W. Heiskell, Charles E. Jackson, James K. P. Jackson, John Johnston, James M. Jones, Walter T. Lenoir, William G. Lillard, Evander Lytle, James D. Martin, McCage M. Oglesby, Edmond E. O'Neill, Gustavus A. Pope, John A. Reid, Robert E. Rogers, James A. Vincent, John W. Wade, Phillip V. H. Weems, Hervey Whitfield, A. J. Williams, James W. Williams, CWVQ.
31. Isaac Butler Day, Samuel B. Clemmons, James P. Caldwell, W. T. Martin,

CWVQ. *See also* E. C. Alexander, Willis Baugh, John D. Bryant, Melmon M. Butts, J. C. Davidson, William C. Dillihay, Meriwether Donaldson, Alexander G. Felts, Elijah T. Hassell, James W. Hendricks, James N. Logan, Daniel W. Long, Robert H. Mosley, William M. Moss, L. B. Odeneal, William A. Phelps, John Thurman, James W. Trusty, Thomas H. Whitfield, James M. Wiser, CWVQ.

32. William A. Vardell, Isaac N. Broyles, George V. Payne, Ezekiel Inman, CWVQ. *See also* Willis Baugh, William D. Beard, John T. Clayton, Robert L. Culps, William E. Deason, James E. Dickinson, John W. Dunnaway, John T. C. Fergus, Isaac W. Grimes, D. M. Hall, George E. Hornberger, J. D. Hughes, T. J. Kersey, John L. McMurty, Julius C. Martin, John R. Mullins, Samuel M. Ray, Samuel N. Reynolds, A. W. Tripp, John S. Welch, Wesley Welch, CWVQ.

33. Herman M. Doak, CWVQ. *See also* Louis J. Bledsoe, Andrew B. Webster, CWVQ.

34. Wesley M. Sheets, CWVQ.

35. Thomas S. Webb, Andrew K. Miller, Elisha H. Taylor, Joshua W. Mewborn, CWVQ.

36. Meriwether Donaldson, Pressley N. Conner, CWVQ. *See also* Robert J. Dew, William T. Porch, CWVQ.

37. Amos B. Jones, Thomas S. Webb, Hervey Whitfield, CWVQ. *See also* Lee T. Billingsley, William W. Carnes, James S. Pearce, John W. Shaw, William Witherspoon, CWVQ.

38. William T. Barnes, Joe C. Brooks, J. W. Keaton, Nimrod Reed, CWVQ.

39. John S. Welch, James J. Carroll, John Wisley Dunavant, J. W. Bradley, James H. Coop, J. M. Davis, Ezekiel Inman, CWVQ. *See also* Ambrose Bennett, A. T. Bransford, William T. Eskew, Thomas S. Glenn, N. C. Godsey, John W. Ketron, James H. McClister, John R. Mullins, James P. E. Nicely, Jonathan K. Rogers, W. M. Willis, CWVQ.

40. James A. Gross, Edward N. Gannaway, CWVQ.

41. William C. Dillihay, Marcus B. Toney, Lewis W. Hayes, CWVQ. *See also* J. P. Dillehay, Robert M. McAlister, CWVQ.

42. William C. Dillihay, CWVQ. *See also* William W. Archer, Russell L. Brown, Charles B. Darden, CWVQ.

43. Ford N. Adams, David F. Watkins, Thomas S. Webb, William Witherspoon, CWVQ.

44. John W. Dunnaway, John T. Duke, John R. Spurlock, Sam H. Smithson, John W. Foster, CWVQ.

45. William M. Moss, CWVQ; Wooster, *Politicians, Planters and Plain Folk*, 113–14.

46. William Mabry, CWVQ.

47. Fesington C. Lowry, CWVQ.

48. Charles A. D. Faris, Napoleon B. Abbott, James S. Tyner, John B. Allen, CWVQ.

49. William M. Moss, Marcus B. Toney, CWVQ.

50. John H. Brawner, Samuel N. Reynolds, CWVQ.
51. William G. Davis, CWVQ.

CHAPTER 5

1. William S. Duggan, John H. Wilson, Carroll Clark, CWVQ.
2. Bryan, "The Civil War in Tennessee," 34–73.
3. D. T. Pinkerton, CWVQ.
4. Walter S. Jennings, Gentry R. McGee, CWVQ.
5. David S. M. Bodenhamer, William Frazier, James Joe Smith, CWVQ.
6. Alexander Teasley, Henry J. Rogers, CWVQ.
7. William W. Carnes, Calvin B. Crook, CWVQ.
8. John A. Fite, CWVQ. *See also* Thomas E. Bradley, Herman M. Doak, W. S. Holmes, Amos B. Jones, Calvin E. Myers, Charles G. Samuel, William P. Timberlake, Phillip V. H. Weems, CWVQ.
9. Carroll Clark, Jesse H. Green, John H. O'Neal, William D. Beard, CWVQ.
10. Escott, "'The Cry of the Sufferers,'" 228–40; Escott, *After Secession*, 94–134; Hahn, *The Roots of Southern Populism*, 116–33.
11. Richard W. Winn, Elias G. Montgomery, G. W. Lamberson, Jeremiah M. McKenzie, CWVQ. *See also* Lemuel J. Beene, George W. McMahan, William L. Morelock, CWVQ.
12. W. L. Shofner, CWVQ. *See also* William Frazier, William J. Gregory, James A. Gross, John N. McKnight, John B. Masterson, James S. Pearce, CWVQ.
13. Harrison W. Farrell, CWVQ.
14. Ibid.
15. Thomas R. Inman, William M. Hunter, William L. Wakefield, John H. Lusk, John B. Tate, William H. Crihfield, Calvin B. Crook, CWVQ. *See also* John H. Bruce, Alfred Friddle, John Gray, James L. Nesbitt, Erasmus G. Osgatharp, James W. Trusty, William Y. Wiley, CWVQ.
16. David Sullins, Sims Latta, Thomas J. Kinser, CWVQ.
17. D. P. Chamberland, J. C. Davidson, John Tallant, William Carnes, James F. Anthony, David F. Watkins, William L. Wakefield, William H. Key, CWVQ. *See also* Robert L. Bowden, John W. Chisum, F. G. Durham, John T. C. Fergus, William S. Hartsfield, James G. Holleman, T. J. Kersey, J. B. King, James M. Langley, James K. P. Webb, CWVQ.
18. Erasmus G. Osgatharp, Edward S. Doe, Ben Moser, Lorenzo J. Sanders, Robert L. Bowden, CWVQ. *See also* Zachary T. Crouch, S. H. Freeze, William D. Latta, William G. Lillard, Joseph K. Marshall, Joshua W. Mewborn, Elvin K. Murdock, CWVQ.
19. William J. Tucker, Isaac Griffith, Demarus P. Cunningham, CWVQ.
20. William H. Yates, CWVQ.
21. James Anthony, CWVQ. *See also* Robert Austin, Hugh L. Ferguson, John D. Givan, Robert P. Lankey, John N. McKnight, CWVQ.

22. Hampton J. Cheney, CWVQ. *See also* Andrew J. Killebrew, John A. Kirby, George W. Lewis, Andrew K. Miller, CWVQ.

23. William S. Hartsfield, Alax I. Underhill, Theodore F. Harris, Robert S. Holman, Hamilton M. Hennessee, Henry C. Guthrie, CWVQ. *See also* Francis M. Dillard, William J. Corn, CWVQ.

24. J. F. Osborne, John R. Dance, Charles S. O. Rice, CWVQ. *See also* Stephen H. Hows, Walter T. Lenoir, James L. Nesbitt, Edwin S. Payne, Milton N. Rowell, Coleman D. Smith, John A. Wilson, CWVQ.

25. Milton Rowell, CWVQ.

26. James T. McColgan, Samuel P. Whitsitt, William A. Johnston, Hampton J. Cheney, Thomas J. Aldrich, CWVQ. *See also* Gideon H. Baskett, John R. McClelland, Lewis B. McFarland, James H. McNeilly, CWVQ.

27. William G. Lillard, Robert A. Parker, CWVQ. *See also* Soloman Brantley, Charles B. Darden, McCage M. Oglesby, CWVQ.

28. Liberty S. Duncan, J. H. Feathers, George W. Brown, CWVQ.

29. William E. Orr, William H. Lucy, John F. M. Mason, CWVQ.

30. G. W. Lamberson, William J. Tucker, Lee Sadler, CWVQ. *See also* W. C. Carden, Thomas J. Corn, M. B. Dinwiddie, Thomas G. Harris, Joseph P. J. Hoover, CWVQ.

31. John Johnston, Christopher W. Robertson, CWVQ.

32. Wesley M. Sheets, Phillip V. H. Weems, CWVQ. These were the only two respondents who died during the war; relatives filled out their questionnaires.

33. C. Rhodes, H. C. Cole, James C. Fly, Harrison H. Neece, James A. Moore, James H. Coop, William H. Key, CWVQ. *See also* J. Press Abernathy, Stokley Acuff, William T. Adams, A. W. Applewhich, A. T. Bransford, George C. Camp, Berenes Carter, Tom Childress, Joseph H. Crouch, F. G. Durham, A. J. Ferrell, Milton E. Head, William L. McKay, William J. McLarrin, Joseph W. Patterson, Franklin F. Wilson, Joseph F. Wilson, CWVQ. Despite his limited vocabulary, Thomas H. Higgason indicated the severity of his injury at Chickamauga: "This was a fierce battle in which I was mortally wounded" (Thomas H. Higgason, CWVQ).

34. Jesse A. Short, Richard W. Colville, Hiram D. Hawk, James Coakley, Pinkney T. Martin, CWVQ.

35. William B. Hollow, F. B. Gause, Benjamin A. Hagnewood, George W. Parks, CWVQ.

36. Amos B. Jones, David S. M. Bodenhamer, Joseph P. J. Hoover, Joel Etheldred Ruffin, CWVQ. *See also* John W. Brown, Moses Garton, Robert L. Jones, Robert P. Lankey, Samuel G. Patterson, Benjamin D. Rogers, James M. Rogers, Lee Sadler, M. D. L. Taylor, CWVQ.

37. William M. Pollard, Hampton J. Cheney, CWVQ. *See also* William W. Carnes, Pressley N. Conner, CWVQ.

38. J. M. Rich, Hiram D. Hawk, Joseph A. Fox, Liberty S. Duncan, CWVQ.

39. Herman M. Doak, Elijah H. Knight, CWVQ.

40. T. R. Ford, CWVQ. For scattered opinions of other general officers see S. H. Freeze, Henry C. Guthrie, H. W. Gwyn, James B. Thompson, CWVQ.

41. H. C. Gwyn, J. H. Ewing, Richard H. Colville, Thomas W. Walthall, Theodore F. Harris, Tennessee M. Hooper, CWVQ.
42. A. J. Williams, Robert E. Rogers, John A. Crawford, M. B. Dinwiddie, Christopher W. Robertson, Jesse H. Green, James H. Morey, Robert F. Street, CWVQ. *See also* William E. Hazelwood, H. A. Humphreys, Henry B. Tally, CWVQ.
43. Theodore F. Harris, Henry C. Dunavant, H. C. Gwyn, CWVQ.
44. Henry C. Dunavant, CWVQ.
45. Hood, *Advance and Retreat,* 296.
46. William E. Reynolds, H. C. Gwyn, James P. Caldwell, Richard W. Colville, CWVQ.
47. Joseph E. Riley, CWVQ.
48. Hesseltine's *Civil War Prisons* remains the only major study of the conflict's prisoner of war policies. A good short summary of the subject appears in McPherson, *Ordeal by Fire,* 450–56.
49. Joseph E. Riley, CWVQ.
50. Joseph P. J. Hoover, CWVQ.
51. Joseph E. Riley, CWVQ.
52. Robert Holman, CWVQ.
53. J. R. Cox, John T. Hinkle, John W. Chisum, Ford N. Adams, Carter Upchurch, James P. Gold, CWVQ. *See also* George W. Crawford, Oakley Deadrick, George W. Gosnell, Thweatt H. McCartney, Jr., CWVQ.
54. Thomas Hatchet, Sam A. Grubb, William M. Hunter, Lucullus C. Atkins, Joseph P. J. Hoover, CWVQ. *See also* Melmon M. Butts, Michel L. Davidson, J. W. Keaton, John A. Kirby, John S. Luna, William B. Moore, James A. Mosley, Erasmus G. Osgatharp, CWVQ.
55. William L. Morelock, Joseph D. Wall, A. M. Bruce, CWVQ.
56. Joseph E. Riley, Jeremiah M. McKenzie, George V. Payne, Claudius Buchanan, CWVQ.
57. Joesph E. Riley, Samuel J. Frazier, Flavius S. Landers, CWVQ.
58. Joseph P. J. Hoover, Asa Johnson, Rody S. Anthony, CWVQ. *See also* John Coffee, Liberty S. Duncan, Abraham Gredig, George E. Hornberger, William T. Jones, John W. Osborne, CWVQ.
59. Archelaus M. Hughes, CWVQ.
60. William J. Mantlo, Charles F. Blackwell, R. W. Michie, CWVQ.
61. Marcus B. Toney, J. C. McCarty, David F. Grable, Andrew J. Jernigan, CWVQ.
62. Joseph E. Riley, Thomas W. Humes, John R. Dance, Andrew J. Bradley, Swimpfield Eidson, Henry C. Moore, CWVQ.
63. J. W. Bradley, John H. Brawner, Augustus G. Buffat, William M. Moss, Francis M. Bunch, Edmond E. O'Neill, CWVQ. Joseph Hoover noted that after Missionary Ridge he and other Rebels were given the opportunity to take the oath to the Union; some accepted and avoided prison. Joseph P. J. Hoover, CWVQ.
64. Joseph E. Riley, Joseph P. J. Hoover, CWVQ. *See also* James M. Nowlin, Erasmus G. Osgatharp, CWVQ.

65. William B. Fonville, George W. Taylor, Robert E. B. Floyd, M. B. Dinwiddie, CWVQ.
66. M. B. Dinwiddie, William J. Tucker, Christopher W. Robertson, Thomas H. Hightower, CWVQ.
67. Statement of Private John Johns[t]on, 3 Feb. 1865, in *War of Rebellion*, Ser. 1, Vol. 46, pt. 2, p. 387. I appreciate Steven V. Ash of Knoxville, Tennessee, who called my attention to Johnston's desertion.
68. J. W. Bradley, Alfred E. Abernathy, R. C. Holmes, John L. Young, William H. Lucy, James A. Gross, CWVQ.
69. W. M. Willis, William Perkins, G. W. Wall, CWVQ. *See also* T. N. Bledsoe, Larkin H. Evans, W. H. Fikes, Lewis F. Gulley, CWVQ.
70. Joseph P. J. Hoover, James Marsh, Joe Sullivan, George Byrne, CWVQ.
71. John Scruggs, John A. Crawford, CWVQ.
72. James L. Singleton, George W. Sharp, Samuel K. Poore, W. H. Harris, J. P. Dillehay, William T. Mays, CWVQ. *See also* Louis J. Bledsoe, John Dickens, Hamilton M. Hennessee, William J. Herbison, J. O. Shaw, CWVQ.
73. James S. Jackson, John A. Pearce, M. B. Tomlinson, J. K. P. Heflin, CWVQ. *See also* William J. Briggs, T. D. Coffey, Robert S. Donaldson, Thompson S. Glenn, William D. Harkleroad, James H. Hinson, CWVQ.
74. William V. Mullins, CWVQ.
75. Josia M. Reams, William A. Langley, Russell L. Brown, CWVQ. *See also* James B. Anderson, Henry C. Arrington, Ridley S. Brown, John W. Dunavant, Alexander G. Felts, John S. Howell, Charles P. Williams, CWVQ.
76. Statement of Private John Johns[t]on in *War of Rebellion*.
77. James B. Bradshaw, CWVQ.
78. Edward M. Gardner, William D. Beard, CWVQ.

CHAPTER 6

1. Henry D. Hogan, Thomas W. Walthall, CWVQ.
2. Edward F. Lee, CWVQ.
3. William E. Hazelwood, CWVQ.
4. Calvin E. Myers, Frank Gilliland, William C. Pullen, William T. Barnes, W. H. Epps, Elijah T. Hassell, CWVQ. *See also* Leander K. Baker, Newton Cannon, Charles E. Jackson, Amos B. Jones, Harrison Randolph, CWVQ.
5. James E. Dickinson, CWVQ. *See also* William M. Fryer, Jesse H. Green, James A. Haymes, Robert T. Lannon, Elias G. Montgomery, George W. Sanford, Andrew C. Taylor, CWVQ.
6. William G. Allen, W. F. Blevins, Hampton J. Cheney, N. C. Godsey, William C. Godsey, CWVQ.
7. Hampton J. Cheney, Henry D. Hogan, Thomas W. Walthall, Lee Sadler,

George E. Donnell, John T. C. Fergus, James W. Hendricks, CWVQ. *See also* James H. McClister, John R. Reagan, John K. Roberts, CWVQ.

8. E. K. Cook, David S. England, Edward W. Woodward, Zachary T. Crouch, John H. Frierson, Thomas H. Williams, CWVQ. *See also* Andrew J. Alexander, John S. Allen, James L. Barry, Felix Bilbrey, G. R. Boles, D. P. Chamberland, Henry S. Cherry, H. C. Denton, William C. Dillihay, Zachary T. Dyer, William W. Elam, Franklin P. Ewton, Mike Farrell, F. F. Fisher, George W. Gann, M. B. Goodrich, George W. Gordon, T. L. Grimes, Robert N. Herbert, William I. Hill, William O. Hollingsworth, Baxter R. Hoover, Theodoric E. Lipscomb, Columbus C. Landon, James P. McCaleb, Henry M. McKenzie, John M. Mitchell, W. M. Montgomery, Robert H. Mosley, William S. Nolen, David Odle, William F. Overall, George W. Park, William H. Rice, Samuel Scoggins, William P. Sims, David F. Watkins, CWVQ.

9. Daniel W. Long, R. P. Lanius, James J. White, William J. Kirkham, George W. Lewis, Isaac A. Bartlett, CWVQ. *See also* John L. Dismukes, Henry D. Hogan, Stephen H. Hows, Ezekiel Inman, CWVQ.

10. William A. Johnston, Josiah S. House, Pressley N. Conner, Hampton J. Cheney, Herman M. Doak, Thomas S. Webb, CWVQ. *See also* William W. Carnes, Thomas J. Firth, Walter T. Lenoir, Robert Z. Taylor, CWVQ.

11. Charles G. Samuel, Victor M. Locke, John A. Wilson, CWVQ.

12. James T. Lasley, CWVQ. *See also* Samuel B. Kyle, George W. Taylor, CWVQ.

13. J. H. Jewell, CWVQ.

14. William T. Durrett, W. T. Askew, Jessie E. Broadaway, CWVQ. *See also* Napoleon B. Abbott, Francis M. Arnold, Thomas V. B. Barry, Lemuel J. Beene, William J. Bennett, James P. Byrne, James K. Clifton, Michael L. Davidson, William Y. Doss, Thomas N. Driver, John T. Hinkle, Robert S. Holman, R. T. M. Jones, Daniel Webster, George F. Wray, CWVQ.

15. Samuel B. Clemmons, Samuel Adkisson, Jack Busly, CWVQ.

16. Powhatan P. Pullen, William T. Baldridge, Samuel J. Frazier, Benjamin A. Hagnewood, CWVQ.

17. R. A. Bryant, John P. Hickman, CWVQ.

18. Joseph E. Riley, CWVQ.

19. Edward N. Gannaway, CWVQ.

20. James A. Holder, James N. Logan, Acey W. Green, William G. Lillard, James F. Anthony, CWVQ.

21. James A. Haymes, John T. Crawford, Elijah H. Wolfe, CWVQ.

22. Ford N. Adams, Berenes Carter, James O. Bass, Elijah H. Knight, A. W. Applewhich, John W. Dunavant, CWVQ. *See also* William R. Arnett, Lewis F. Gulley, Napoleon B. Johnson, Samuel C. Odom, Calvin J. Orr, William J. Tucker, Thomas S. Webb, Pleasant T. Williams, James L. Wylie, CWVQ.

23. Robert H. Kittrell, Robert E. Moss, James A. Haymes, Josia M. Reams, CWVQ.

24. Joseph F. Wilson, Constantine P. Nance, CWVQ.

25. G. R. Boles, Franklin F. Wilson, Theodoric E. Lipscomb, W. H. Lamastus, William P. Baker, Tom Childress, CWVQ. *See also* Stokley Acuff, George L. Alexander, Joe C. Brooks, John W. Carpenter, Calvin B. Crook, Jeptha M. Fuston, William B. Hollow, William D. House, William L. McKay, Julius C. Martin, James W. Swinny, Hervey Whitefield, CWVQ.

26. Henry B. Tally, Hampton J. Cheney, Charles S. O. Rice, CWVQ.

27. H. A. Humphreys, Lewis C. Howse, Lee T. Billingsley, M. B. Dinwiddie, CWVQ.

28. Thomas Blackwell, W. H. Kearney, Robert J. Brunson, Robert L. Morris, Marcus B. Toney, Amos B. Jones, CWVQ.

29. John H. O'Neal, CWVQ.

30. W. C. Carden, J. B. King, CWVQ.

31. Franklin S. Leonard, James M. Harris, William J. Kirkham, William E. McElwee, CWVQ.

32. A. M. Bruce, M. D. L. Taylor, Henry A. Parrott, George W. McMahan, Abraham Gredig, Augustus H. Gotham, Swimpfield Eidson, CWVQ. *See also* John Coffee, Zachary T. Crouch, James A. Delozier, J. P. Funk, Thomas H. Hightower, John N. Johnson, William S. Rogers, Thomas C. Wright, CWVQ.

33. James T. McColgan, James Morey, William G. Taylor, Nathaniel Harris, CWVQ.

34. Allen W. Gibbs, A. T. Bransford, Samuel M. Ray, CWVQ.

35. Charles Mison, CWVQ.

36. Andrew J. Beaner, D. Frank Duckworth, George V. Payne, Ezkiel Inman, George E. Hornberger, Elijah C. Barnes, CWVQ.

37. Robert S. Holman, William H. Roach, Thomas W. Wood, Robert H. Mosley, CWVQ. *See also* William Grant, Elijah T. Hassell, Joseph Marshall, John M. Mitchell, John S. Prather, Pleasant T. Williams, CWVQ.

38. Isaac N. Rainey, Charles S. O. Rice, Lauchlan Donaldson, Joshua W. Mewborn, Alexander W. McKay, CWVQ. *See also* George W. Alexander, E. K. Cook, M. D. Dinwiddie, Jesse W. Embry, Joshia S. House, H. A. Humphreys, Walter S. Jennings, John M. Mitchell, CWVQ.

39. Benjamin F. Hawkins, A. W. Applewhich, Newton Cannon, CWVQ.

40. George W. Lewis, Carrick W. Heiskell, James J. Womach, John A. Kirby, Aratus T. Cornelius, John R. Dance, Milton E. Head, Gideon H. Baskett, Charles W. Hubner, Samuel G. Sparks, William W. Carnes, William P. Timberlake, William H. Sebring, Thomas S. Webb, Thomas H. Williams, CWVQ.

41. Robert N. Herbert, Hamilton Parks, John R. McClelland, Lewis B. McFarland, Robert L. Morris, John Nettleton Johnson, Lycurgus W. Taylor, James A. Carringer, James M. Jones, Lemuel H. Tyree, CWVQ. *See also* Meriwether Donaldson, William H. Halbert, John P. Hickman, B. P. Hooker, B. B. Hooper, Elijah H. Knight, Walter T. Lenoir, William G. Lillard, William S. Nolen, J. F. Osborne, Christopher W. Robertson, Da-

vid Sullins, Robert Z. Taylor, William G. Taylor, J. G. Williamson, Jacob Young, CWVQ.

CHAPTER 7

1. William P. Timberlake, CWVQ.
2. Clipping from *Jackson Sun* in ibid.
3. W. M. Willis, CWVQ.
4. Arthur Davis, Moses Garton, George Hodge, Halyard Wilhite, CWVQ. *See also* James Aiken, William W. Archer, William Ary, James K. Clifton, F. M. Copeland, William Y. Doss, John G. Herbert, James P. Warner, CWVQ.
5. David Odle, CWVQ.
6. W. A. Duncan, Timothy Leigon, Alan Underhill, Richard Rigsby, CWVQ.
7. William Moss, Ephriam O. Randle, John W. Garren, CWVQ.
8. Thomas L. Bryan, James L. Cooper, George A. Rice, CWVQ. *See also* Henry C. Arrington, John Wolfe, CWVQ.
9. David L. Buckner, James P. Coffin, John T. Crawford, CWVQ. *See also* David S. M. Bodenhamer, John C. Eskew, James A. Carringer, Gentry R. McGee, Robert L. Morris, J. F. Osborne, Samuel G. Sparks, CWVQ.
10. Benjamin D. Rogers, CWVQ.
11. Edward W. Love, Charles G. Samuel, Robert H. Mosley, CWVQ.
12. Holston Roddy, James Coakley, Alexander Teasley, Albert M. Townsend, J. K. P. Thompson, H. C. Furry, Alan Underhill, CWVQ. *See also* Julius C. Martin, G. W. Miller, Daniel Webster, John S. Welch, CWVQ.
13. Ozias Denton, S. H. Clayton, James McKnight, CWVQ. *See also* George W. Alexander, William P. Baker, Jack Busly, Samuel B. Clemmons, William T. Fields, Harrison Randolph, James L. Singleton, John B. Tate, John P. Verhine, CWVQ.
14. David Watkins, CWVQ.
15. Owsley, *Plain Folk*, 142–43.
16. William E. Reynolds, CWVQ.
17. Ibid.
18. Marcus B. Toney, CWVQ.
19. Charles G. Samuel, CWVQ.
20. Jacob Slinger, George W. Willing, Thomas Booker, CWVQ.
21. James M. Rogers, Samuel N. Reynolds, CWVQ.
22. Napoleon B. Johnson, Stephen H. Hows, William M. Pollard, L. H. Russe, Walter T. Lenoir, CWVQ. *See also* Lee T. Billingsley, James L. Nesbitt, Charles S. O. Rice, CWVQ.
23. Charles S. O. Rice, William B. Bates, Nathaniel Harris, Herman M. Doak, CWVQ.
24. James P. Warner, CWVQ.
25. Robert Z. Taylor, CWVQ; Vanderwood, "Night Riders," 129–30.

26. Robert Z. Taylor, CWVQ.
27. Vanderwood, "Night Riders," 133–35.
28. Ibid.
29. Ibid.
30. "A Dramatic Trial of Night Riders," *Current Literature* 46 (Feb. 1909), 126.
31. Vanderwood, "Night Riders," 135–140.

BIBLIOGRAPHY

INTERVIEWS

Linden, Fabian. Interview with author. New York, New York, 3 Sept. 1983.
Weaver, Herbert, and Blanche Clark Weaver. Interview with author. Nashville, Tennessee, 17 May 1983.

MANUSCRIPT SOURCES

Bryan, Tom. Papers. Tennessee State Library and Archives, Nashville, Tennessee.
The Civil War Veterans Questionnaires. Tennessee State Library and Archives, Nashville, Tennessee.
Country Store Journals. Mississippi Valley Collection, Memphis State Library, Memphis, Tennessee.
Dyer, Gustavus W. Folder. Vanderbilt University Library, Nashville, Tennessee.
Gardner, Edward M. Memoir. Tennessee State Library and Archives, Nashville, Tennessee. Typescript.
Moore, John Trotwood. Papers. Tennessee State Library and Archives, Nashville, Tennessee.
Owsley, Frank L. Papers. Vanderbilt University Library, Nashville, Tennessee.
Prior Family Papers. Tennessee State Library and Archives, Nashville, Tennessee.
Southern Review Papers. Yale University Library, New Haven, Connecticut.
Stephenson, Wendell H. Papers. Duke University Library, Durham, North Carolina.

NEWSPAPERS

Knoxville Sentinel. 1926.
Nashville Banner. 1948.
Nashville Tennessean. 1948.

PUBLISHED SOURCES

Ash, Steven V. "Civil War, Black Freedom, and Social Change in the Upper South: Middle Tennessee, 1860–1870." Ph.D. diss., University of Tennessee, 1983.

———. "Middle Tennessee Society in Transition, 1860–1870." *The Maryland Historian* 13 (Spring 1982): 14–38.

Bailey, Fred A. "Caste and the Classroom in Antebellum Tennessee." *The Maryland Historian* 13 (Spring 1982): 39–54.

———. "Class and Tennessee's Confederate Generation." *Journal of Southern History* 51 (Feb. 1985): 31–60.

———. "The Poor, Plain Folk, and Planters: A Social Analysis of Middle Tennessee Respondents to the Civil War Veterans Questionnaires." West Tennessee Historical Society *Papers* 34 (1982): 5–24.

———. "Tennessee's Antebellum Society from the Bottom Up." *Southern Studies* 22 (Fall 1983): 260–73.

Blassingame, John W. *The Slave Community: Plantation Life in the Antebellum South.* New York: Oxford University Press, 1972.

Bradford, Melvin E. "What We Can Know for Certain: Frank Owsley and the Recovery of Southern History." *The Sewanee Review* 78 (Oct. 1970): 664–69.

Bryan, Charles F., Jr. "The Civil War in East Tennessee: A Social, Political, and Economic Study." Ph.D. diss., University of Tennessee, 1978.

Burnett, Edmund C. "The Hog Drivers' Play-Song and Some of Its Relatives." *Agricultural History* 23 (July 1949): 161–68.

———. "Hog Raising and Hog Driving in the Region of the French Broad River." *Agricultural History* 20 (Apr. 1946): 86–103.

Burton, Orville Vernon. *In My Father's House Are Many Mansions: Family and Community in Edgefield, South Carolina.* Chapel Hill: University of North Carolina Press, 1985.

Campbell, Randolph B. *A Southern Community in Crisis: Harrison County, Texas, 1850–1880.* Austin: Texas State Historical Society, 1983.

Campbell, Randolph B., and Richard G. Lowe. *Wealth and Power in Antebellum Texas.* College Station: Texas A & M University Press, 1977.

Carnoy, Martin, ed. *Schooling in a Corporate Society: The Political Economy of Education in America.* New York: Longman, 1972.

Cash, Wilbur J. *The Mind of the South.* New York: Alfred A. Knopf, 1941.

Clark, Blanche Henry. "The Agricultural Population in Tennessee, 1840–1860: With Special Reference to the Non-Slaveholders." Ph.D. diss., Vanderbilt University, 1939.

———. *The Tennessee Yeomen, 1840–1860.* Nashville, Tenn.: Vanderbilt University Press, 1942.

Coles, Harry L., Jr. "A History of the Administration of Federal Land Policies and Land Tenure in Louisiana, 1803–1860." Ph.D. diss., Vanderbilt University, 1949.

———. "Some Notes on Slaveownership and Landownership in Louisiana, 1850–1860." *Journal of Southern History* 9 (Aug. 1943): 381–94.

Couch, William T., ed. *Culture in the South*. Chapel Hill: University of North Carolina Press, 1935.

Daniel, Pete. *The Shadow of Slavery: Peonage in the South, 1901–1969*. London: Oxford University Press, 1972.

Davis, Allison; Burleigh B. Gardner; and Mary R. Gardner. *Deep South: A Social Anthropological Study of Caste and Class*. Chicago: University of Chicago Press, 1941.

Dodd, Donald B. "Unionism in Confederate Alabama." Ph.D. diss., University of Georgia, 1969.

Dunning, William A. *Reconstruction, Political and Economic: 1865–1877*. New York: Harper and Brothers, 1907.

Dyer, Gustavus W. *Democracy in the South before the Civil War*. Nashville, Tenn.: Methodist Publishing House, 1905.

_____. "My Experiences on the Stump." *Vanderbilt Alumnus* 3 (Feb. 1918): 113–15.

_____. "Social Tendencies in the South." In *The South in the Building of the Nation* 10:654–72. Richmond, Va.: Southern Historical Publications, 1909.

Dyer, Gustavus W., ed. *Library of American Lives: Tennessee Edition*. Washington, D.C.: Historical Records Association, 1949.

Eaton, Clement. *The Growth of Southern Civilization: 1790–1860*. New York: Harper and Row, 1961.

Escott, Paul D. *After Secession: Jefferson Davis and the Failure of Confederate Nationalism*. Baton Rouge: Louisiana State University Press, 1978.

_____. "'The Cry of the Sufferers': The Problem of Welfare in the Confederacy." *Civil War History* 23 (Sept. 1977): 228–40.

_____. *Many Excellent People: Power and Privilege in North Carolina, 1850–1900*. Chapel Hill: University of North Carolina Press, 1985.

_____. *Slavery Remembered: A Record of Twentieth-Century Slave Narratives*. Chapel Hill: University of North Carolina Press, 1979.

Elliott, Colleen M., and Louise A. Moxley, comp. *The Civil War Veterans Questionnaires*. 5 vols. Easley, S.C.: Southern Historical Press and Company, 1985.

"Faculty Notes." *Vanderbilt Alumnus* 7 (Apr. 1922): 137.

Foner, Eric. "The Causes of the American Civil War: Recent Interpretations and New Directions." *Civil War History* 20 (Sept. 1974): 197–214.

Genovese, Eugene D. "Medical and Insurance Costs of Slaveholding in the Cotton Belt." *Journal of Negro History* 45 (July 1960): 141–55.

_____. *Roll, Jordan, Roll: The World the Slaves Made*. New York: Vintage Books, 1972.

_____. "Yeomen Farmers in a Slaveholders' Democracy." *Agricultural History* 49 (Apr. 1975): 331–42.

Green, Claud B. *John Trotwood Moore: Tennessee Man of Letters*. Athens: University of Georgia Press, 1957.

Green, Fletcher M. "Democracy in the Old South." *Journal of Southern History* 12 (Feb. 1946), 3–23.

Hahn, Steven. *The Roots of Southern Populism: Yeomen Farmers and the Transfor-

mation of the Georgia Upcountry, 1850–1890. New York: Oxford University Press, 1984.

Helper, Hinton R. *The Impending Crisis of the South.* New York: A. B. Burdick, 1857. Reprint. Cambridge, Mass.: Harvard University Press, 1968.

Hesseltine, William B. *Civil War Prisons: A Study in War Psychology.* Columbus: Ohio State University Press, 1930.

Holst, Hermann Von. *Constitutional and Political History of the United States.* 7 vols. Chicago: Callaghan and Company, 1872–92.

Hood, John B. *Advance and Retreat.* New Orleans: Hood Orphan Memorial Fund, 1880. Reprint. Bloomington: Indiana University Press, 1959 [1880].

I'll Take My Stand: The South and the Agrarian Tradition. New York: Harper and Brothers, 1930.

Kraus, Michael. *The Writing of American History.* Norman: University of Oklahoma Press, 1963.

Linden, Fabian. "Economic Democracy in the Slave South." *Journal of Negro History* 32 (Apr. 1946): 140–89.

_____. Review of *Mississippi Farmers, 1850–1860,* by Herbert Weaver. *American Historical Review* 52 (Jan. 1947): 338–40.

Litwach, Leon F. *Been in the Storm So Long: The Aftermath of Slavery.* New York: Vintage Books, 1979.

McDonald, Forrest, and Grady McWhiney. "The Antebellum Southern Herdsman: A Reinterpretation." *Journal of Southern History* 41 (May 1975): 147–66.

McMaster, John Bach. *A History of the People of the United States.* 8 vols. New York: D. Appleton and Company, 1883–1913.

McPherson, James M. *Ordeal by Fire: The Civil War and Reconstruction.* New York: Alfred A. Knopf, 1982.

McWhiney, Grady. "Historians as Southerners." *Continuity: A Journal of History,* no. 9 (Fall 1984): 1–31.

_____. Introduction to *Plain Folk of the Old South,* by Frank L. Owsley. Baton Rouge: Louisiana State University Press, 1982.

_____. "The Revolution in Nineteenth-Century Alabama Agriculture." *The Alabama Review* 31 (Jan. 1978): 3–32.

Meier, August. *Negro Thought in America, 1880–1915.* Ann Arbor: University of Michigan Press, 1969.

Mooney, Chase C. *Slavery in Tennessee.* Bloomington: Indiana University Press, 1957.

_____. "Slavery in Tennessee." Ph.D. diss., Vanderbilt University, 1939.

Moore, Emily. "The Tennessee State Library in the Capitol." *Tennessee Historical Quarterly* 12 (Mar. 1953): 3–22.

Newby, Idus A. *Jim Crow's Defense: Anti-Negro Thought in America, 1900–1930.* Baton Rouge: Louisiana State University Press, 1965.

O'Brien, Michael. *The Idea of the American South, 1920–1941.* Baltimore, Md.: Johns Hopkins University Press, 1979.

Owens, Harry P., ed. *Perspectives and Irony in American Slavery.* Jackson: University of Mississippi Press, 1976.

Owsley, Frank L. Letter to editor. *American Historical Review* 52 (July 1947): 845–49.

———. *Plain Folk of the Old South.* Baton Rouge: Louisiana State University Press, 1949.

———. Review of *Origins of Class Struggle in Louisiana,* by Roger W. Shugg. *Journal of Southern History* 6 (Feb. 1940): 116–17.

Owsley, Frank L., and Harriet C. Owsley. "The Economic Structure of Rural Tennessee, 1850–1860." *Journal of Southern History* 8 (May 1942): 161–81.

Owsley, Harriet C., ed. *The South: Old and New Frontiers, Selected Essays of Frank Lawrence Owsley.* Athens: University of Georgia Press, 1979.

Phillips, Ulrich B. "The Central Theme of Southern History." *American Historical Review* 34 (Oct. 1929): 30–43.

———. *Life and Labor in the Old South.* New York: Little, Brown and Company, 1929.

———. Review of *Democracy in the South Before the Civil War,* by G. W. Dyer. *American Historical Review* 11 (Apr. 1906): 715–16.

Raper, Arthur F. *Preface to Peasantry.* Chapel Hill: University of North Carolina Press, 1936.

Roark, James L. *Masters Without Slaves: Southern Planters in the Civil War and Reconstruction.* New York: W. W. Norton and Company, 1977.

Rhodes, James Ford. *History of the United States from the Compromise of 1850.* 9 vols. New York: Macmillan, 1892–1909.

Savitt, Todd L. "The Special Problem of Slavery." Paper presented at The Second Barnard-Millington Symposium on Southern Science and Medicine: Medicine in the Old South, 19 Mar. 1983, at The University of Mississippi, University, Mississippi.

Schouler, James. *History of the United States Under the Constitution.* 6 vols. New York: Co-operative Publication Society, 1890–99.

Sensing, Thomas. "Dr. Gus Dyer Dies at 81." *Vanderbilt Alumnus* 33 (Apr.–May 1948): 2.

Shapiro, Edward S. "Frank L. Owsley and the Defense of Southern Identity." *Tennessee Historical Quarterly* 34 (Spring 1977): 75–94.

Shugg, Roger W. *Origins of Class Struggle in Louisiana.* Baton Rouge: Louisiana State University Press, 1939.

Stampp, Kenneth M. *The Peculiar Institution: Slavery in the Antebellum South.* New York: Vintage Books, 1956.

Temple, Oliver P. *Notable Men of Tennessee from 1833 to 1875.* New York: Cosmopolitan Press, 1912.

Tennesseans in the Civil War. 2 vols. Nashville, Tenn.: Civil War Centennial Commission, 1964.

Tilly, Betty B. "Aspects of Social and Economic Life in West Tennessee before the Civil War." Ph.D. diss., Memphis State University, 1974.

U.S. Bureau of the Census: *Eighth Census: Population Schedule, 1860.* Washington, D.C.: U.S. Government Printing Office, 1864.

Vance, Rupert B. *The Negro Agricultural Worker.* 1934.

Vanderwood, Paul J. "Night Riders of Reelfoot Lake." *Tennessee Historical*

Quarterly 28 (Summer 1969): 126–40.

War of Rebellion: Official Records of the Union and Confederate Armies. 70 vols. Washington, D.C.: U.S. Government Printing Office, 1880–1909.

Weaver, Herbert. "The Agricultural Population of Mississippi, 1850–1860." Ph.D. diss., Vanderbilt University, 1941.

———. *Mississippi Farmers, 1850–1860.* Nashville, Tenn.: Vanderbilt University Press, 1945.

Wiener, Jonathan M. *Social Origins of the New South: Alabama, 1860–1885.* Baton Rouge: Louisiana State University Press, 1978.

Wilson, Clyde. Introduction to *Recovering Southern History.* Special issue of *Continuity: A Journal of History*, no. 9 (Fall 1984): i–x.

Wilson's Tennessee Farmer's Almanac for the Year 1827. Nashville, 1827.

Woodward, C. Vann. *The Strange Career of Jim Crow.* London: Oxford University Press, 1955.

Wooster, Ralph A. *Politicians, Planters and Plain Folk: Courthouse and State House in the Upper South, 1850–1860.* Knoxville: University of Tennessee Press, 1975.

Wright, Gavin. *The Political Economy of the Cotton South: Households, Markets, and Wealth in the Nineteenth Century.* New York: W. W. Norton and Company, 1978.

INDEX